6/-

2/6

THE SCOTTISH REFORMATION

Yes always cordially
Alex. F. Mitchell

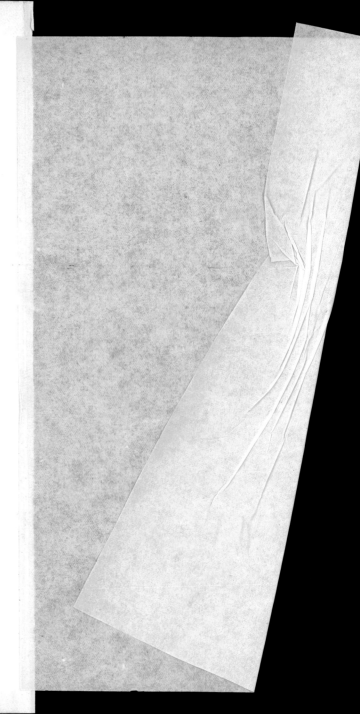

THE
SCOTTISH REFORMATION

Its Epochs, Episodes, Leaders, and Distinctive Characteristics

(Being the Baird Lecture for 1899)

BY THE LATE

ALEXANDER F. MITCHELL, D.D., LL.D.

EMERITUS PROFESSOR OF CHURCH HISTORY
IN ST ANDREWS UNIVERSITY

EDITED BY

D. HAY FLEMING, LL.D.

WITH A BIOGRAPHICAL SKETCH OF THE AUTHOR
BY JAMES CHRISTIE, D.D.

WILLIAM BLACKWOOD AND SONS
EDINBURGH AND LONDON
MDCCCC

47112

PREFACE.

FEW men have shown more indomitable application to an arduous duty, amid physical weakness and bodily pain, than did the author of these Lectures in their preparation and revision. In the MS. there are a goodly number of additions and minute alterations in his own hand—some of them very tremulous, some of them in ink, some of them in pencil. He intended to revise them still more carefully ere they were published; but expressed the desire that, if he were not spared to do so, I would see them through the press. The Master, whom he served so long and so faithfully, having released him from the work he loved so well, and from the suffering he so patiently endured, the final revision has devolved upon me.

On the suggestion of Professor Robertson the book has been arranged in chapters. The sixth lecture having temporarily gone amissing before its delivery, Dr Mitchell prepared a rescension of it. The original and the rescension are now combined in chapter x. He intended to devote an extra lecture to Alesius, and another to Andrew Melville, but unfortunately was unable. The chapter on Alesius is therefore taken from two of his class-lectures, some of the longer extracts being thrown into appendices, and a few passages being slightly compressed. This is at once the fullest and the best account of Alesius that has yet been published. The facts concerning Melville in chapter x. are supplemented to a small extent in the paper quoted in Appendix A.

Comparatively few of the authorities were entered in the MS. when it was placed in my hands. I have filled in many, and have taken care, in almost every instance where volume and page are given, to check the quotations with the originals. My notes, and my additions to Dr Mitchell's notes, are enclosed within square brackets; but when I have merely supplied authorities, they are not so distinguished. The

list which he had drawn up of the works of
Alesius was partly in an obsolete form of short-
hand, which to me was quite undecipherable.
Having been privileged to examine a good many
of these rare treatises in various public libraries,
I have been able, though only to an inconsider-
able degree, to supplement the list; these additions being marked like those in the notes and
other appendices. In revising the Lectures themselves, I have corrected a number of trifling slips,
but have made no alteration of which Dr Mitchell
would not have cordially approved had his attention been drawn to it.

In preparing the Lectures, Dr Mitchell availed
himself of elaborate articles he had written at
various times for periodicals and other publications. The present volume is valuable in several
ways, not the least of these being that it embodies, on many obscure and important points,
the matured views of one of the most competent
and cautious of historical students—of one who
grudged no time and spared no labour in elicit-
ing and elucidating the truth.

D. H. F.

December 1899.

CONTENTS.

APPENDICES.

BIOGRAPHICAL SKETCH

OF

THE VERY REV. ALEXANDER FERRIER MITCHELL,
D.D., LL.D., PROFESSOR OF ECCLESIASTICAL HISTORY IN
ST MARY'S COLLEGE, ST ANDREWS.

———————

A PATHETIC and almost melancholy interest attaches to this volume of the Baird Lectures. Their scholarly and accomplished author may be said to have entered on the last stage of the malady to which he succumbed when they were read for him in Blythswood Parish Church, Glasgow, by his friend and former student, Professor Robertson, the closing one, indeed, having been delivered but a few days before his death. In proof of the deep interest which he took in the subject of these Lectures, and of his desire to present them in as perfect a form as possible, it may also be mentioned that he employed his time in revising them while confined to bed during the protracted and painful illness through which he passed.   The editing of them he intrusted to another friend, Dr Hay Fleming of St Andrews, with whom he had much in common—similarity of tastes and interest in the same literary pursuits having led to an intercourse between them which ripened into mutual confidence and esteem.   Had Professor Mitchell lived to see the work through the press himself, there is hardly room to doubt that, as in the case of most of his other publications, additional explanatory and supplementary notes on obscure points would have been appended by him.   As it is, the editor in executing his task has done what he could in this respect.

When the decease of the venerable Professor took place at St Andrews towards the end of March of this year, it was felt that the Church of Scotland had been bereft not only of one of her ablest and most trusted leaders, but of one of the wisest and warmest friends of her missions ; and the many tributes paid to his memory, both from the pulpit and in the press, were all expressive of the high regard in which he was held, and of the sense of public loss caused by his removal.   But the loss was not that of his own Church alone, nor of the University with which his name had been so long and so honourably associated. There are those in other communions who had learned to look upon him as " a master of Israel,". and in all Presbyterian Churches especially he was recognised as one of the ablest and most learned exponents of the principles which they hold in common, and as one of the most earnest defenders of "the faith once delivered to the saints."

As many of those who are familiar with Professor Mitchell's writings may know little or nothing of his personal history, it has been suggested that a short biographical sketch of him would form an appropriate introduction to this posthumous volume. The particulars woven together in the following narrative have been collected from various sources, some of them having been furnished by members of his own family.

Alexander Ferrier Mitchell was born on 10th September 1822 in the old ecclesiastical city of Brechin, with which his ancestors had had an honourable connection for several generations. His grandfather, Alexander Mitchell, and his father, David Mitchell, were both known as Convener Mitchell, probably as having succeeded each other in the convenership of the local guilds. On the maternal side he was descended from another Brechin family, some of the members of which had in their day served in various capacities abroad, one of his granduncles, Alexander Ferrier, after whom he was named, having been a doctor in India, and another, Captain David Ferrier, "a brave and bold sailor,"—in memory of whom there is a tablet on the east door of the old Cathedral,—having made a voyage round the world in the Dolphin, in which also he ran the

blockade in time of war into some of the French
ports.   Elizabeth, daughter of James Ferrier at
Broadmyre, the Professor's mother, was a woman
of good judgment and deep piety, and from her
he seems to have inherited some of the most
prominent features of his character.   He was one
of a family of three, his brother and sister having
died, the former at Bloemfontein in South Africa,
many years ago.   In childhood he had a narrow
escape, a cart having run over his body.   He was
picked up and carried home by the minister of
the Episcopal church.   As a boy he passed
through more than one severe illness, and when
taken for a change to Glenesk one summer he
was described by a sympathetic friend as "a
deein' laddie."   To a mother's unwearied care
and attention he owed, under the divine blessing,
the recovery of his health, and to a mother's
religious training he owed in no small degree
that knowledge of the Holy Scriptures and that
pious disposition by which he was distinguished
from his earliest years.   His elementary education he received at the grammar-school of his
native town, and when fifteen years of age he
proceeded to St Andrews to prosecute his studies
with a view to the Christian ministry.

In those days the journey thither was not
made with the comfort and facility with which
it is now accomplished; and the Professor himself has told how, on landing from the North off
the ferry-boat at Newport, he walked all the way

to St Andrews—a distance of eleven miles—along with the carrier's son by the side of the cart which conveyed his luggage to its destination. Widely different as were the future careers of those two youths, there were various interesting points of contact in their lives, the one becoming an eminent doctor in the University, and the other filling the honourable position of a magistrate in the ancient city, while both were associated as members of the kirk-session of the Town Church.

At the very outset of his career at St Andrews the young student from Brechin gained the highest distinction, having won the first bursary open to students entering the University, as the result of a competitive examination in classical scholarship. Throughout his course, both in Arts and Divinity, he maintained a highly honourable place in all the classes, distinguishing himself particularly by proficiency in Hebrew and other Oriental languages; while he won the commendation of his professors and the esteem of his fellow-students not more by his attainments in learning than by the sterling integrity of his character and the example of his consistent Christian life. Among his contemporaries at College were not a few who in after-life rose to prominent positions in the Church, one of these being his future colleague, the late Principal Tulloch, with whom he continued to have most cordial relations during a lifelong friendship.

On completing the usual curriculum of study

at the University, Mr Mitchell was in 1844 licensed to preach the Gospel, and after acting for some time as an assistant, first to the minister of the parish of Meigle and then to the minister of the parish of Dundee, he was in 1847 ordained by the Presbytery of Meigle to the pastoral charge of the parish of Dunnichen in his native county.

The Professor had been no passive spectator of the exciting and momentous events which were taking place in the Church of Scotland in the years which immediately preceded and followed his entrance on the work of the ministry; and in his address as Moderator of the General Assembly, four decades afterwards, he gives a graphic account of the impressions made upon him by his visits to the Supreme Court of the Church during that period of acrimonious controversy and painful separation. He says: " My first view of the General Assembly was gained in 1840, where from the public gallery of the Tron Church, in near proximity to Dr John Ritchie, of the Potterrow (whose thoughts were already running in the same direction as those of his successors are now), I listened to the thrilling eloquence of Chalmers, and the calm, thoughtful utterances of Cook, and witnessed the first of those titanic encounters between Cunningham and Robertson, which the pen of Hugh Miller and the histories of the period have made classical. My next glimpse of the Assembly was in 1843, when, from the students' gallery of St

Andrew's Church, beside my friend William Smith, afterwards of North Leith, I witnessed that sad sight which was never to fade from our memories, nor cease to influence the course of our thought and action—the scene when Welsh, Chalmers, Gordon, and many more good and devoted ministers, abandoning in despair the contest of ten years, withdrew from the Church of their fathers, to rear another in which they hoped to enjoy greater freedom and peace. My next view of the Assembly was in 1848, when, along with Dr Tulloch, and two or three other college friends, I took my place for the first time as a member of the House, and when my old preceptor, then Professor of Church History in St Mary's College, filled the chair. The Church at that time was but slowly recovering from the staggering blow she had received in '43, and the great Dr Robertson was shaping out the splendid scheme which was to constitute her mission for the immediate future, and give to her the consciousness and confidence of reviving life. There were plenty of aged men there, whose lives had been honourably worn out in her service; a goodly band of young men, with not a little of the ardour and enthusiasm of youth; not a few of riper years, who, after weary waiting, had at last been promoted to pastoral charges. But that class which is the mainstay of a Church— the men who have attained to experience by years of labour in her service, and are still able to bear the burden and heat of the day — was more scantily represented."

The young minister, with so many conspicuous gifts and graces, was not allowed to remain long in the quiet pastoral charge at Dunnichen, where his ministry had been very acceptable; and in 1848 — only one year after his ordination, and when not more than twenty-six years of age—he was appointed to the chair of Hebrew in St Mary's College, St Andrews, through which he had so recently passed as a student. He has himself told of the cordial welcome which he received from the venerable Principal Haldane and the other members of the professorial staff, and of the harmony with which they co-operated in the work of the College.

It was not then a common thing that so young a minister should be called to occupy such a position of dignity and responsibility, nor was Hebrew then so popular a branch of study as it has, for various reasons, since become in our Divinity Halls; but the ability and success with which the Professor discharged the duties of his chair, and the salutary influence which he exerted in many ways upon the students, more than justified the appointment. He was one of the first in Scotland to introduce a scientific method in the teaching of Hebrew, and his class-room became a place of very real work, necessitating careful preparation on the part of the students. Some of these, perhaps, thought him rather exacting, and the strict discipline which he enforced was not altogether to their liking; but there were very few who did not value his good opinion, or who would not have considered it a kind of degradation to incur his displeasure; while many, imbued with something of his own spirit, attained under his guidance to such a degree of proficiency in the knowledge of the sacred tongue as made the reading of the Old Testament in the original a source of interest and pleasure to them in subsequent years. Dr William Wright, one of the greatest of Orientalists, was one of his students, and two others of them are occupants of Hebrew Chairs in Scottish Universities.

The appointment of the Professor to the Convenership of the Committee on the Mission to the Jews in 1856 marked a new era in its history, in respect both of the method of its operations and the field in which these have ever since been carried on. One of the results of the Crimean war, which had then but recently closed, was the opening of the Turkish empire for evangelistic enterprise; and it may be said that the Professor laid the foundations of the Mission in the Levant at the several stations occupied by the Church of Scotland, which are now known not only as places of great historic interest but as important centres of missionary activity in which the Church bears an honourable part. In the autumn of 1857 he undertook a journey to the East at the request of the Committee, and in the course of his travels there visited not only the principal Turkish cities on the coast, but Jerusalem and other places in Palestine and Syria, collecting information with a view to find openings for the planting of the Mission at suitable stations in addition to the two which had been already occupied. The report which he presented on his return led by degrees to a great expansion of the Mission, and several of his own students and others were through his influence induced to enter the service of the Committee. With many other claims on his attention, he ungrudgingly gave up a great part of his time to the administration of the affairs of the Mission, over which for nineteen years he continued to preside with great zeal and wisdom, pressing its claims on the members of the Church, and guiding and encouraging the missionaries by an intelligent and sympathetic interest in their arduous work. When in 1875 he retired from the Convenership, the General Assembly expressed its sense of the value of the distinguished services which he had rendered to the Church in this department of her work in the following terms: " The Assembly are satisfied that the present prosperity of the Jewish Mission, and the remarkable progress which it has made, has been mainly owing to the great labour, the learning, enthusiasm, and warm and intelligent Christian interest which Dr Mitchell has devoted during these years to the cause of Jewish conversion in connection with the Church of Scotland." After his retire-

ment from the Convenership he but seldom attended the meetings of the Committee, for the
reason, as he was once heard to say, that he did
not wish to appear to hamper his successors; but
he never ceased to take a deep interest in the
Mission, and none rejoiced more than he in its
growing prosperity.

While the Professor still occupied the Hebrew
Chair, he had shown a special aptitude for another
branch of learning, in which he was yet to make
a reputation for himself in the Churches not only
of Britain but of America. In 1866 he published
a lecture, primarily addressed to his students, on
'The Westminster Confession of Faith: A Contribution to the Study of its Historical Relations
and to the Defence of its Teaching,' which, as a
reply to views then current in certain quarters,
attracted no little notice at the time of its
publication, and which is not only of special
interest as illustrating his theological standpoint,
and the calm and temperate, yet earnest and
vigorous, manner in which he could defend it,
but is of permanent value as a contribution to
the literature of the subject with which it deals.
In the following year he published 'The Wedderburns and their Work, or the Sacred Poetry of
the Scottish Reformation in its Relation to that
of Germany'—a subject which was treated by
him much more fully in one of his most recent
works.

The Professor was known to possess a most

extensive and accurate knowledge of Church History in general, and of Scottish Church History in particular; and when in 1868 he was called to occupy the Chair of Ecclesiastical History in St Mary's College, the appointment was hailed with satisfaction alike by the University and the Church. With an absorbing interest in his subject, and with the true instinct of the historian, he was most painstaking in ascertaining historical facts, never reaching his conclusions but as the result of patient and careful investigation; and those who knew him intimately can tell how little he grudged the trouble of a journey to Edinburgh or London, or even of an occasional excursion to the Continent, in order to prosecute his researches. in libraries there with the view of verifying a statement, or of obtaining indubitable evidence on some controverted point. Besides those who had the privilege of listening to his prelections from the professorial chair, there are many in the Churches on both sides of the Atlantic who have profited by his great erudition; and his published writings, which all bear the impress of a master-hand, will always be reckoned standard works in Ecclesiastical History.

It is no part of the purpose of this notice to describe his various works in detail, but the mere enumeration of them will show what a life of unremitting study he lived. Besides those already referred to, he edited, along with the late

Dr Struthers, in 1874, 'The Minutes of the Westminster Assembly from November 1644 to March 1649,' to which is prefixed an elaborate Historical Introduction written by himself; in 1882 he wrote a 'Historical Notice of Archbishop Hamilton's Catechism' (first printed at St Andrews in 1551), prefixed to Paterson's black-letter reprint of the same; in 1883 he published his Baird Lecture, 'The Westminster Assembly: Its History and Standards'; in 1886 he published 'The Catechisms of the Second Reformation'; in 1888 he edited, for the Scottish Text Society, 'The Richt Vay to the Kingdome of Heuine,' by John Gau, the earliest known prose-treatise in the Scottish dialect setting forth the doctrines of the Reformers; and in 1897, for the same Society, 'The Gude and Godlie Ballatis,' reprinted from the edition of 1567, with a full and most interesting Introduction. For the Scottish History Society he also edited in 1892 and 1896, along with the writer of this sketch, two volumes of 'The Records of the Commissions of the General Assembly,' covering the period 1646-1650, from the original manuscript in the Assembly library, with an introduction, notes, and appendices by himself. To these must be added the present volume of the Baird Lecture, 'The Scottish Reformation.'

The Baird Lecture on the Westminster Assembly was received with great favour in America as well as in this country, and a new edition of it was published at Philadelphia in 1897, in a notice of which in the 'Presbyterian and Reformed Review' the following statement occurs: "The book at once took its rank as the most trustworthy and sympathetic account of the Westminster Standards in existence, and rapidly ran out of print. The public is to be congratulated that Dr Mitchell has permitted himself to be persuaded by the [Presbyterian] Board to revise the text and allow a new edition to be issued to meet the present demand. The revision does not much alter the text. A phrase is more felicitously turned here or rendered a shade more exact or emphatic there; a few additional references are added in the notes; and a few additional citations and remarks incorporated in them: that is about all. But so good a book needed only these little touches of betterment."

The Professor also contributed to various journals and encyclopædias many important articles, chiefly on historical topics relating to Scotland, which, if collected, would form a volume of miscellaneous papers of great interest and value. The most important of these are included in the subjoined list: In the 'British and Foreign Evangelical Review,' January 1872, "Our Scottish Reformation: Its Distinctive Characteristics and Present-Day Lessons," pp. 87-128; October 1875, "Dr Merle D'Aubigné on the Reformation in Scotland," pp. 736-760; October 1876, "Killen's Ecclesiastical History

of Ireland," pp. 713-741: in the 'Catholic Pres-
byterian,' March 1879, "Calvin and the Psalmody
of the Reformed Churches": in the 'Scottish
Church,' November 1886, "St Andrews in Covenanting Times": in the 'Year - Book of the
Church of Scotland,' 1886, "Brief Sketch of the
History of the Reformed Church of Scotland":
in 'St Giles' Lectures,' First Series, 1880-81,
"Pre - Reformation Scotland"; and in Fourth
Series, 1883-84, "The Primitive or Apostolic and
Sub - Apostolic Church," being the first of the
lectures entitled, "The Churches of Christendom." To Dr Schaff's Encyclopædia he contributed separate articles on "St Columba," "The
Culdees," "Patrick Hamilton," "Iona," and
"The Keltic Church"; and to the 'Presbyterian
and Reformed Review,' published at Philadelphia,
he contributed a review of Dr Hume Brown's
'John Knox.' Besides many Reports on various
matters presented to the General Assembly,
he issued for special purposes a "Statement
regarding the Eldership," and a "List of
Acts of the Scottish Parliament, and of Acts,
Overtures, and Resolutions of the General Assembly of the Church of Scotland, adopted at
various times for the Acknowledgment of the
True Reformed Protestant Religion, the Main-
tenance of Sound Doctrine, and the Subscription
of the Confessions of Faith of 1560 and 1647."
When at Geneva, on one of his visits to the
Continent, he prepared for private circulation,

from the original, which is still preserved among
the historical treasures in the Hotel de Ville,
"Livre Des Anglois, or Register of the English
Church at Geneva under the pastoral care of
Knox and Goodman, 1555-1559," with a Prefatory
Notice and a Facsimile of pp. 49, 50. To this
list of his minor works may be added a sermon on
"The Unsearchable Riches of Christ," published
in 1879.

The Professor accorded a generous and helpful
sympathy to those who were workers in the field
in which he laboured himself with so great assi-
duity and success; and he was not only a member both of the Scottish History Society and of
the Scottish Text Society, but took an active
interest in their affairs. He was also one of the
representatives of the Church of Scotland in the
General Presbyterian Alliance from the date of its
formation, and took part in the business of all its
General Councils, at the first of which, held at
Edinburgh in 1877, he laid on the table a paper
which he had drawn up on "The Harmony between the Bibliology of the Westminster Confession and that of the earlier Reformed Confessions, exhibited in parallel columns." He was
appointed Convener of the Committee on the
Desiderata of the History of the Presbyterian
Churches; and at the following General Council,
held at Philadelphia in 1880, it fell to him, in
consequence of the death of Principal Lorimer,
who was Convener of the British section of the

Committee on Creeds and Formulas of Subscription, to give in the report containing " Answers
to Queries regarding Creeds and Confessions."
The Answers as regards the Church of Scotland,
which had been prepared by himself, are to be found
in the Report of the Proceedings of the Council,
pp. 969-984.   When in America he also delivered
a course of lectures at Alleghany. His connection
with the Alliance brought him into close contact
with some of the leading Presbyterian divines of
Britain and America, with whom his opinions on
the history of the doctrine, worship, and government of the Church carried great weight; and Dr
Schaff has acknowledged his obligations to him,
among others, in his well-known work entitled
' The Creeds of Christendom.'

In 1885 the Church showed her appreciation of
the Professor's character and work by electing
him to the Moderatorship of the General Assembly, an office which he filled with a union of
dignity and authority which reflected honour
upon the Church. If there are parties in the
Church of Scotland, he never identified himself
with any of them, and had learned to call no man
master but Christ. He knew his own mind, and
could give forcible expression to his convictions
when occasion required. Naturally of an un-
assuming disposition and unobtrusive manners, he
never courted popularity nor sought to thrust his
opinions upon others; and it was for this reason,
perhaps, that he was deferred to even by those

d

whose views were in some respects widely diverg-
ent from his.   It was doubtless for this reason
also, as well as for others, that he wielded so great
an influence in the counsels of the Church, and
probably few men had more to do than he with the
shaping of her policy in recent years.   In paying
a tribute to his memory at a meeting of the Presbytery of Edinburgh a few days after his decease, the
Very Rev. Dr Scott of St George's said that " by
Professor Mitchell's death the Church had lost
a laborious, faithful, successful, and honoured
minister and professor, and perhaps one of the
soundest and wisest counsellors that the Church
ever had.   He was a man who had friends in all
the Churches.   He knew how powerfully his influence had told in the Church—always for conciliation, not only so far as those without their own
Church were concerned, but those within the
Church also.   Had it not been for Dr Mitchell's
influence the relaxation of the formula regarding the subscription of elders would never have
been carried through."

A man of a very catholic spirit, and a lover of
peace and concord, the Professor, like many
others who longed for a comprehensive union of
the Scottish Churches, would willingly have made
all reasonable concessions for the attainment of
so desirable an object.   But he was too loyal a
son of the Church of Scotland to consent to any
unworthy compromise, and in the hour of danger
no one was more ready than he to exert all the

influence at his command in her defence. Readers
of Dr Boyd's 'Twenty-five Years of St Andrews'
may remember the account there given of the
impression made by the Professor's sermon in
the Town Church in the height of the contest
in 1885, when the question of Disestablishment
was brought so prominently before the electors
of the St Andrews Burghs. Dr Boyd says: "It
had been intimated at the services during the day
that Dr Mitchell, our Professor of Church History,
would lecture in the parish church in the evening
on 'Some aspects of the Church Question deserving of consideration in the present crisis.' Dr
Mitchell was that year Moderator of the Kirk:
and he very seldom preaches. The church was
filled by a great congregation. I should not in
the least degree have been surprised to hear Dr
Mitchell preach wisely and devoutly: that is his
usual way. But it did surprise me to find that
man of calm and well-balanced mind fire up into
a pathos and vehemence which I have rarely seen
equalled and never surpassed. The question of
disestablishment had been raised: and one was
made to realise how it stirs the blood of good
men here. And not merely were there this
evening a fire, a keenness, a power of stirring a
multitude to the depth of their nature, which are
rare indeed, but an incisive severity of denuncia-
tion which few had expected from that calm,
cautious man. And if the preacher was at white-
heat, so was the congregation long before he was

done.   Several times there would have been loud applause, had it not been hushed."

The attitude which the Professor maintained in regard to the doctrine and worship of the Church was a strictly conservative one, and may be best described in his own words, taken from an article included in the list of his minor works.   In that article, after quoting the advice tendered by an eminent minister of the Church of England to a minister of the Church of Scotland—" Stick by your own Kirk: it is an honest Kirk, one of the few that has fairly rid itself of sacerdotalism and ritualism, and you have no cause to be ashamed of it "—he goes on to say: " The advice is not unneeded in the present day by others than he to whom it was originally tendered, and I give it this publicity for the benefit of all whom it may concern.   The Reformed Church of Scotland from the first rid herself of these medieval corruptions, and the attempt to bring her again under the yoke issued in dire disaster to those who made it. This surely is no time for the Presbyterian Churches to swerve from the testimony they have so long and resolutely borne against all such errors.   When we think of the mischief they are now causing in the Church of England, and the grief they are occasioning to many of her most loyal sons, rather does it become us to bear more decided testimony to the truths, that under the New Testament there is but one Priest, who ever liveth to make intercession for us, and one sacrifice once offered, which perfects for ever them that are sanctified; that He has not communicated His priestly office to His ministers either by succession or delegation, nor authorised them to repeat or continue that sacrifice which is the propitiation for sin; and that He has neither Himself imposed, nor warranted others to impose, a load of 'fondly' invented ceremonies in His worship."

If the Professor thus strenuously opposed sacerdotalism on the one hand, he had as little sympathy with Broad Churchism on the other. The non-natural sense in which the narratives of the New Testament miracles are understood and interpreted by some of the modern critics he rejected as subversive of Christian truth, a common saying of his being, "If the Gospel is not true historically, it is not true at all: 'If Christ be not raised, your faith is vain'"; and while he mellowed with advancing years, he never wavered in his deep religious convictions, nor for a moment relaxed the tenacious grasp which he had of the doctrines of Christianity as set forth in the standards of the Reformed Churches. One of his latest sayings was, "I die in the faith which I have always professed."

From his *Alma Mater* the Professor had received the degree of D.D. in 1862, and in 1892 the University of Glasgow conferred upon him the degree of LL.D. in recognition of his eminence as a teacher and an author. A young minister of the Church, himself one of his most distinguished students, has drawn a picture of him as he appeared about the latter of these dates, which is so true to the life that no excuse is needed for introducing it here. He says: " St Andrews and Professor Mitchell are inseparable. For forty-four years he has taught in the University: first the Hebrew Tongue; next the History of the Church of Christ. As a Professor, Dr Mitchell comes into contact with a comparatively small number of students. The classes in St Mary's are diminutive—in some ways a source of much gratification to the writer and others — consequently he is little known by most men here. Of course, all are familiar with the Figure pacing the town in the bright of the forenoon; or, arm-in-arm with a youthful Professor, walking as far as the Swilcan; or, at a Graduation Ceremony, scanning the audience, if perhaps he may get a glimpse of some old pupil among the crowd of interested spectators. For many of his students have risen high: and some of them have a weight of years to bear. But all are not aware that in the Church History Class-Room English is spoken as she is nowhere else in St Andrews. The beautifully rounded and perfectly balanced sentences, and the elegance of the language, will hardly be excelled. To make the study of Church History what is called popular is one of the few impossibilities of life, but there is no man living who can invest the subject with more interest;

for Professor Mitchell is thoroughly up to date with all his facts, and loses no opportunity of visiting the great German authorities. . . . To be re-proved in class by the Professor is not to be desired : to be 'spoken to' in his ante-room still less so. Many men stand in awe of him—I have always thought unnecessarily so."

The Professor continued to take a warm interest in his students after they had left the Divinity Hall, and had entered on the work of the ministry ; and when attending the General Assembly he could generally tell how many of its members had passed through one or other of his classes in St Mary's College. When he retired from the duties of his Chair in 1894, the occasion was regarded as affording a suitable opportunity of giving public expression to the esteem in which he was held by his friends, and to their grateful appreciation of his services both to the Church and the University; and in 1895, while the General Assembly was in session, he was presented, in name of a large number of his former students and other friends, with an illuminated address, a cheque for 200 guineas, and his portrait by Sir George Reid —acknowledged to be one of the best that have yet come from the studio of the President of the Royal Scottish Academy. The Right Hon. James A. Campbell of Stracathro, M.P., with whom he had long had intimate relations, presided at the ceremony and made the presentation. The reply of the Professor, as containing many interesting reminiscences, and as showing the view which he took himself of his life and work, is here inserted *in extenso*.   He said :—

"Mr Campbell, I thank you, sir, with all my heart, for the many kind things—far more kind than I deserve—which you have just said of me, and for the many kind services which you have rendered to me in the course of our lifelong friendship; and I thank, with all my heart, you, my many esteemed friends and pupils, who have united in presenting me with this address ex-pressive of your warm affection, this speaking likeness and munificent gift.   Kindness far more than I have merited has followed me all my life through—never more conspicuously than at the close of my public career; and now in retiring from the professorial work I loved, and from the College for which almost for half a century I lived and laboured, it is a consolation to me to know that I carry with me into my retirement the esteem of so many honoured friends and the affectionate regard of so many former pupils. Some have been speaking lately of the loneliness of a Scottish student's college life.   I can only say for myself that the years I spent as a student in St Mary's College were among the happiest of my life, and that the friendships then formed within the little band of my fellow-students were among the most valued and lasting of those I have enjoyed.   I have but to name John Robert-son, afterwards minister of Glasgow Cathedral;

John Tulloch, afterwards Principal of St Mary's
College; William Milligan, afterwards Professor
of Biblical Criticism in Aberdeen; William Dick-
son, afterwards Professor of Divinity in Glasgow;
Drs W. H. Gray, Gloag, and Herdman, and with
these some who afterwards joined the Free
Church: Dr Thomson, long at the head of the
Free Church Jewish Mission at Constantinople;
Dr Thomas Brown, younger brother of my late
colleague, Dr William Brown, agent for the
Turkish Missions Aid Society; and Edward
Cross, afterwards Free Church minister at Moni-
fieth, with whom I laboured in happiest intercourse in Dundee, he being assistant to the
Free Church minister in the same district of
the town when I was assistant to the Parish
minister. When in my twenty-sixth year I returned as a Professor in the College where so
shortly before I had been a student, I can never
forget the kindness with which I was received
by my aged instructors there, especially by Principal Haldane, whose kind counsels were then
invaluable to me, nor the kindness of Professors
Duncan and Alexander, the only two of my instructors remaining in the Old College. St
Andrews about that time had the reputation of
being rather a hot place. The conviction that
I was a man of rather placid temper, who would
not add fuel to the flame, I believe weighed considerably with Lord Advocate Rutherfurd in
finally recommending me for the Chair. Within

St Mary's College we were a happy family, and the youth of twenty-six and the two aged Professors beyond threescore and ten continued to work in unbroken harmony—the youth deeming it a special privilege to aid the venerable Principal in his class-work during the last year of his life, as well as to aid him and his aged colleague in their pulpit work. It was soon after this that I began to take an active part in Church work, attending the General Assembly as an elder and as Convener of the Jewish Mission—doing what I could to reorganise it in Turkey, first in conjunction with such venerable fathers as Drs Muir, Hunter, Grant, and James Robertson, and with several brethren nearer my own age, who were bearing the burden and heat of the day — Drs Crawford, Nicholson, Nisbet, William Robertson, and Elder Cumming, and such laymen as Sheriff Arkley, David Smith, Henry Cheyne, John Elder, John Tawse, and the good Edmund Baxter, all now gone to their rest and their reward. Principal Haldane was succeeded by my old class-fellow, Principal Tulloch, in harmony with whom I wrought for thirty years in the College, occasionally taking part of his work, as I had of his predecessor's, when he was laid aside by ill-health, and also taking part with him in Church work, especially in the work of the Anti - Patronage Committee, on whose success so many in the Church had set their hearts. After his untimely removal, though I had served for seven or eight

years beyond the statutory thirty, I continued at
my post, and in the most kind and cordial relations both in Church and University work with
his successor, Principal Cunningham, heartily
co-operating with him in the repeal of what has
been termed the Black Act of 1711, and in the
restitution of the old formula for ministers and
elders, which are now so generally welcomed,
and have been acknowledged by one at least of
the three who protested against the change to
be a great boon. I have often spoken of the
pleasure I have had in superintending the work
of my students, and my gratification at the zest
with which they took to the study both of Hebrew and Church History. The circumstances
which led to my resignation are already well
known to you all, and I need only say that it was
to me a very regretful necessity. I leave in each
of the three other Divinity Faculties at least one
distinguished pupil, and in St Mary's College two
who, with their younger colleagues, I trust will
strive to make it more than ever a School of the
Prophets, a nursery for earnest, faithful, scholarly,
and devoted ministers, who shall set high above
all passing isms Christ the personal Saviour, and
those great truths as to His divine nature, incarnation, atoning death, and glorious resurrection,
to which the historic Church of Christ through
so many centuries has clung as her life and
strength and joy. Christ before, Christ behind,
—according to St Patrick's prayer,—Christ above,

Christ beneath, Christ in the heart, Christ in the home. I heartily thank you all for your great kindness, and especially Principal Stewart and Mr Wenley, and one who once said I had been as a father to him, and of whom I may truly say that he has been as a son to me."

In 1852 the Professor married the eldest daughter of the late Mr Michael Johnstone of Archbank, near Moffat, who belonged to an influential yeoman family that has been connected with Annandale for the last two hundred years. The late Mr Peter Johnstone, brother of Mrs Mitchell's father, who was a proprietor as well as a large farmer, is still remembered as having done a great deal to promote the cause of education in the district where he resided; and her brother, the late Mr James Johnstone, was tenant of Bodsbeck farm, which is the scene of the Ettrick Shepherd's well-known Covenanting story—" The Brownie of Bodsbeck." How much Mrs Mitchell did to brighten the life and to minister to the happiness of the Professor can be known only to those who have had the privilege of being admitted into the inner circle of their friends, and there are not a few who have very pleasant reminiscences of delightful intercourse with them in their house at 56 South Street, where the duty of entertaining strangers seemed never to be forgotten. Their family of four sons and two daughters all survive, with the exception of the eldest son, Robert Haldane, who died several years ago in Australia, to which he had emigrated along with his brother Johnstone.

Probably few are aware that the Professor spent many of his happiest days, and did much of his literary work, at Gowanpark, his country residence near Brechin, which, with its charm of seclusion and restfulness, no one who has visited it can ever forget, and which his family came to regard as their home almost as much as St Andrews. There he found relaxation in the interest which he took in the work of his little farm, which was his own property, and as long as he had health he enjoyed a ramble among the neighbouring hills, or a walk, varied by an occasional drive, along the quiet country roads. His home in the country, however, was with him no mere place of recreation, still less of idleness, and there, as elsewhere, he never failed to find his chief source of pleasure in the prosecution of his favourite studies.

When the Professor retired from the duties of his Chair he did not cease to take an interest in the affairs of the College, of which he was an ornament while he lived, and with which, as was said in a notice of him at the time of his death, his name will always be associated—like those of Andrew Melville, Samuel Rutherford, and others in remote and troublous times, and that of Principal Tulloch in our own more peaceful days. Nor did he cease to interest himself in the work of the Church which he loved so well and had served so faithfully. Perhaps it was to show his love for

the Church as much as to gratify his own feelings
that, amid great bodily infirmity, he undertook
the journey to Edinburgh, in May 1898, to attend
the General Assembly. He was unable, indeed,
to be present there more than once or twice, and
when on one occasion he occupied the Moderator's chair for a few minutes, a thrill of respectful
sympathy passed through the House. In a letter
written a few days after his return home he says,
"I am very pleased to have been able to give
even such limited attendance," adding, with a
touch of pathos, as if anticipating that the visit
would be his last, "in the fiftieth year since Mr
John Tulloch and Alex. F. Mitchell were first
returned as members."

Soon afterwards he removed to his loved retreat
at Gowanpark, but his health did not improve,
and he was but seldom able to leave the house.
Most of the letters he wrote at this time, some of
them in pencil, with his head resting on the pillow,
were evidently intended to be his parting words
to those to whom they were addressed. In one
of these, written in the middle of September, he
says, "For the first fortnight after I came here
I was able to go out of doors, and in my invalid
chair bask in the sun for an hour a-day. I am
still keeping my bed in the hope of being able
to return without risk to St Andrews in the end
of the month;" and then, alluding to a subject
his interest in which seems to have helped to
keep him alive, he says, "I have got five of

my six Baird Lectures transcribed. Of course I must get some one to read them for me."

When he returned to St Andrews, the burden of his infirmities grew heavier, and as the spring approached it was manifest that he was nearing the end. He was greatly affected by the tidings of the tragic death of Dr Boyd, who had paid him a visit shortly before his departure for the south. On the Monday before he died he re- peated the words of the second paraphrase in a clear, strong voice, and quoted almost the last recorded words of St Paul, " I have fought a good fight, I have finished my course, I have kept the faith." On Tuesday evening he desired some one to sing to him, and as Miss Mitchell was unable to control her feelings to do so, Mr Smith, his amanuensis, who had come in, was asked by him to sing " Jesus, Lover of my Soul." When this was done he turned to Miss Mitchell, and said, " What would you like ? " and they sang together " Rock of Ages." With uncomplaining patience he had suffered much, but welcome rest came to him on the morning of Wednesday, 22nd March. Having served his own generation by the will of God, he fell asleep amid the tender regrets of his family, leaving behind him a memory that will always be held in honour, and an example of laborious service, of deep piety, and of fervent trust in Christ.

In compliance with his own wish, his remains were conveyed to Brechin, where they were laid to rest beside those of his fathers under the shadow of the old Cathedral, the members of the local Presbytery, in token of their respect, being present on the occasion. "The world passeth away, and the lust thereof: but he that doeth the will of God abideth for ever."

GILMERTON MANSE, *December* 1899.

THE SCOTTISH REFORMATION.

CHAPTER I.

THE NATURE AND NEED OF THE REFORMATION.

WITH the single exception of the period which covers the introduction and first marvellous triumphs of Christianity, the Reformation of the sixteenth century must be owned as perhaps the greatest and most glorious revolution in the history of the human race. And the years of earnest contendings and heroic sufferings which prepared the way for its triumph in many lands and issued in its cruel suppression in others, and the story of the men who by God's grace were enabled to bear the brunt of the battle and to lead their countrymen on to victory or to martyrdom, will ever have a fascination for all in whose hearts

A

faith in the great truths, then more clearly brought to light, has not yet altogether evaporated. The movement then initiated was no mere effort to get quit of acknowledged scandals, which had long been grieved over but never firmly dealt with ; no mere desire to lop off a few later accretions, which had gathered round and obscured the faith once delivered to the saints ;[1] no mere "return to the Augustinian, or the Nicene, or the Ante - Nicene age," but a vast progress beyond any previous age since the death of St John—a

[1] As Lord Acton has so well said, "The modern age did not proceed from the medieval by normal succession, with outward tokens of legitimate descent.   Unheralded, it founded a new order of things, under a law of innovation, sapping the ancient reign of continuity.   In those days Columbus subverted the notions of the world, and reversed the conditions of production, wealth, and power. . . . Luther broke the chain of authority and tradition at the strongest link ; and Copernicus erected an invincible power that set for ever the mark of progress upon the time that was to come.   .   .   . It was an awakening of new life ; the world revolved in a different orbit, determined by influences unknown before.   After many ages, persuaded of the headlong decline and impending dissolution of society, and governed by usage and the will of masters who were in their graves, the sixteenth century went forth armed for untried experience, and ready to watch with hopefulness a prospect of incalculable change " (Lecture on the Study of History, 1895, pp. 8, 9). "There are no true 'cycles' in human development; history never repeats itself; the Greco-Roman world has only distant analogies with the Feudal-Catholic world, just as this has only distant analogies with the Revolutionary world.   The great phases of human civilisation are contrasted rather than compared ; they differ as infancy, childhood, manhood, and senility differ in the individual" (Harrison on "Freeman's Method of History," in the 'Nineteenth Century' for November 1898).

deeper plunge into the meaning of revelation than had been made by Augustine, or Anselm, or St Bernard, or À Kempis, or Wycliffe, or Tauler. Its object was to get back to the divine sources of Christianity,—to know, and understand, and appropriate it as it came fresh and pure from the lips of the Son of God and His inspired apostles, not excluding that chosen vessel to whom the grace had been given " to preach among the Gentiles the unsearchable riches of Christ." It was, in fact, a return to the old Gospel so attractively set forth by him in his Epistles, and verified to the reformers by their own inmost spiritual experience under deep convictions of sin and shortcoming. The cry of their awakened consciences had been, How shall we sinners have relief from our load and be justified before God ? And this, as has been said, was just the old question put to the apostle himself by the jailer at Philippi, What must I do to be saved ? And the answer their own experience warranted them with one accord to proclaim was still, Believe in the Lord Jesus Christ, believe in the riches of His pardoning mercy, in the merit of His atoning death, in the freeness and power of His efficacious grace. By believing, however, they meant, and were careful to explain that they meant, not a mere intellectual assent to the truth of the facts, but such an assent as drew with it the trust of the heart and the personal surrender of the soul to Christ ; or—to use language of somewhat later origin—the individual *appropriation* of the freely offered Saviour, with all His fulness of blessing, pardon, and righteousness by His one offering once offered, and renewal into His own image by the continuous indwelling of His Holy Spirit.

Such was the animating principle which gave power to the teaching of the reformers in all lands, and which constitutes still the central article of a standing or a falling church to all their true-hearted successors—Christ crucified for our sins, raised again for our justification, and now exalted to the right hand of the Majesty in the heavens as Prince and Saviour, to give repentance and remission of sin and all needed grace to those who thus believe in Him, and are brought into union with Him. And the Reformed Church will never perish or decay while it continues to set forth this Gospel, and is honoured by its divine Head to bring it home to the hearts and consciences of men, with the same power as its first teachers were honoured with in the brave days of old. For it must never be forgotten, I repeat, that the Reformation movement was not only the introduction of a more scriptural and scientific method of exhibiting Christian doctrine, and simple unfolding of its teaching

as to man's fallen state and the remedy their
heavenly Father had in His love provided for
them; not only the reassertion of the supremacy
of the written Word of God over human tradi-
tions, as well as of the right of all Christian men
and women to have direct access to that blessed
Word; not only the translation into the vernacular—German, English, Danish, Dutch, French,
Italian, Spanish—and the circulation throughout
Western Europe of that which for ages had been
to the Christian laity as a book that is sealed;
but it was also, above all this, the infusion of a
new and higher life into the churches. We fall
short of a full comprehension of the movement
if we fail to recognise that the God of all grace
and blessing was then pleased to "send a plentiful rain to confirm His inheritance when it was
weary," to grant a second Pentecost to the church,
to make the people willing in the day of His
power, and to pour out His Spirit in rich abundance upon men.

With all the conscious and unconscious preparation which had paved the way for them, the
men who were God's chosen instruments at that
crisis were made deeply to feel and humbly to
own that it was God Himself who had led them
on—at times by ways they had not thought of;
that it was He who had upheld them in their
extremity when all human power seemed to be

arrayed against them; that it was He who, when their resources were exhausted, was pleased, in the day when they cried unto Him, to hear their prayer and revive their hopes by the plentiful outpouring of His Spirit. How feelingly this was acknowledged by Luther at various crises in his life is known to all who are in any measure acquainted with his thrilling story. No one could have more constantly in his heart or more frequently on his lips the Hebrew psalmist's song of holy confidence, "God is our refuge and strength, a very present help in trouble. Therefore will not we fear, though the earth be removed, and though the mountains be carried into the midst of the sea. . . . There is a river, the streams whereof shall make glad the city of God." There was also that other which, under reverses and discouragements, was the solace of our own reformer, "If it had not been the Lord who was on our side, when men rose up against us: then they had swallowed us up quick. . . . Blessed be the Lord, who hath not given us as a prey to their teeth." As they mused the fire burned and found expression in such songs of holy confidence as—

> "A sure stronghold our God is He,
>   A trusty shield and weapon;
>   Our help He'll be, and set us free
>   Whatever ill may happen.

.   .   .   .

Through our own force we nothing can,
　Straight were we lost for ever,
But for us fights the proper Man,
　By God sent to deliver.
　　　Ask ye who this may be?
　　　Christ Jesus named is He,
　　　Of Sabaoth the Lord
　　　Sole God to be adored,
'Tis He must win the battle." [1]

" If God were not upon our side
　When foes around us rage,
Were not Himself our help and guide
　When bitter war they wage,
Were He not Israel's mighty shield,
To whom their utmost crafts must yield,
　We surely must have perished." [2]

By the time at which reforming influences began manifestly to show themselves in Scotland, that grand medieval organisation, which had supplanted the simpler arrangements of the old Celtic church, had in its turn exhausted its life powers, and shown unmistakable signs of deep-seated corruption and hopeless decay. Whatever good it may have been honoured to do in times past,—in keeping alive the knowledge of God and of things divine in the midst of "a darkness which might be felt," in promoting a higher civilisation than the Celtic, in alleviating the evils of the feudalism which Anglo-Norman settlers

[1] Miss Winkworth's Christian Singers of Germany, pp. 110, 111.
[2] Ibid., p. 117.

had brought in, in founding parishes and universities and some other institutions which, with
a purified church and revived Christian life, were
to be a source of blessing after it was swept away,
—yet now at last it had grossly failed to keep alive
among the common people true devotion, or to
give access to the sources at which the flame
might have been rekindled; it had failed to provide educated men for its ordinary cures, to raise
the masses from the rudeness and ignorance in
which they were still involved, and even to maintain that hearty sympathy with them and that
kindly interest in their temporal welfare which its
best men in its earlier days had shown. It continued to have its services in a language which
had for ages been unintelligible to the bulk of the
laity, and was but partially intelligible to not a
few of its ordinary priests. It had no catechisms
or hymn books bringing down to the capacities
of the unlettered the truths of religion, and freely
circulated among them.[1]   It did not, when the
invention of printing put it in its power, make
any effort to circulate among them the Holy
Book, that they might read therein, in their own
tongue, the message of God's love.   No doubt it
had its pictures and images, its mystery plays and

[1] [Hamilton's Catechism, which was not intended for indiscrim-
inate circulation among the laity, was not published until 1552;
and The Twopenny Faith was not issued until the spring of 1559.]

ceremonies, which it deemed fit books for children and the unlearned. But it forgot that these
children were growing in capacity, even if allowed
to grow up untrained; that " to credulous simplicity was succeeding a spirit of eager curiosity,
an impatience of mere authority, and a determination to search into the foundation of things";
and that, if it was to maintain its place, it must
not only keep abreast but ahead of advancing
intelligence and morality. But the old church
began greatly to decline just as the laity began
to rise. Bishop Kennedy, I suppose, was almost
its last preaching bishop; and the character of
the preaching, so far as preaching was still continued by the friars and some of the inferior
clergy, was not generally fitted to supply the lack
of Bibles and catechisms, and other vernacular
books of instruction. It never grappled, as it
ought, with the problem of lightening the burdens
it had long exacted of the peasantry; but refused
almost to the last moment to ease even the most
galling of them. It never grappled, as it ought,
with the problem of the education of the masses;
and what was done for those of the community
in more fortunate circumstances was done more
by the efforts of a few noble-minded individuals
than by any corporate action of Church or State.
There is not among all its codes of canons anything approaching to the clear ringing utterances

of our First Book of Discipline concerning the
necessity and advantages of education.[1]

Not only had the life powers of the medieval
church been exhausted and decay set in, but
corruption, positive and gross corruption, had
reached an alarming height. There were the indolence and neglect of duty which wealth too
often brings in its train; the covert secularising
of that wealth, just as in the old Celtic church,
by various devices, to get it into the hands of
unqualified men and minors; luxury, avarice,
oppression, simony, shameless pluralities, and
crass ignorance; and above all that celibate system, which nothing would persuade them honestly
to abandon, though it had proved to be a yoke
they could not bear, and was producing only too
generally results humiliating and disastrous to
themselves and to all who came under their influence. The proof of this does not rest merely
or even mainly on the statements of Knox,
Alesius, and Spottiswood, nor on the representa-
tions of Lindsay and the Wedderburns. The
fact, as both the late Dr David Laing and Dr
Joseph Robertson have shown, and the late
Bishop Forbes has sorrowfully acknowledged, is
confessed and deplored in the canons of their
councils, in the Acts of the Scottish Parliament,

---

[1] [For these utterances see *infra*, chap. viii. sec. iv.]

and in the writings of their own best men.[1] The harsh measures to which men themselves so vulnerable had recourse to maintain their position, the relentless cruelties they perpetrated on men of unblemished character, amiable disposition, deep-seated conviction and thorough Christian earnestness, could not fail in the end to turn the tide against them, and arouse feelings of indignation which on any favourable opportunity would induce the nation to sweep them away.

The corruptions in the doctrine of the church were hardly less notable than those in the lives of its clergy.　The sufficiency and supremacy of

[1] Because of its permanent importance, I deem it best to insert here a note from my Introduction to ' The Gude and Godlie Ballatis,' p. lxiv : " We do not need to call in Knox, or Lindsay, or the satirists, in evidence of this humbling fact.　The testimony of their own councils, of the Acts of Parliament, and of some of their best men, as Principal Hay in his congratulatory address to Cardinal Betoun, and Ninian Winzet in the sad appeals and confessions inserted in his ' Tractates,' as well as that of impartial modern historians like Tytler and Dr Joseph Robertson, is more than sufficient to establish it beyond contradiction.　The testimony of Conæus, who died when about to be raised to the purple, covers almost all that Alesius and Knox have averred : ' In multorum sacerdotum aedibus scortum publicum . . . nec a sacrilego quorundam luxu tutus erat matronarum honos aut virginalis pudor.'　More notable still is the representation given in the ' Memoire ' addressed to the Pope by Queen Mary and the Dauphin, evidently at the instance of Mary of Guise, in which the spread of heresy is expressly attributed to the ignorance and immorality of the clergy.　See Appendix B, vol. ii., of Mr Hume Brown's recent biography of Knox."

the written Word of God were denied, and co-ordinate authority was claimed for tradition. The Virgin Mary and the saints departed were asserted to share the office which Scripture reserves for the one Mediator between God and man. Penances and other external acts of work-righteousness were alleged to co-operate in the pardon of sin with the "one obedience" by which "many are made righteous." The sacraments were asserted to produce their effect *ex opere operato*,—not by the working of the Spirit in them that by faith receive them. Belief in the literal transubstantiation of the bread and wine in the Lord's Supper was rigidly enforced and substituted for that spiritual presence and spiritual manducation which the earlier church had maintained. The doctrine of a purgatory after this life was invented, and the virtue of masses for the dead therein detained was persistently taught and required to be believed. The Roman church was affirmed to be the mother and mistress of the churches, and its head to be the successor of St Peter and the Vicar of Christ.

Yet it must never be forgotten that, even in these degenerate days, there were those among the ministers of the church who wept in secret over the abominations that were done, who longed for the dawn of a better day, and, in their parishes or cloisters or colleges, sought to prepare the way for it, and who succeeded in doing so with many of their younger comrades, and only made up their minds in the end to abandon the old church when all their efforts for its revival proved vain. Nay, the men who initiated and carried to a successful issue the struggle for a more thorough reformation than the others desired, the martyrs, confessors, and exiles, were almost all from the ranks of the priesthood of the old church—from the regular as well as from the secular priesthood; from the Dominican and Franciscan monasteries as well as from the Augustinian abbeys; and from none more largely than the Augustinian Priory of St Andrews, and the College of St Leonard founded in connection with it, notwithstanding that its prior for the time being was so far from what he ought to have been. At least twenty priests joined the reformed congregation of St Andrews in 1559-60, and among them more than one who had sat in judgment on the martyrs and assisted in their condemnation.[1] A much larger number were ultimately admitted as readers in the Reformed Church.

[1] [So early as the 23rd of June 1559, Knox wrote to Mrs Anna Lock : " Diverse channons of Sanct Andrewes have given notable confessiouns, and have declared themselves manifest enemies to the pope, to the masse, and to all superstitioun " (Laing's Knox, vi. 26). In all probability some of these canons were included among the fourteen canons of St Andrews Priory who are mentioned as Protestants in January 1571-72, and of whom twelve were then parish

How was the great revolution which was to bring the church back from these corruptions of life and doctrine prepared for? Ebrard supposes that witnesses for holy living and simple faith, but partially connected with the dominant church, were never from Celtic times entirely wanting in Britain; and it may have been that, through Richard Rolle and a few other hermits, the feeble spark in the smoking wick continued to smoulder on till it was blown into a flame by Wycliffe. At any rate it was blown into a flame by him and his poor priests; and from their time witness after witness arose to contend for the right of the laity to read the Word of God, and to maintain that men were saved by the merits of Christ and should pray to Him alone, that there was no purgatory in the popish sense, and that the pope was not the Vicar of Christ. Wycliffe's poor

ministers ('Booke of the Universall Kirk,' Bannatyne Club, i. 222). None of these fourteen is found signing the General Band of 13th July 1559, which in St Andrews was adopted as "the letters of junctioun to the Congregatioun"; but eighteen priests did sign it; and of the other thirteen ecclesiastics who there made sweeping recantations, at least six may be held to have joined the congregation, for they not only confessed that "we haif ower lang abstractit ourselfis and beyne sweir in adjuning us to Christes Congregatioun," but they promised "in tyme cuming to assist in word and wark with unfenyiet mynde this Congregatioun" ('Register of St Andrews Kirk-Session,' Scot. Hist. Soc., i. 10-18). In 1573 it was stated that "the most part of the persons who were channons monks and friars within this realme have made profession of the true religion" ('Booke of the Universall Kirk,' i. 280).]

priests, when persecuted in the south, naturally
sought shelter among the moors and mosses of
the north. The district of Kyle and Cunningham
was "a receptakle of Goddis servandis of old,"
where their doctrines were cherished till the dawn
of the Reformation. In 1406 or 1407 James
Resby, one of these priests, is found teaching as
far north as Perth, and for his teaching he was
accused and condemned to a martyr's death. A
similar fate is said to have befallen another in
Glasgow about 1422, in all probability the Scottish Wycliffite whose letter to his bishop has
recently been unearthed in a Hussite MS. at
Vienna ; and in 1433 Paul Craw or Crawar, a
Bohemian, for disseminating similar opinions,
was burned at the market cross in St Andrews.
These were not in all probability the only grim
triumphs of Laurence, Abbot of Lindores, one of
the first rectors in the University of St Andrews,
who during so many years "gave no rest to
heretics," but they are all of whom records have
been preserved to our time. The fact that every
Master of Arts in the University of St Andrews
had to take an oath to defend the church against
the Lollards,[1] and the other fact that the Scottish
Parliament in 1425 enjoined that every bishop
should make inquiry anent heretics and Lollards,

---

[1] [Enacted by the University on 10th June 1416 (M'Crie's Melville, 1824, i. 420).]

and that where any such were found, they should be punished as the law of holy church requires,[1] speak more significantly of the alarm they had occasioned than these sporadic martyrdoms. Still more, perhaps, does the abuse Fordun, or rather his continuator, heaps on them, bear witness to the alarm they had caused. Yet at the very close of the century, and in the old haunt, we find no fewer than thirty processed, and through the kindness of the king more gently dealt with than the ecclesiastical authorities wished; three of the most resolute — namely, Campbell of Cessnock, his noble wife, and a priest who officiated as their chaplain and read the New Testament to them — being released when at the stake.

Reforming tendencies in the sixteenth century, it has been said, first showed themselves in Scotland in the reassertion of "those principles, catholic but anti-papal," which had been maintained in the preceding century in the Councils of Constance and Basle. The decisions of the former were received in Scotland in 1418, and allegiance to Benedict XIII. was finally renounced.[2] A Scottish doctor[3] had taken a rather prominent

---

[1] [Enacted by Parliament on 12th March 1424-25 (Acts of Parliament, ii. 7).]

[2] Robertson's Concilia Scotiæ, vol. i. p. lxxviii.

[3] [For an account of this Scottish cleric—Thomas, Abbot of Dundrennan—who so greatly distinguished himself at the Council of Basle, see 'Concilia Scotiæ,' vol. i. pp. xcvii-xcix.]

part in the proceedings of the latter, though the Scottish Church, like the others, ultimately fell away from that council and the pope elected by it, and under Bishop Kennedy was reconciled to the Roman See and to Pope Eugenius.[1] Scotland had had no Grosteste, no Anselm or Bradwardine among its prelates in the middle ages, no Wycliffe among its priests. Duns Scotus, the one theologian before the sixteenth century who claimed Scottish birth and European fame, never seems to have taught in his native land. Chief among its doctors in the beginning of the sixteenth century stood John Major, a native of East Lothian, who taught with distinguished success, first in Paris, then in Glasgow, after that in St Andrews, then once more in Paris, and finally in St Andrews again. Melanchthon, while ridiculing his scholastic ways, places him at the head of the doctors of the Sorbonne. The remembrance of his early labours in Montaigu College had not died out when Calvin entered it, and probably he had returned to it before Calvin left. Patrick Hamilton and Buchanan may possibly have been brought into contact with him while there, as they, Alesius, and John

---

[1] [The bull of Eugenius the Fourth, addressed to Bishop Kennedy, and dated 6th July 1440, orders the excommunication of the followers of the anti-pope, Felix the Fifth, elected by the Council of Basle, to be published in Scotland (Ibid., p. c.)]

Wedderburn afterwards were in St Andrews, and John Hamilton and Knox in Glasgow. He was a true disciple of D'Ailly and Gerson, but like them was warmly attached to the dominant church and opposed to the heretics of his time. He taught, as they had done, that the church, assembled in general council, may judge and even depose a pope and reform abuses in the church; that papal excommunications have no force unless conformed to justice, and do not necessarily prevent a man who dies under them from going to heaven. He sharply censured the vices of the Roman court, and of the bishops and clergy of his time, particularly those of his native land. He is especially severe in censuring their immorality and ignorance; and, like Wycliffe, condemns the monks and friars for inveigling into their order young novices who had no vocation for a celibate life, and ought rather to have been encouraged to enter into honest wedlock. But he was a stern opponent of heresy—Lutheran as well as Wycliffite—a subtle defender of Roman doctrine; and in dedicating to Archbishop Betoun his Commentary on St Matthew's Gospel, he congratulated him on the success of his cruel measures against Hamilton and the heretics.[1]

---

[1] [Dr Mitchell, no doubt, had the Commentary itself before him. Those who have not access to it will find the dedication in the Appendix to Constable's 'Major,' Scot. Hist. Soc., pp. 447, 448.]

CHAPTER II.

PATRICK HAMILTON.

IT has not been very clearly ascertained how or when the opinions and writings of Luther were first introduced into Scotland. M. de la Tour, who in 1527 suffered in Paris for heresy, was accused of having vented various Lutheran opinions while in Edinburgh in attendance on the Duke of Albany. This, of course, must have been before 1523. On the 9th June 1523, the same day that John Major was received as Principal of the Pædagogium, or St Mary's College,[1] Patrick Hamilton was incorporated into the University of St Andrews;[2] and on 3rd October 1524 he

---

[1] See Appendix A.

[2] [The entry in the Register of the University occurs at the bottom of a page, and is preceded and followed by entries of 1521, as if it had been inserted there to save space. The entries of 1521 are distinct and easily read, but in this of 1523 the ink is very faint, and the surface of the vellum has a rubbed appearance. It runs thus : " Die nono mensis Junii anno Domini I^m V^c xxiij incorporatus erat venerabilis vir Magister noster Magister Johannes Major doctor

was admitted as a member of the Faculty of
Arts. If he did not from the latter date act as
a regent in the University, he probably took
charge of some of the young noblemen or gentle-
men attending the classes. At that date he was
probably more Erasmian than Lutheran, though
of that more earnest school who were ultimately
to outgrow their teacher, and find their congenial
home in a new church.

Patrick Hamilton was born in 1503 or 1504 at
Stonehouse in Lanarkshire, or at Kincavel near
Linlithgow. His father, a natural son of the
first Lord Hamilton, had been knighted for his
bravery, and rewarded by his sovereign with
the above lands and barony. His mother was
a daughter of Alexander, Duke of Albany, the
second son of James II., so that he had in
his veins the noblest blood in the land. His
cousins, John and James Hamilton, were in due
time raised to episcopal rank in the unreformed
church of Scotland, and several others of his
relations received high ecclesiastical promotion.
Marked out for a similar destiny, Patrick was
carefully educated, and, according to the corrupt
custom of the time, was in his fourteenth year
appointed to the Abbacy of Ferne in Ross-shire,

theologus in Parisiensis et thesaurarius capelle regis. Eodem die
incorporati sunt Magister Patricius Hamilton et Magister Robertus
Laudar in nostra Universite" (*sic*).]

to enable him to maintain himself in comfort while continuing his studies abroad. Like many of his aristocratic countrymen he went first to the University of Paris, and probably to the College of Montaigu, where Major, the great Scottish scholastic doctor, was then teaching with much *eclat,* and gathering round him there, as afterwards at St Andrews, an ardent band of youthful admirers, several of whom in the end were to advance beyond their preceptor, and to lend the influence of their learning and piety to the side of Luther and the reformers. Before the close of 1520 he took the degree of M.A. at the University of Paris, and soon after left Paris for Louvain, to avail himself of the facilities for linguistic studies provided there, or to enjoy personal intercourse with Erasmus, the patron of the new learning. He is said while there to have made great progress in the languages and in philosophy, and to have been specially attracted towards the philosophy of Plato. With the Sophists of Louvain, as Luther terms them, he could have had no sympathy. But there were some there, as well as at Paris, whose hearts God had touched, to whom he could not fail to be drawn. He may even have met with those Augustinian monks of Antwerp whom these Sophists so soon after his departure sent to heaven in a chariot of fire, and whose martyrdom un-

sealed in Luther's breast the fount of sacred
song. In the autumn of 1522, or the spring of
1523, he returned to Scotland, and, after a brief
visit to his relatives in Linlithgowshire, appears
to have come on to St Andrews. Probably,
along with Alesius, Buchanan, and John Wedderburn, he there heard those lectures on the Gospels which Major afterwards published in Paris
and dedicated to the Archbishop of St Andrews
and other prominent churchmen in Scotland.
But his sympathies were more with the young
canons of the Augustinian priory than with the
Old Scholastic; and probably it was that he
might take a place among the teachers of their
daughter college of St Leonard's that he was
received as a member of the Faculty of Arts.
Skilled in the art of sacred music, which the
alumni of that college were bound specially to
cultivate, he composed what the musicians call
a mass, arranged in parts for nine voices, and
acted himself as leader of the choir when it was
sung in the cathedral. He is said to have taken
on him the priesthood about this time, that he
might be formally admitted " to preach the word
of God." But he was not then of age for priests'
orders, and Dr David Laing is doubtful if he
was in orders at all, and certainly no mention
is made of his degradation from orders before
his martyrdom, and the final summons of Betoun

seems to imply that he had never been authorised to preach at all.

The years 1525 and 1526 were very unquiet
years in Scotland, various factions contending
with varying success for the possession of the
person of the young king. It was on the 17th
July of the former year that his Parliament passed
its first Act against the new opinions, in which,
after asserting that the realm had ever been clean
"of all sic filth and vice," it enacted, "that na
maner of persoun strangear that hapnis to arrife
with their schippis within ony part of this realm
bring with thaim ony bukis or werkis of the said
Lutheris his discipillis or servandis, desputt or
rehers his heresyis or opunyeouns bot geif [*i.e.*,
unless] it be to the confusioun therof, and that
be clerkis in the sculis alanerlie, under the pane
of escheting of ther schippis and gudis and putting of ther persouns in presoun."[1] In consequence of a letter from the pope, urging the
young king to keep his realm free from stain of
heresy, the scope of the Act was extended in 1527
by the chancellor and Lords of Council so that
it might apply to natives of the kingdom as well
as to strangers resorting to it for purposes of
commerce.[2]

---

[1] Acts of the Parliaments of Scotland, ii. 295.
[2] [The Act as thus extended was ratified on the 12th of June 1535
(Ibid., ii. 342).]

In 1526 the primate, Archbishop James Betoun, uncle of the cardinal, having taken a keen part in the political contentions of the day with the faction which lost, had to escape for a time from St Andrews, and, disguised as a shepherd, to tend a flock of sheep for three months on the hills of Fife, on the high grounds of Kennoway, immediately to the east of where the railway now reaches its summit level.[1] It was at this juncture that copies of the New Testament of Tyndale's translation were brought over from the Low Countries by the Scottish traders to the seaports of Aberdeen, Montrose, St Andrews, and Leith. Most of them are said to have been taken to St Andrews and put in circulation there in the absence of the archbishop. One was present there at that time who had long treasured the precious saying of Erasmus, "Let us eagerly read the Gospel, but let us not only read, but live the Gospel"; and who seized the golden opportunity to impress the saying on others, and invite longing souls to quench their thirst at those wells of living water which had so marvellously been opened to them for a season. During the months when the primate was in concealment, and in those which followed his return, Patrick Hamilton came out more earnestly than he had done before as an evangelist and an advocate of the great

[1] Pitscottie's History, 1778, p. 216; Lesley's History, p. 136.

truths, for which ultimately he was to be called to lay down his life. His conduct could not long escape the notice of the returned archbishop. I do not suppose that he was naturally cruel, nor after his recent misfortunes likely, without consideration, to embroil himself with the Hamiltons, with whom in the tortuous politics of the times he had often acted. But he had those about him who were less timid and more cruel, especially his nephew, the future cardinal. He was himself ambitious and crafty, and about this very time was exerting all his influence to obtain special favours from the pope without the sanction of the king.[1] He knew that the holy father had written the sovereign requiring him to keep his realm free from heresy, and no doubt he and his scheming nephew thought that by their zeal in this matter they would discredit the opposition of the king and his advisers to their ambitious schemes at the papal court. Still, he was anxious to perform the ungrateful task in the way least offensive to the Hamiltons. So while issuing his summons against the reformer to appear and answer the charges which had been brought against him, he did not at-

[1] Soliciting legatine powers over the whole of Scotland, instead of over his own province of the archdiocese, so as to render nugatory the exemption granted to the king's old tutor and favourite prelate the Archbishop of Glasgow.

tempt at once to restrain his personal liberty;
he would rather, if he could, rid the kingdom
of his presence without imbruing his hands in
his blood.   And that was the result actually
attained.

Some of Hamilton's opponents even, touched
by his youth, his illustrious descent, his engaging
manners and noble character, joined with his
friends in urging him to avoid by flight the
danger which impended.   He yielded to their
counsels, and, along with two friends and a servant, made his escape to the Continent.   The
story of his residence there has been graphic-
ally told by Principal Lorimer and Dr Merle
D'Aubigné; and the latter has the merit of explaining why Hamilton did not carry out his
original intention of visiting Luther and Melanchthon at Wittenberg, as well as Frith, Tyndale, and Lambert at Marbourg.   At the very
time he arrived on the Continent, the plague was
raging in Wittenberg.   "Two persons died of
it in Melanchthon's house."   Luther himself was
suddenly taken ill.   "All who could do so, and
especially the students, quitted the town." [1]   Thus
the absence of documents bearing on his alleged
sojourn at the Saxon university is naturally explained.   He went to the younger University of
Marbourg in Hesse, and prepared there, and

[1] D'Aubigné's Reformation in the Time of Calvin, vi. 42, 43.

publicly disputed, those theses that most fully
and systematically set forth the doctrines which
he mainly taught, and for which at last he suffered. He was warmly beloved by Lambert of
Avignon, who was then the most distinguished
theological professor in the infant university, as
well as by others with whom he was brought
into contact; and he would have been gladly
retained by them, could he have been persuaded
to remain in Germany: but his heart yearned
to return to his native land, and once more proclaim there the truths which had now become
to him more precious and engrossing than before.
His faith had been confirmed, and his spirit
quickened, by living for a time among earnest
and decided Christians; and in the autumn of
1527 he set out once more for Scotland, prepared for any fate that might await him, not
counting even life dear unto him if he might
finish his course with joy, and bear faithful witness to his Master's truth, where before he had
shrunk back from an ordeal so terrible. He appears first to have resorted to his native district,
and made known to relatives, friends, and neighbours about Linlithgow that Gospel of the grace
of God which gave strength and peace to his own
spirit. In his discourses and conversations he
dwelt chiefly on the great and fundamental truths
which had been brought into prominence by the

reformers, and avoided subjects of doubtful disputation. His own gentle bearing gained favour
for his opinions and success in his labours, and
it won for him the heart of a young lady of noble
birth, to whom he united himself in marriage,
following in this the example of Luther and others
of the German reformers.

Archbishop Betoun being then on the other
side of the Forth, in the neighbouring abbey of
Dunfermline, could not fail to hear of his doings
or to desire to silence him. But neither could
he fail, in the state of the political parties in
Scotland at the time, to recognise " that a heretic
with the power of the Hamiltons at his back was
more to be dreaded than Luther himself," and
must be dealt with very cautiously. It was long
supposed that, if not at the king's express desire,
as Bishop Lesley seems to suggest,[1] then certainly
from his own wariness, the archbishop did not
at first venture formally to renew his old summons, but invited the reformer to St Andrews
to a friendly conference with himself and other

---

[1] [The only passage, so far as I know, in which Lesley speaks
of the king in connection with the martyr is the following : " Suae
pertinaciae, ac flagitii poenas igni luebat, adhortante magno Catho-
licae Religionis protectore Rege ipso, quem et sanguinis propin-
quitate attigerat " (Lesley's ' De Origine,' 1578, p. 427 ; 1675, p.
407). This is rendered by Dalrymple : " For his obstinacie and
wickednes committed, he is burnte at command of the king selfe
gret Catholik protectour, to quhom Ferne als was neir of kin and
bluid " (Dalrymple's Lesley, Scot. Text Soc., ii. 215, 216).]

chiefs of the church on such points as might seem to stand in need of reform, and that Hamilton accepted the invitation. At first, it has been said, he was well received: "All of them displayed a conciliatory spirit; all appeared to recognise the evils in the church; some of them seemed even to share on some points the sentiments of Hamilton."[1] He left the conference not without hope of some other than the sad issue he had at first anticipated. He was permitted for nearly a month to move about with freedom in the city, to dispute in the schools of the university, and privately to confer with all who chose to resort to him at the lodging which had been provided for him. It was evidently the intention of those who were deepest in the plot against him, that he should have ample time allowed him to express his sentiments fully and unmistakably, and even should be tempted by dissemblers, like Friar Campbell, to unbosom himself in private on matters as to which he refrained from saying much in public—the many alterations required in doctrine and in the administration of the sacraments and accustomed rites.

It is said that the archbishop still desired that he should again save himself by flight, and there is nothing in the summons flatly inconsistent

[1] D'Aubigné's Reformation in the Time of Calvin, vi. 57.

with this ;[1] but he and his friends took the credit
of the terrible deed as promptly as if they had
planned and intended it from the first.   They
also assembled their armed retainers, that when
the days of truce had expired they might be able
to hold their prisoner against all attempts to
rescue him.   The reformer refused to flee, affirming that he had come to the city for the very
purpose of confirming, if need be, by the sacrifice
of his life, the doctrines he had taught.   He even
anticipated the time fixed for his appearance, and
had one more conference with the archbishop
and his doctors, who even then had come to a
formal decision that the articles charged against
him were heretical.   The same evening he was
seized and imprisoned in the castle, and next
day was brought out for public trial and condemnation in the Abbey Church or cathedral of
St Andrews.

---

[1] In an old manuscript book of forms used in ecclesiastical processes by the archbishops of St Andrews before the Reformation, I
found and have been able to decipher the recorded copy of the summons issued by Archbishop James Betoun against Hamilton after
his return from Germany.   It is addressed specially to the Dean of
the Lothians, and refers only to the preaching of the reformer in
West Lothian, so that there can no longer be any doubt that his
compearance in St Andrews before the date appointed in the summons must be regarded as a resolute avowal of his determination to
defend his teaching at all hazards.   The summons is inserted at
length in Appendix B.   [For an account of the manuscript Formu-
lare see Robertson's ' Concilia Scotiæ,' vol. i. pp. cxcv, cxcvi.]

Among the articles with which he was charged, and the truth of which he admitted and maintained, the most important were: "That a man is not justified by works, but by faith alone;" "That faith, hope, and charity are so linked together, that he who hath one of them hath all, and he that lacketh one lacketh all;" and "That good works make not a good man, but that a good man doth good works."[1]   On being challenged by his accuser with having avowed other heretical opinions, he affirmed it was not lawful to worship images or to pray to the saints; and maintained that "it is reason and lcisome to all men that have a soul to read the Word of God, and that they may understand the same, and in special the latter-will and testament of Christ Jesus."[2] These truths, which have been the source of life and strength to many, were to him the cause of condemnation and death; and on the last day of February 1527-28, the same day the sentence was passed, it was remorselessly executed before the gates of St Salvator's College. "Nobly," as I have said elsewhere, "did the martyr confirm the minds of the many godly youths he had gathered round him, by his resolute bearing, his gentleness and patience, his steadfast adherence to the truths he had taught, and his heroic endur-

---

[1] Spottiswoode's History, i. 124, 125.
[2] Pitscottie's History, 1778, p. 206.

ance of the fiery ordeal through which he had to pass to his rest and reward." The harrowing details of his six long hours of torture have been preserved for us by his friend Alesius, himself a sorrowing witness of the fearful tragedy. " He was rather roasted than burned," he tells us. It may be that his persecutors had not deliberately planned thus horribly to protract his sufferings— though such cruelty was not unknown in France, either then or in much later times. They were as yet but novices at such revolting work, and all things seemed to conspire against them. The execution had been hurried on before a sufficiency of dry wood had been provided for the fire. The fury of the storm, which had prevented the martyr's brother from crossing the Forth with troops to rescue him, was not yet spent. With a fierce wind from the east sweeping up North Street, it would be a difficult matter in such a spot to kindle the pile and keep it burning, or to prevent the flames, when fierce, from being so blown aside as to be almost as dangerous to the surrounding crowd as to the tortured victim. They did so endanger his accuser, the traitor Campbell, and " set fire to his cowl, and put him in such a fray, that he never came to his right mind." But, through all his excruciating suffer- ings, the martyr held fast his confidence in God and in his Saviour, and the faith of many in the truths he taught was only the more confirmed by witnessing their mighty power on him.[1]

[1] The older sources for the facts of Patrick Hamilton's career and martyrdom are the references to them by his friend Alesius in two or three of his works, and especially in his 'Commentary on the First Book of Psalms,' under Psalm xxxvii.; by Lambert in his 'Commentary on the Apocalypse'; and by Gau in the latter part of his treatise on 'The Richt Vay to the Kingdom of Heuine'; and after those by Foxe, Knox, Calderwood, Pitscottie, and Spottiswoode in their histories. The only satisfactory formal biography of him is that by Principal Lorimer entitled, 'Patrick Hamilton, the first Preacher and Martyr of the Scottish Reformation.' His story has also been told by Dr Merle D'Aubigné, in his own dramatic way; and still more recently it has been made the subject of a veritable drama by the Rev. T. P. Johnston, minister of Carnbee.

CHAPTER III.

THE OPPRESSED AND THE OPPRESSORS.

ARCHBISHOP BETOUN thought that by Patrick
Hamilton's death he had extinguished Lutheranism in Scotland. The University of Louvain
applauded his deed; and so also, I regret to say,
did John Major, the old Scottish Gallican, then
resident at Paris, and preparing for the press his
Commentary on the Gospels, the first part of
which was to be dedicated to his old patron in
Scotland, and was emphatically to express his
approval of what that patron had done to root out
the tares of Lutheranism.[1] But, according to the
well-known saying, "the reek of Patrick Hamilton
infected all on whom it did blow."[2] His martyr
death riveted for ever in the hearts of his friends

[1] *Supra*, p. 18, n.
[2] [The saying in slightly different forms may be found in Laing's
Knox, i. 42; Calderwood's History, i. 86; Spottiswoode's History,
i. 130.]

the truths he had taught in his life. This was
especially the case with the younger *alumni* in the
colleges, and the less ignorant and dissolute inmates of the priory and other monastic establishments in the city. As at a later period it was felt
certain that a stern Covenanter had been detected
when a suspected one refused to own that the
killing of Archbishop Sharp was to be regarded
as murder, so in these earlier days it was thought
a sufficient mark of an incipient Lutheran if he
could not be got to acknowledge that Hamilton
had deserved his fate. On the charge that he
had a copy of the English New Testament, and
had been heard to say that Hamilton was no heretic, Henry Forrest was subjected to a rigorous
imprisonment and a violent death. Forrest was
a native of the county of Linlithgow, and had
associated with Hamilton in St Andrews, and
was the first to share his bloody baptism there.
He was burned at the north kirk-style of the
Abbey Church, that the heretics of Angus might
see the fire and take warning from his fate.[1] One
for simply touching in his sermons with a firm
hand on the corruptions of the clergy had to
escape for his life.[2] Another, whose history after
being long forgotten has been again brought to

[1] [Various dates, ranging between 1529 and 1533, have been
assigned for Forrest's martyrdom.]

[2] [William Arth.]

light in our own day, for a similar offence was
subjected to cruel imprisonment, and at last forced
to flee from his native land.

The name of this confessor was Alexander Alane,
and it is so entered in the Registers of St Andrews
University; but it is by the name of Alexander
Alesius, imposed on him by Melanchthon, that he
has been chiefly known to posterity. It may
admit of some doubt whether he was absolutely
the first after the death of Hamilton to abandon
his country [1] and all he held dear, rather than
renounce the faith the martyr had taught him,
or crouch before the lecherous tyrant who had
destined him to a filthy dungeon and a lingering
death. But it admits of no doubt that he was
the most notable of all the band of young Scottish
exiles who had to leave their native country between the martyrdom of Hamilton and that of
Wishart, and who were honoured to do faithful
service in the cause of the Reformation in England and on the Continent. The story of Alesius,
of the shameless cruelties which drove him from
his native land, of the hardships he had to bear
in the earlier years of his exile, of the high place
he gained in the affections of Melanchthon and
Beza, and the great work he was to do by his writings and prelections for the Protestant churches
of Germany, is one of the most interesting in the

---

[1] [It was probably in 1530 that he left Scotland.]

great movement of the age. But to be appreciated it must be told in detail, and as most of his work was done out of Scotland, I have decided to reserve it for a supplementary lecture. I must not, however, omit to mention here one special service which he was honoured to do for the cause in his native land soon after he left it, as it casts fresh light on the origin of the Reformation in Scotland. His first publication, printed in 1533, was entitled 'Alexandri Alesii Epistola contra decretum quoddam episcoporum in Scotia, quod prohibet legere Novi Testamenti libros lingua vernacula.' It brought into bold relief, and set high above all minor issues, what had been taught by Wycliffe in the fourteenth century, and maintained by the Lollards of Kyle in the fifteenth, and what had actually been urged as an additional charge against Patrick Hamilton. Save for this epistle of Alesius, and the controversy it occasioned, we might not have known that even in ignorant Scotland the bishops had been so far left to themselves as to issue such a decree.[1] It

[1] [Howard and Barlo, in writing from Edinburgh on the 13th of May 1536, say, that to the Scots the reading of God's Word "in theyr vulgare tonge is lately prohybitede by open proclamation" (Lemon's State Papers, v. 48). Norfolk, writing to Crumwell from Berwick on the 29th of March 1539, says : "Dayly commeth unto me some gentlemen and some clerkes, wiche do flee owte of Scotland as they saie for redyng of Scripture in Inglishe ; saying that, if they were taken, they sholde be put to execution" (Ibid. v. 154). In the Epistle to James VI. prefixed to the Bassandyne

is still more melancholy to think that even among
the better informed controversialists of Germany
one was found to champion their cause, and to
maintain that there was nothing at variance with
sound doctrine in the decree; that nothing but
harm could come from the practice of allow-
ing laymen to read the Scriptures in their own
tongue; and that it could not fail to make them
bad Christians and bad subjects, as Luther's
translation had done in Germany.

From the time that Alesius fled from Scotland
down to the death of James V. in the end of
1542, there was almost continual inquisition made
for those who were suspected of having in their
possession heretical books, including the New
Testament in the vernacular, or who otherwise
betrayed a leaning towards the new opinions. In
1532, we are told, "there was ane greit objura-
tioun of the favouraris of Mertene Lutar in the
Abbay of Halyrudhous;"[1] and of course their
goods were forfeited to the crown. In 1534 a
second great assize against heretics was held in

Bible, it is said : "The false namit clergie of this realme, abusing
the gentle nature of your Hienes maist noble gudschir of worthie
memorie, made it an cappital crime to be punishit with the fyre
to have or rede the New Testament in the vulgare language."
One of the charges on which Sir John Borthwick was condemned,
on the 28th of May 1540, was that he possessed a copy of the New
Testament in the vernacular ('Register of St Andrews Kirk Session,'
Scot. Hist. Soc., i. 98).]

[1] Diurnal of Occurrents, p. 15.

the same place. The king, as the great Justiciar
of the realm, was present in his scarlet robe, and
took a prominent part in the proceedings. Betoun was also present and taking part. About
sixteen are said to have been convicted and to
have had their goods forfeited. James Hamilton,
brother of the martyr, had been ordered by the
king to flee the country, as he could not otherwise
save him. His sister was persuaded to submit to
the church. Two were reserved for a fiery death
—Norman Gourlay and David Stratoun. Gourlay
was a priest in secular orders, and "a man of
reassonable eruditioun," [1] who had been abroad,
and there imbibed the new opinions. These he
abjured, [2] and was, it seems, really burned for the
greater crime of having married a wife. [3] Stratoun
was the brother of the Laird of Laureston in the

[1] Laing's Knox, i. 58.

[2] [Foxe alleges that Gourlay and Stratoun were condemned and
burned, "because, after great solicitation made by the king, they
refused to abjure and recant" (Cattley's Foxe, iv. 579) ; but, on the
other hand, the writer of the Diurnal of Occurrents (p. 18) and Bishop
Lesley (History, 1830, p. 149) assert that Gourlay did abjure.]

[3] Such was the punishment meted out to him for endeavouring
to do in a scriptural way what rulers of the church were doing in
disregard of the laws of Scripture as well as the laws of their church.
Pitscottie knew no other cause why he was burned save that "he was
in the East-land, and came home, and married a wife contrary to
the form of the pope's institution because he was a priest ; for they
would thole no priest to marry, but they would punish and burn him
to the dead ; but if he had used ten thousand whores he had not
been burnt " (Pitscottie's History, 1778, p. 236).

Mearns, and had been reclaimed from his former godless life by his neighbour, Erskine of Dun, but by some free speeches had incurred the resentment of the notorious Prior Hepburn. They were burned at the Rood of Greenside, on the northern side of the Calton Hill. In the same year, Willock, M'Alpine, and M'Dowal had to escape into England. In 1536, when the king and Betoun were abroad, there was comparative peace. In 1537 several were convicted at Ayr, and had their goods forfeited, among whom was Walter Steward,[1] son of Lord Ochiltree. In 1538-39 many were accused and convicted in various burghs in which by that time reformed opinions were spreading, and many had to seek safety in flight. Among these last were Gavin Logie, principal regent in St Leonard's College,[2] who for a number of years had been exercising a marked influence on the students under him; John Fyfe, who under the designation of Joannes Faithus matriculated at Wittenberg in 1539, and under that of Joannes Fidelis was incorporated into the University of Frankfort on the Oder, and appointed Professor of Divinity there in 1547; George Buchanan, who

---

[1] [In the letter, dated 29th December 1537, granting his escheat to his father, he is described as "*umquhill* Walter Stewart" (M'Crie's Knox, 1855, p. 316). Calderwood places his recantation and accidental death in 1533 (History, Wodrow Society, i. 104).]

[2] [Gavin Logie is usually spoken of as Principal of St Leonard's (Laing's Knox, i. 36, n.).]

at the king's command had exposed the hypocrisy of the friars; and George Wishart, who had taught the Greek New Testament in Montrose; also Andrew Charters, John Lyne, and Thomas Cocklaw, John and Robert Richardson and Robert Logie, canons of the Augustinian Abbey of Cambuskenneth. Nearly all of these fugitives took refuge in England. Cocklaw, Calderwood tells us, for marrying a wife had been mewed up within stone walls, but his brother came with crowbars and released him. His goods, as well as those of his wife, were forfeited to the Crown. Large numbers of the wealthy burgesses, even after they had consented to abjure their opinions, were stripped of their possessions, among whom the burgesses of Dundee were conspicuous. "Nor was the good town of Stirling far behind Dundee in the same race of Christian glory. She had less wealth to resign, . . . but she brought to the altar a larger offering of saintly blood."[1] On 1st March 1538-39, no fewer than four of her citizens were burned at one pile on the Castle Hill of Edinburgh. On the same day with them, and in the same place, perished one of the most sainted and interesting of Scotland's martyrs—Thomas Forret, canon of the Augustinian Abbey of Inchcolm, and thereafter vicar of Dollar, who was universally admired for his attractive character.

[1] Lorimer's Scottish Reformation, 1860, p. 51.

He taught his parishioners the ten commandments, penned a little catechism for their instruction, and caused a child to commit it to memory
and to repeat it publicly, that it might be impressed on the hearts of his parishioners who
could not read.   He succeeded in leading several
of the younger monks in the abbey to more evangelical views; but the old bottles, he said, would
not take in the new wine.   He preached every
Sunday to his people on the epistle or gospel for
the day, and showed them, in opposition to the
teaching of the friars, that pardon for sin could
only be obtained through the blood of Christ.

During all these anxious years the severe
measures against the reformers had really been
directed by the man who comes more prominently
into public view toward their close.   This was
David Betoun, the nephew of the primate, and,
like him, a younger scion of the house of Balfour
in Fife, who by this time was not only Abbot of
Arbroath and Bishop of Mirepoix in France, but
also coadjutor to his aged uncle in the Archbishopric of St Andrews, and cardinal, with the
title of St Stephen on the Cœlian Mount.   " Paul
III.," says D'Aubigné, "alarmed at seeing the
separation of England from Rome, and fearing lest
Scotland—as she had a nephew of Henry VIII. for
her king—should follow her example, was anxious
to have in that country one man who should

be absolutely devoted to him. David Betoun
offered himself. The pope created him cardinal
in December 1538, and thenceforth the *red*—a
colour thoroughly congenial with him—became
his own, and, as it were, his symbol. Not that
he was by any means a religious fanatic: he was
versed neither in theology nor in moral philosophy.
He was a hierarchical fanatic. Two points, above
all, were offensive to him in evangelical Christians:
one, that they were not submissive to the pope;
the other, that they censured immorality in the
clergy, for his own licentiousness drew on himself similar rebukes. He aimed at being in Scotland a kind of Wolsey, only with more violence
and bloodshed. The one thing of moment in his
eyes was that everything in church and state
should bend under a twofold despotism. Endowed with large intelligence, consummate ability,
and indomitable energy, he had all the qualities
needed to ensure success in the aim on which
his mind was perpetually bent without ever being
diverted from it. Passionately eager for his pro-
jects, he was insensible to the ills which must
result from them. One matter alone preoccupied
him, the destruction of all liberty. *The papacy
divined his character and created him cardinal!*" [1]

[1] D'Aubigné's Reformation in the Time of Calvin, vi. 131.—Like
his predecessor Archbishop Forman, who—thirty years before, in the
interests of France, which had richly rewarded him with the Arch-

This is one of the few attempts made fairly to estimate the character of the man whom one party seemed to have thought they must make out to be a very monster of iniquity, and of whom the other party seemed to have felt that the less they said the better; and to a certain extent D'Aubigné's estimate is correct, but it requires to be supplemented. The cardinalate was rather eagerly sought by him and his friends on the ground of what he had already done, and was expected yet to do, for pope and king, than voluntarily offered by the pope. Two, if not three, letters, extremely urgent, were written regarding it by the king to the pope, to the King of France, and to Cardinal Farnese, in the favour of all of whom he stood high.[1] The pope consented to bestow on him the cardinalate he so much coveted; but the office of legate *a latere*, without which the other was rather an office of dignity than of power, was not granted till 1544,[2] by which time neither

bishopric of Bourges—had so cruelly embroiled Scotland with England and almost courted the disaster of Flodden, Betoun never ceased either during the life or after the death of James V. to sow the seeds of discord between the two realms, and so to court reverses to the Scottish arms, and destruction to the Scottish monasteries near the southern border. He shunned no risk, shrank from no cruelty, to remove out of the way those who thwarted his schemes or favoured the better policy which in the end was to carry the day.

[1] Theiner's Vetera Monumenta Hibernorum et Scotorum, 1864, pp. 608-612.

[2] [Betoun's Commission as Legate is dated 30th January 1543-44 (Lemon's State Papers, v. 443; Thorpe's Calendar, i. 46).]

the papacy nor any others needed to divine his character. Betoun was a man not only of large intelligence, high ability, unremitting energy, and unbounded ambition, but also of considerable scholarly attainments. He did not belong, it is true, to the school of Pole and Contarini, who would have made concessions to the reformers in regard to doctrine, nor to that of the disciples of D'Ailly and Gerson, who were pressing for a reformation within the old church in regard to morals. His associations and sympathies were rather with the laxer Italian and French humanist school, both in their virtues and vices, and he seems to be lightly referred to in their gossip as *ille latinus Juvenalis.*[1] He was a great stickler for the liberties of holy church, and for years refused to pay the tax imposed on him for the support of the College of Justice.[2] It was no doubt by his counsel that heretical processes from the first were carried on under the canon law, and that that code and French consuetudinary ecclesiastical law were more completely natural-ised in Scotland than they had been before. Most of his time from 1514 to 1524 was passed abroad —the later years in the diplomatic service of his country; and he had acquitted himself with much

[1] [There is such a reference to him in Theiner's Vetera Monu-menta, p. 608.]

[2] Robertson's Concilia Scotiæ, vol. i, p. cxxxvi, n.

credit and success. He had been subsequently employed in the negotiations for the marriage of the king, first with the daughter of the King of France, and after her death with Mary of Guise, and in both missions had given high satisfaction to his sovereign. He had no sooner returned home in 1524-25, than the same measures of cruel restraint against the reformers began to be adopted here which had already been put in practice in France; and he was a member of the various Parliaments in which the rigour of these measures had been increased. Even some of the hardest sayings of the Scottish king against heretics were but the echo of those of his father-in-law, the King of France.

Like too many of the high dignitaries of the Scottish church of his time, Cardinal Betoun was of notoriously incontinent habits;[1] but he was never, so far as I know, guilty of such shameless excesses as were the boast of his comrade, Prior Hepburn, nor did he ever allow himself to sink into the same indolence and unredeemed sensuality. He was above all a " hierarchical fanatic," devoted to the cause of absolutism, who would shrink from no measures, however cruel, to preserve intact the privileges of his order, and to stamp out more earnest and generous thought, whether that thought was aiming at the reforma-

[1] See Appendix C.

tion of the old church or the building up of another on her ruins. If we may not say that he
had sold himself to France—which had pensioned
him with a rich bishopric and helped him to his
honours—we must say he had lived so long in
it, and had got so enamoured of it, that he was
at any rate three parts French, and all popish.
He had mingled not only with her scholars but
with her nobles, loved and determined to imitate
their ways even down to their scandalous laxity
of morals and merciless treatment of so-called
heretics. He made no earnest effort to reform
the old church, and so help her to weather the
gathering storm; and it was not till towards the
close of his life that he laid out on the building
of St Mary's College part of the money which
his uncle had carefully hoarded for that purpose.

For the forcible suppression of the new opinions
the cardinal needed the unflinching support of
his sovereign, and he spared no efforts to gain
him over completely to his side, and to detach
him from his nobility,—turbulent and self-willed,
but fondly clinging to what remnants of liberty
were still left to them,—and to alienate him from
his uncle, not unfrequently well-meaning but always over-impetuous, and often in his later years
selfish and untrustworthy. There was much in
the king's character to encourage such efforts.
With good natural abilities and a frank and ami-

able disposition, he had for their own selfish ends been encouraged by his early guardians in sensual pleasures, and never to the last freed himself from his evil habits. " Dissolute as a man, prodigal as a king, and superstitious as a Catholic, he could not but easily fall under the sway of superior minds," [1] who undertook to free him from the worries of business, to provide him with money, and to regard his failings with indulgence, and on easy terms to absolve him from those grosser excesses which could not fail at times to trouble his conscience. These things Betoun and his clerical party endeavoured to do; and, lest he should be tempted to follow the example of his uncle, and appropriate the property of the mon- asteries and other religious institutions, or set the church lands to feu, as he had threatened, they once and again presented lists to him of those who were suspected of heresy, urging that they should be prosecuted without delay, and their goods, on conviction, be escheated to the Crown. They made large contributions from their own revenues to aid him in the wars with England, which obedience to their counsels had brought on him. They procured dispensations from the papal court to enable his sons, though illegitimate and infants, to hold any ecclesiastical benefices inferior to bishoprics, and on reaching

[1] D'Aubigné's Reformation in the Time of Calvin, vi. 132.

a certain age to hold even the highest offices in
the church. In this way they largely added to
his revenues during the minority of his sons,
and buoyed him up with the hope that when
these sons came to years, and were formally in-
vested with their dignities, he would have wealthy
allies on whom he could thoroughly depend in
his contests with his nobles.

But though James showed little indulgence to
the reformers, and little favour for their doctrines,
he seems to the last to have had less real liking
for the priests of the old faith. No bribery, no
flattery, no solicitations could reconcile him permanently to those who for their own selfish ends
dragged him into courses from which his own
better impulses at times made him revolt. "He
incited Buchanan to lash the mendicant friars in
the vigorous verse of the 'Franciscanus.' He
encouraged by his presence the public performance
of a play" which, by its exposure of the vices of
the clergy, contributed greatly to weaken their influence. "He enforced the object of that remarkable drama by exhorting the bishops to reform
their lives, under a threat if they neglected his
warning that he would deal with them after the
fashion of his uncle of England" or his cousin of
Denmark. "He repeated the exhortation in his
last Parliament, declaring that the negligence, the
ignorance, the scandalous and disorderly lives of

the clergy, were the causes why church and churchmen were scorned and despised." [1]

So, notwithstanding all measures of repression, the desire for a reformation quietly grew and spread throughout the nation, especially among the smaller landed proprietors in Angus and Mearns, in Perthshire and Fife, in Kyle and Cunningham, as also among the more intelligent burgesses in the various burghs, and, above all, among the *élite* of the younger inmates of the monasteries and of the *alumni* of the University. When the poor monarch, as much sinned against as sinning, at last died of a broken heart,[2] and the Earl of Arran, who claimed the regency, looked about for trusty supporters to defend his claims against the machinations of the cardinal and the queen dowager, he deemed it politic to show not a little countenance to the friends of the Reformation and of the English alliance. We are not warranted to assert that he meant to declare himself a Protestant; but he chose as his chaplains preachers who showed themselves favourably inclined to the new faith. He encouraged the chief men among the Protestants to frequent his court, and he ventured to lay hands on the unscrupulous cardinal, who had striven to exclude him from the regency. He consented to pass through Parliament an Act expressly permitting

---

[1] Concilia Scotiæ, vol. i. pp. cxxxix, cxl.   [2] [14th Dec. 1542.]

the people to have and to read the Scriptures of
the Old and New Testaments in the vulgar tongue,
and despatched messengers to all the chief towns
to make public proclamation of the Act. The
little treatises of Alesius had thus done their
work, and he himself thought of returning and
completing what he had so well begun.

The friends of the Reformation imagined that
the hour of their triumph was at hand. They did
not know on what a treacherous prop they were
leaning, or what sore trials were yet in store for
them ere that triumph should be gained. They
knew the regent to be weak and timid; they did
not know him to be deceitful—so deceitful that,
within six weeks after the last of the messengers
were despatched with the above-named proclamation, immediately on the return from France of
his brother, the Abbot of Paisley, others were
secretly sent off to inform the holy father of his
accession to the regency, to put himself and the
kingdom under his protection, and to ask permission to have under his control the income of the
benefices of the king's sons till they should come
of age.[1] The love of money was with him the
root of this evil; as the fear of man was of others
which soon followed, and were fraught with dire
calamities to the nation. And so he went from

---

[1] [His letter to the Pope is dated 10th May 1543 (Theiner's Monumenta Hibernorum et Scotorum, pp. 614, 615).]

bad to worse, till in the dim light of the Franciscan chapel at Stirling,[1] "that weak man, to whom
people had been looking for the triumph of the
Reformation in Scotland, fondly fancying that he
was performing a secret action, knelt down before
the altar, humbly confessed his errors, trampled
under foot the oaths which he had taken to his
own country and to England, renounced the evangelical profession of Jesus Christ, submitted to the
pope, and received absolution of the cardinal."[2]

Even in June he had entered in the books of
the Privy Council an Act against Sacramentaries
holding opinions on the effect and essence of the
Sacraments tending to the enervation of the faith
catholic, in which they were threatened with
"tinsale of lif, landis, and gudis."[3]   He had not
dared to proclaim this openly, though perhaps his
ally, Henry VIII., would not have blamed him
greatly for doing so.   But no sooner was he in
league with, and under the power of, the cardinal,
than he showed in open Parliament "how thair is

---

[1] [On the 8th of September "he was enjoyned to passe to the
Freres in Stirling, . . . and there received open pennance and a
solempne othe, in the presence and hereing of all men that was
there, that he shulde never doo the same againe, but supporte and
defende the professon and habit of mounkes, freres, and such other ;
and therupon, being absolved by the Cardinall and the Busshoppes,
herde masse and received the sacramente" (Hamilton Papers, ii.
38).]

[2] D'Aubigné's Reformation in the Time of Calvin, vi. 206.

[3] Concilia Scotiæ, ii. 294.

gret murmure that heretikis mair and mair risis
and spredis within this realme, sawand dampnable
opinionis incontrar the fayth and lawis of Haly
Kirk, actis and constitutionis of this realm"; and
exhorted all prelates and ordinaries "to inquir
upon all sic maner of personis and proceid aganis
thame according to the lawis of Haly Kirk";
promising to be ready himself to do therein at all
times what belonged to his office.[1] This promise
he was soon obliged cruelly to fulfil.

On the 20th January 1543-44 he set out in
company of the cardinal, the Lord Justice and
his deputy, with a band of armed men and artillery, to Perth, where a great assize was held.
Several were convicted of heresy, and their goods
forfeited. Several were condemned to die. The
governor himself was inclined to spare their lives,
but the cardinal and the nobles who were with
him threatened to leave him if he did this. So
on St Paul's day (25th January) 1543-44, Robert
Lamb, James Hunter, William Anderson, and
James Ranaldson were hanged; and the wife of
this last, who had refused when in labour to pray
to the Virgin Mary, was denied the consolation of
being suspended from the same beam with her
husband, and put to death by drowning, after she
had consigned to the care of a neighbour the

---

[1] Acts of Parliament, ii. 443. [This was on the 15th of December
1543.]

infant she carried in her arms. Dundee was next
visited, but it was found that the suspected citizens—who in the previous autumn had sacked
and destroyed the Grey Friars and the Dominican
monasteries—had taken the alarm and fled from
their homes.

The weak and inconstant man continued to be
regent in name, but from that hour he was domin-
ated by the imperious cardinal almost as completely
as King James had been. He wrote to the pope
that the cardinal's devotion to the holy see and
to the interests of his native country was so great
that he deserved the praise, or at least no small
part of the praise, of preserving its liberty and
extinguishing heresy.[1] That last work, however,
was by no means so nearly accomplished as the
regent in his letter to the pope had boasted.
In fact, within two months after we find the
cardinal himself confessing in a letter to the
pope that he was still in the thick of the fight,
and all but worn out—" *vigiliis, laboribus, atque
sumptibus* " — not only in contending with foes
without, but also with traitors within, the camp.[2]
The regent himself was obliged to confess, in a
subsequent letter, that they were then in a miserable plight; and that, unless material assistance

---

[1] [This letter is dated 20th May 1545 (Theiner's Monumenta, p.
616).]

[2] Theiner's Monumenta, p. 617. [This letter is dated 6th July
1545.]

came to them from abroad,—and in particular from his holiness, when almost all their other friends were growing cold,—it would be hard for them to maintain the struggle against the English king. The balance of parties at this critical juncture was more nearly equal than is generally supposed. "An active minority of the nobles and gentry saw in the government of Beaton not only their own personal ruin, but the giving away of the country to a power more dangerous to its liberties than England itself. . . . With those who favoured England were naturally associated those who desired a reformation of religion,—a body now so numerous in the opinion of a papal legate [Grimani] who visited the country in 1543, that, but for the interposition of God, Scotland would soon be in as bad a case as England itself."[1] These appeals for foreign help, and the hopes raised by them, intensified the struggle, and retarded for years the triumph of a really national party resolved to set the interests of Scotland above those of France and Rome as well as of England.

[1] Hume Brown's Knox, i. 64, 65. Grimani's opinion, as sent from Stirling, is thus summarised by Father Stevenson : "The realm is in such confusion, so divided, so full of heresy that, but for the interposition of God, it will soon become as bad as England. The queen and the cardinal have spent all their money in the common cause ; and the clergy are unable to assist, for the fruits of their benefices have been seized by the Lutherans" (Mary Stuart, 1886, p. 51).

CHAPTER IV.

GEORGE WISHART.

IT was about this time that a new evangelist
arrived in the country, singularly fitted to impress on the hearts of men the lessons of the
Holy Book to which they had now access in
their native tongue. This was George Wishart,
a younger son or nephew of Sir James Wishart,
laird of Pittarrow in the Mearns. He appears
to have been born about 1512-13, and to have
received his university training in King's College,
Aberdeen, then presided over by a distinguished
humanist skilled both in Latin and Greek. He
acquired a knowledge of Greek—at that time a
very rare accomplishment in Scotland — either
from the Principal of King's College, or from
a Frenchman teaching languages in Montrose.
From his early years he seems to have been intimate with John Erskine, laird of Dun, and at
that time also provost of the neighbouring burgh

of Montrose. The earliest notice we have of him is as attesting a charter granted in favour of Erskine.[1] This lends confirmation to the tradition which Petrie, himself a native of the town, says he had heard from ancient men (who in their youth had seen and known the reformer) that then, or soon after, he was employed as assistant or successor of Marsillier, the Frenchman Erskine had brought from France to teach the languages, and that, like him, he read the Greek New Testament with some of his pupils. John Hepburn, then Bishop of Brechin, would not naturally have been quick-scented to detect heresy in one who stood so high with his good friend Erskine of Dun; but David Betoun, Abbot of Arbroath, often resided at the mansion-house of Ethie, half-way between Arbroath and Montrose, and he was both more lynx-eyed and more anxious to stamp out any approach to heresy, and he urged the bishop on.

Wishart in consequence was summoned by Hepburn, but instead of appearing in answer to the summons, he, like many others in that year of grievous persecution, sought safety in England, and it is said that he was forthwith excommunicated and outlawed. He found shelter under

---

[1] [The charter is dated at Montrose on the 20th of March 1534-35. The Martyr's signature, as " M. Geo. Wischert," proves that he had already taken his degree (Register of Great Seal, iii., No. 1462).]

Bishop Latimer, whose diocese comprehended Gloucester and Bristol, as well as Worcester; but in the following year he fell into fresh trouble at Bristol—not, as was at one time supposed, by denying the merits of the Virgin Mary, but by denying the merits of Christ Himself. For this he was duly convented before Archbishop Cranmer, and, after conference with him, was persuaded to recant and bear his faggot. Soon after the enactment of the bloody statute of the six articles, he, like most of the Scottish refugees, left England and sought shelter among the reformed churches on the Continent, especially those of Zürich, Basle, and Strassburg, and brought home with him, and ultimately translated into English, the First Helvetic Confession,[1] composed and agreed on by the chief theologians of these churches.

He returned to England about the close of 1542, and soon after entered into residence in Corpus Christi or Benet College, Cambridge, with the view of studying and teaching there. In one of the windows of the common-room in that college, above the arms of archbishops and nobles, distinguished *alumni* of the college, stands the name of George Wishart, with the martyr's crown over it; and it is to Emery Tilney, his

[1] [His translation is reprinted in the Wodrow Miscellany, pp. 7-23.]

pupil during the year he was in residence there,
that we are indebted for our fullest description
of his appearance and habits. He was, he tells
us, "a man of tall stature, polled-headed, and
on the same a round French cap of the best;
judged to be of melancholy complexion by his
physiognomy; black haired, long bearded, comely
of personage, well spoken after his country of
Scotland, courteous, lowly, lovely, glad to teach,
desirous to learn, and was well travelled; having
on him for his habit or clothing never but a
mantle or frieze gown to the shoes, a black
Millian [*i.e.* Milan] fustian doublet, and plain
black hosen, coarse new canvas for his shirts,
and white falling bands and cuffs at his hands,—
all the which apparel he gave to the poor, some
weekly, some monthly, some quarterly, as he
liked, saving his French cap, which he kept the
whole year of my being with him. . . . His
charity had never end, night, noon, nor day, . . .
infinitely studying how to do good unto all, and
hurt to none." [1]

Such, according to his pupil, was the evangelist
who—in 1543 according to some, in 1544 according to others—returned to his native land, and
for two years testified of the gospel of the grace
of God throughout Angus and Mearns, Ayrshire
and the Lothians, but whose favourite fields of

[1] Cattley's Foxe, v. 626.

labour were to be central Angus and Mearns,
the towns of Montrose and Dundee. A portrait
of him, as well as one of his great opponent, has
been preserved in the Roman Catholic College of
Blairs, and the expression of the face harmonises
well with the description his pupil gives of him.
Another portrait, deemed by Dr Laing not unworthy of Holbein, is in possession of a descend-
ant of the Wisharts.[1]

It is supposed that for a short time after his
return to Scotland he lived quietly at Pittarrow,
in the parish of Fordoun, where the shrine of St
Palladius was preserved; and being an accomplished artist, occupied himself with adorning the
ancestral mansion with several beautiful fresco
paintings, which, after being long covered over
by the wainscot, were again brought to light in
the present century, but unfortunately were destroyed before their value was perceived. Dr
Leslie of Fordoun, who saw them, has thus described the most remarkable of them : " Above
the largest fireplace in the great hall was a paint-
ing of the city of Rome, and a grand procession
going to St Peter's. . . . The Pope, adorned with
the tiara, and mounted on horseback, was attended by a large company of cardinals on foot,
richly dressed, but all uncovered. At a little distance, directly in front of the procession, stood a

[1] [This is now in the National Portrait Gallery, Edinburgh.]

beautiful white palfrey, finely caparisoned, held by some persons who were well dressed, but uncovered. Beyond them was the Cathedral of St Peter, the doors of which appeared to be open. Below the picture were written the following lines :—

"IN PAPAM.

"Laus tua, non tua fraus, virtus non gloria rerum
    Scandere te fecit hoc decus eximium ;
Pauperibus dat sua gratis nec munera curat
    Curia Papalis, quod more percipimus.
Haec carmina potius legenda, cancros imitando." [1]

---

[1] [Cook's History of the Reformation, 1811, i. 272, 273 ; 1819, i. 273. Dr Cook says that Dr Leslie, minister of Fordoun, "got a short view of them," and favoured him with the account which he wrote. In a very similar notice of the paintings by Dr Leslie, it is stated that they were discovered when the old house of Pittarrow was being pulled down in 1802 ('New Statistical Account of Kincardineshire,' p. 81).] As Dr Cook long ago surmised, the lines of covert sarcasm on the pope are not original. One evening as I returned to Guildford Street after a long day in the British Museum, I had occasion to pass through Red Lion Square and the alley to the east of it, where I saw exposed in a pawnbroker's window a little antique volume, in a very dilapidated state, opened at the page which contained these lines almost *verbatim.* I at once purchased it, and on further examination I found it had been published at Basle in 1537—*i.e.*, a few years before Wishart was there. [The little collection which Dr Mitchell thus refers to bears the title : " Pasqvilli de Concilio Mantuano Iudicium. Qverimonia Papistarum ad Legatum Pontificium in comicijs Schmalcaldianis. Mantua uæ miseris nimium uicina Papistis. MDXXXVII."

The colophon runs thus : "Impressum Romae in porta Angelorum. M.D.XXXVII."

Wishart evidently found his lines in the following :—

" Lavs Romani Pontificis. Scripta ad placitum Romanae curiae per

Wishart began his work as a preacher in Montrose, the scene of his early scholastic labours, expounding the rudiments of the Christian faith and practice as set forth in the Ten Commandments, the Lord's Prayer, and the Apostles' Creed. At that time Montrose was frequented by many of the landed gentry in the surrounding districts who were favourable to the Reformation and the English alliance, and their hearts could not fail to be cheered and their courage raised by the exhortations of the evangelist. Dundee, however, was the chief and favourite scene of his ministrations; and it was from the great success attending them that it gained the name of the Scottish Geneva. It was even more decidedly attached to the new opinions and the English alliance than

uenerabilem dominum Doctorem Ioannem Coċhleum, Theutonicae Doctor Rotzloffel, et Georgium VVicelium cognomento, Meister Lugenmaul, Romanae Ecclesiae propugnatores egregios.

> " Pauperibus sua dat gratis nec munera curat
> Curia Papalis quod modo percipimus
> Laus tua non tua fraus, Virtus non copia rerum
> Scandere te fecit, hoc Decus eximium
> Conditio tua sit stabilis nec tempore paruo
> Viuere te faciat hic Deus omnipotens.

" Quos uersiculos pessimus quidam haereticus, Lutheranus, iuuenilis fortasis Poeta VVittembergensis, ita de uerbo ad uerbum inuertit.

> " Percipimus modo quod Papalis curia curat
> Munera, nec gratis dat sua pauperibus
> Eximium decus hoc fecit te scandere rerum
> Copia, non uirtus, fraus tua, non tua laus.
> Omnipotens Deus hic faciat te uiuere paruo
> Tempore, nec stabilis sit tua conditio."]

Montrose; and a reformation, as it was called—
including the sacking of the monasteries in the
town and neighbourhood—had taken place in the
autumn of 1543. The governor confessed, when
put to penance, that this had been done with his
permission.[1] The martyr cannot with any cer-
tainty be connected with it, much less made to
bear the blame of it; though another George
Wishart, a citizen and bailie of Dundee, with
whom the martyr has been recklessly confounded,
was afterwards put on his trial for having taken
a leading part in it.[2] If the martyr could, his
enemies would hardly have failed to have brought
it against him at his trial.

He preached for a time in Dundee with great acceptance, expounding systematically that Epistle
to the Romans, the full significance of which the
recently published Commentary of Calvin had
deeply impressed on the minds of his co-religionists in various lands where Wishart had been.
At length he was charged by one of the magistrates in the queen's name and the governor's to
desist from preaching, to depart from the town,
and trouble it no more. This was intimated to
him when he was in the pulpit, surrounded by
a great congregation, and with a significant re-

[1] Hamilton Papers, ii. 38.
[2] Maxwell's Old Dundee prior to the Reformation, 1891, pp. 92,
395.

minder that he had already been put to the horn,
and that there was no intention to relax the law
in his favour. Thereupon he called God to witness that he intended not their trouble but their
comfort, and felt sure that to reject the Word of
God, and drive away His messenger, was not the
way to save themselves from trouble; adding,
" God shall send unto yow messengeris who will
not be effrayed of hornyng nor yitt for banish-
ment." [1] He left the town forthwith, and with
all " possible expeditioun passed to the west-
land." [2] There he pursued his labours in the
same kindly spirit, refusing to allow his followers to dispute possession of the churches by force
of arms with the authorities, and choosing rather
to preach in the open air wherever he found
a convenient place and audience fit to listen to
him.

Soon after he left Dundee, the plague, which
that year was raging in several of the towns of
Scotland, extended its ravages to that place.
This naturally led the citizens to bethink themselves of the treatment they had allowed the evangelist, who had laboured so devotedly among
them, to suffer at the hands of his enemies, as
the news of what they were suffering led him to

---

[1] Laing's Knox, i. 126. [Calderwood (i. 186) and Spottiswoode
(i. 150) have *burning* for *hornyng*.]

[2] Laing's Knox, i. 126.

think compassionately of his friends who were
now in trouble, and stood in need of comfort.
He returned to the afflicted town, and its inhabitants received him with joy. He announced
without delay that he would preach to them ; but
it was impossible he could do so in a church.
Numbers were sick of the plague; others in attendance on them were regarded as infected, and
must not be brought into contact with those who
were free from infection. The sick were crowded
in and about the lazar-houses near St Roque's
Chapel, outside the East or Cowgate Port of the
town. Wishart chose as his pulpit the top of
that port, which, in memory of the martyr-
preacher, has been, it is said, carefully preserved,
though — like Temple Bar, so long tolerated in
London—it is now in the heart of the town, and
an obstruction to its traffic.[1] The sick and suspected were assembled outside the port, and the
healthy inside. The preacher took for the text
of his first sermon the words of Psalm cvii. 20 :
" He sent His word and healed them ; " and,

[1] [Knox calls it "the East Porte of the Toune" (Laing's Knox, i.
129). Maxwell says that the Port which stood in the Seagate would
alone correspond to that described by Knox ; and he adds : "The
Port yet standing in the Cowgate—which, because of its association
with the honoured name of George Wishart, only was left when some
of the others were demolished—really cannot be identified as his
preaching-place, and should not carry the inscription which has been
recently put over its archway " ('History of Old Dundee,' 1884, pp.
220-222).]

E

starting on the key-note that it was neither herb nor plaster, but God's Word which healeth all, " He maist comfortablie did intreat [*i.e.* treat of] the dignitie and utilitie of Goddis Woord; the punishment that cumis for the contempt of the same; the promptitude of Goddis mercy to such as trewlye turne to Him; yea, the great happynes of thame whome God tackis from this miserie evin in His awin gentill visitatioun, which the malice of man cane neyther eak nor paire." [1] By this sermon, Knox tells us, he so raised up the hearts of all who heard him, that they regarded not death, but judged those more happy that should depart than those that should remain behind, considering that they knew not whether they should have such a comforter with them at all times.

No doubt John Wedderburn, as well as the others who had been suspected of heresy and had fled from the town in the persecution of 1539, had before this time returned, and were co-operating with Wishart in his work; and then, in all probability, was prepared that beautiful funeral hymn which passed from the Bohemians to the Germans, and from the Germans to the Scotch; and which, in addition to the original stanzas, contains in the Scottish version certain new verses having unmistakable reference to the circum-

[1] Laing's Knox, i. 130.

stances in which they originated—in a plague-stricken town which had just before been occupied by the soldiers of the cardinal and the regent, and might well dread a similar visitation for its determined adherence to the new evangelist.

> " Thocht *pest or sword* wald vs preuene,
>   Befoir our hour, to slay vs clene,
>   Thay can nocht pluk ane lytill hair
>   Furth of our heid, nor do vs deir.
>
>   Quhen fra this warld to Christ we wend,
>   Our wratchit schort lyfe man haif end
>   Changeit fra paine, and miserie,
>   To lestand gloir Eternallie.
>
>   End sall our dayis schort, and vaine,
>   And sin, quhilk we culd nocht refraine,
>   Endit salbe our pilgremage,
>   And brocht hame to our heritage." [1]

Wishart concerned himself not only about the souls but also about the bodies of his hearers in that sad time, fearlessly, like Luther on a similar occasion, exposing himself to the risk of infection, that he might minister to the diseased and the dying, and taking care that the public funds for the relief of the destitute should be properly administered. He forgot himself only too much, and the terrible risks to which, as an excommunicated and outlawed man, he was exposed

---

[1] Gude and Godlie Ballatis, 1897, p. 165.

in so near proximity to the cardinal, who was so eager to get him out of the way.

One day as the people were departing from the sermon, utterly unconscious of the peril menacing their favourite preacher, Knox tells us that a priest, bribed by the cardinal, stood waiting— with his whinger drawn in his hand under his gown — at the foot of the steps by which the preacher was descending from the top of the port. Wishart, most sharp of eye and swift of judgment, at once noticed him, and, as he came near, said, " My freind, what wald ye do?" and at the same moment seized the hand in which he held the dagger, and took it from him. The priest fell down at his feet and confessed the whole truth. Immediately the rumour spread that a priest had attempted to assassinate their favourite preacher, the sick outside burst open the gate, crying, " Deliver the tratour to us, or ellis we will tack him by forse." But the preacher put his arms around his would-be assassin, exclaiming, " Whosoevir trubles him shall truble me, for he has hurte me in nothing, bot . . . hes lattin us understand what we may feare in tymes to come"; and so, says Knox, he saved the life of him that sought his.[1]

---

[1] Laing's Knox, i. 130, 131. The name of this priest is given as Sir *John* Wightone, or Weighton, by Knox, Calderwood, and Spottiswoode. Maxwell cannot find a priest of this name among

Like Drs Laing, Lorimer, and Weir, I cannot persuade myself that the man who spoke and acted thus is the same as "a Scottish man called Wysshert," who is mentioned in a letter of the Earl of Hertford in April 1544, as privy to a conspiracy to apprehend or assassinate Cardinal Betoun, and as employed to carry letters between the conspirators and the English court.[1] There were other Wisharts in Scotland. Yea, as Dr Laing has shown, another George Wishart in Dundee, who was a zealous friend of the English alliance—not only after the conspirators got possession of St Andrews castle, but from the earlier date when the monasteries in Dundee were destroyed and sacked.[2] There was probably another about St Andrews who, while the martyr was yet a boy, was called in to attest a charter by the notorious friar Campbell in 1526. I will not venture to affirm that, with all his gentleness,

those ministering in Dundee in 1550 ('Old Dundee prior to the Reformation,' 1891, p. 87, n.) The *James* Wichtand who was reader at Inchture and Kinnaird in 1574 (Wodrow Miscellany, p. 353) is said to have held a chaplaincy in Dundee before the Reformation. But Dr Laing holds that there was a Sir *John* Wighton, a chaplain in Dundee, who obtained the vicarage pensionary in the parish church of Ballumby in 1538, and who appears to have been incarcerated in St Andrews Castle in the cardinal's absence in 1543 (Laing's Knox, vi. 670).

[1] Lemon's State Papers, v. 377.

[2] Laing's Knox, i. 536. [Maxwell gives a detailed account of this other George Wishart in his 'Old Dundee prior to the Reformation,' 1891, pp. 91-95.]

Wishart might not have been tempted to maintain that violence and murderous intent—such as
Betoun had twice shown to get rid of him privately
—might be lawfully met and restrained by force,
though even that is hardly in keeping with all we
know of his gentle ways; but we may be sure that
had such thoughts been cherished by him, he, like
Knox, would have said this openly, and not have
engaged in any secret reprisals.   As an outlawed
man he came down to Scotland under protection,
and never seems to have travelled in it save under
protection; and so he was one of the last men
likely to be chosen for a secret mission to England.   If anything more than the able essay of
the late Professor Weir in the 'North British
Review' for 1868 were needed to prove that the
" pure lustre of the martyr's fame is still un-
sullied," it seems to me to be supplied by himself
in his affecting address at the stake.   " I beseech
Thee, Father of heaven ! to forgive them that
have of any ignorance, or else have of any evil
mind, *forged any lies* upon me.   I forgive them
with all my heart." [1]   The cardinal was not ignorant of the volcano on which he was sitting or
of the plots that had been hatched against him;
and he may have suspected Wishart of being in
the conspiracy.   That may have been the reason
why he sent two friars to him to get his last

[1] Cattley's Foxe, v. 635.

confession, and, when they failed to do so, allowed Wynram to go, as the reformer had requested. Wynram, after hearing it, returned to the cardinal and his abettors, and assured them that Wishart was innocent. This can only refer to such a suspicion of conspiracy, not to the charge of heresy which was confessed and acknowledged; and Mr Andrew Lang has failed as completely as the cardinal in his laboured attempt to produce a tittle of evidence against him.

From the time of Wighton's attempt the reformer had a clearer view of the perils which beset him, and a mournful conviction of the issue which awaited him if he would not flinch or flee. By his success in Dundee the rage of his adversaries was lashed into a fury which appalled his friends in various districts; but none of these things moved him that he might finish his course with joy, and make full proof of his ministry. As soon as the plague abated in the city, heedless of the new proofs he then had of the cardinal's relentless determination to capture or trepan him, and the earnest warnings of his northern friends that they could not be answerable for his safety, he took his last farewell of his kirks in Montrose and Dundee. At all hazards he was determined to fulfil his engagement to meet his western friends in Edinburgh, to prosecute his work there under their promised protection, and to seek a public disputation with some of the popish clergy who about that time were to meet in Synod in the capital. Disappointed of the presence and protection of the western men, he laboured for a brief season in Leith, Inveresk, and East Lothian without much success. At last, forsaken by many of those who should have stood by him, he was seized at Ormiston, under cover of night and promise of safe keeping, by the Earl of Bothwell, Sheriff Principal of the county. The Earl pledged his honour not to give him up to his enemies, but was soon persuaded to deliver him to the governor, as was the governor to hand him over to the cardinal, though he finally protested against his being tried or condemned by the churchmen in his own absence. A full account of his labours during these days of despondency has been given by Knox, who got from him, it is said, the first rudiments of Greek, and who— having rendered his first service to the cause of the Reformation by bearing the two-handed sword for his protection—was dismissed on the night of his betrayal with the significant words, " One is sufficient for one sacrifice," showing what fate he now anticipated for himself.

I cannot enlarge on these things, nor on the sad scenes which took place at St Andrews on the last day of February and 1st of March 1545-46, when the cardinal, regardless of the remon-

strances of the regent and the murmurs of the
people, but with the assent of the Council which
he had adjourned from Edinburgh to St Andrews,
condemned him to the stake. Throughout all
these trying scenes he comported himself as nobly
as Patrick Hamilton had done; and not less plenti-
fully did his blood prove the seed of the church,
verifying his words, that few would suffer after
him before the glory of God evidently appeared.
No doubt his cruel martyrdom hastened the removal of that tyrant who set himself above all
restraint of civil law, and breathed forth threatenings against the saints of God,—though that removal had not been plotted by him, nor would
have been approved by him. The words attributed to him at the stake by Buchanan and
Lindsay of Pitscottie, foreshadowing his persecutor's approaching fate, are not generally regarded
as authentic. Knox says nothing of them, nor
Foxe, nor Spottiswoode; nor does Sir David
Lindsay, in his 'Tragedy of the Cardinal,' make
any reference to them. It seems better authenti-
cated that he made the following general statement : " I beseech you, brethren and sisters, to
exhort your prelates to the learning of the Word
of God, that they at the last may be ashamed to
do evil and learn to do good, and if they will not
convert themselves from their wicked error, there
shall hastily come upon them the wrath of God,

which they shall not eschew."[1] It is easy to see —especially after the events which so speedily occurred—how a statement which referred to the prelates generally should come to be applied specifically to their imperious chief, just as the example of Eli had, in a well-known ballad, been similarly used for warning by the Reformation poet to the aged James Betoun for his weak indulgence to his nephew and the younger Prior Hepburn, notwithstanding their scandalous excesses.[2]

Such was the end of the life and ministry of George Wishart, one of the most zealous and winning evangelists, and one of the most heroic and steadfast confessors, that our country has ever produced. The remembrance of him was fondly cherished, especially in that district where he chiefly laboured, and where he wrought a work not less memorable than that which M'Cheyne and Burns were honoured to do in our own day. His influence was but deepened by his cruel fate, and he "lived again," as Dr Lorimer has eloquently said, "in John Knox. . . . The zealous disciple, who had counted it an honour to be allowed to carry a sword before his master, stood

---

[1] Cattley's Foxe, v. 635. [Foxe is here quoting the account in the black-letter tract printed in or about 1547, which Knox deemed important enough to copy from Foxe into his own pages.]

[2] Gude and Godlie Ballatis, 1897, p. 180.

forth immediately to wield the spiritual sword which had fallen from the master's grasp, and to wield it with a vigour and trenchant execution superior even to his."[1]

It may not be inappropriate to state how far the organisation of the Reformed Church had by this time advanced in Scotland. Patrick Hamilton seems to me to have laboured to the last for the revival of Scriptural teaching and Christian living within the old church rather than apart from her. Alesius, and some others of his disciples, were for a time reluctant to separate from her, if her rulers could have been persuaded seriously to set about repairing acknowledged evils and defects. But Wishart, and those who came under his influence, seem to have abandoned this struggle, and to have striven for the formation of a new organisation apart from the old one. He formed kirks or congregations—at least in Montrose and Dundee ; the former consisting probably mainly of the lesser gentry in the adjacent districts of Angus and Mearns, and the latter chiefly of the substantial burghers of the town of Dundee. I suppose that some forms of discipline began to be put in practice in the Dundee congregation, and that it was on that account, as well as from the remarkable revival which had taken place under his ministrations, that the town came to

[1] Lorimer's Scottish Reformation, 1860, pp. 153, 154.

be spoken of as "the Scottish Geneva." The New Testament of Tyndale's translation had been introduced both there and in Montrose as early as 1526; and by this time the subsequent editions had been largely imported, and since 1543 might be openly read.[1] John Wedderburn was then in his native city, and I suppose by that date had published, in its most rudimentary form, his 'Psalms and Spiritual Songs,' largely translated from the German. John Scott, the printer, was also there, and under suspicion of the authorities in Edinburgh. Of the psalms and hymns, one, as I have already mentioned, bears unmistakable reference to the *pest* then infesting the town of Dundee; another was sung by Wishart that evening on which he was apprehended in East Lothian; a third is certainly referred to in the 'Complaynt of Scotland,' which, being published as early as 1549, is a guarantee for the earlier existence of the hymn.[2] This rudimentary collection of 'Psalms and Spiritual Songs' was the book of praise in family and social gatherings of the reformed until the 'Genevan Psalter' came into use.[3] The earliest editions of it have per-

---

[1] Wedderburn and Wishart seem also to have been acquainted with Coverdale's Bible of 1535.

[2] See my Introduction to 'The Gude and Godlie Ballatis,' 1897, p. xxxviii, n.

[3] No doubt the initial Catechism was in use also. It has been conjectured that the Catechism may even have been printed separ-

ished. A nearly complete copy of the edition of 1567 has, however, been preserved, and now at last reprinted.[1]

The translation of the First Helvetic Confession, which Wishart made, was no doubt meant as the Confession of the churches he formed, though it may only have been extant then in manuscript, and not published till 1548. That fragment of the Communion Office which was used by Knox in the administration of the Lord's Supper at Berwick in 1550, and perhaps had been used by him at St Andrews in 1547—and which was recently brought to light again by Dr Lorimer from among the MSS. in Dr Williams' library in London[2]—was almost certainly derived from Wishart, for part of it is translated from the Office of the Church of Zürich, with which he could not fail to have become acquainted during his residence there, and part from other German Offices, which were more likely to have fallen in his way (who had been a traveller on the Continent) than in Knox's. It may even have been used by Wish-

ately, and that the first part of the following entry may refer to it : "The catechisme in two partes ; the first in Scotch poetry, having a kalender before it. The second part in Latin and Scotis prose, entituled Catechismus ecclesiae Geneuensis. . . . Edinburgh : Imprinted by John Ross for Henrie Charteris, 1574" (Dickson and Edmond's Annals of Scottish Printing, 1890, p. 334).

[1] [Reprinted under the editorial care of Dr Mitchell in 1897 for the Scottish Text Society.]

[2] Lorimer's Knox and the Church of England, 1875, pp. 290-292.

art in 1545, when he dispensed the communion in both kinds at Dun. The same may be said of that interesting burial-service which purports to have been used in the kirk at Montrose, and has been reprinted in the Miscellany of the Wodrow Society;[1] though probably this, as we now have it, may not be the original form, but a recension of it, made later, under the auspices of Erskine of Dun, superintendent of Angus and Mearns. The foundations of the superstructure that was to be were thus laid by Wishart. It was reserved to his successor to raise it, as the martyr had predicted it would be raised, even to the copestone.

[1] Wodrow Miscellany, pp. 295-300.

CHAPTER V.

KNOX AS LEADER OF OUR REFORMATION.

As stated towards the close of my last lecture, the sword-bearer of Wishart stood forth at once " to wield the spiritual sword which had fallen from the master's grasp, and to wield it with a vigour and trenchant execution superior even to his."

At this time Knox was full forty years of age, having been born at Giffordgate, in Haddington, in 1505. He probably received the rudiments of his education there, and matriculated at the University of Glasgow in 1522. Some suppose that he may have followed Major to St Andrews in 1523, or may have come there later, to study theology or to act as a private tutor to some young men studying at that university. But there is no reference to him in the university books, nor mention of his presence by any one then resident. From 1522 up to 1545-46, when he appears as sword-bearer to Wishart, his life is to us almost a blank. But as Minerva was said to have come full armed from the brain of

Jupiter, so did Knox then start up as leader of our Reformation, fully equipped and singularly matured. Whatever his early training may have been, he had by that time thoroughly mastered the subjects in controversy between the two churches, and possibly, as Bayle supposes, had made himself aquainted in his retirement with the writings of that great doctor of the western church to whom Luther, Calvin, and Alesius were largely indebted. I believe no man in recent times has in brief space sketched his character, both on its brighter and darker sides, with less partisan feeling than Dr Merle D'Aubigné, when he says: " The blood of warriors ran in the veins of the man who was to become one of the most intrepid champions of Christ's army. . . . He was active, bold, thoroughly upright and perfectly honest, diligent in his duties, and full of heartiness for his comrades. But he had in him also a firmness which came near to obstinacy, an independence which was very much like pride, a melancholy which bordered on prostration, a sternness which some took for insensibility, and a passionate force sometimes mistakenly attributed to a vindictive temper." [1]   According to Calderwood, he received his first " taste of the truthe " from the preaching of his fellow - countryman, Thomas Guilliame or Williams, a black friar, who in 1543 became one of the chaplains of the

[1] D'Aubigné's Reformation in the Time of Calvin, vi. 17.

regent, and shortly after, being inhibited to preach, retired into England.[1] The good seed sown by him was watered by Wishart, and grew up apace, "first the blade, then the ear, after that the full corn in the ear."

On 29th May 1546, while the applause of priests and friars was still ringing in his ears, and he was proudly congratulating himself on the progress of his new fortifications, and the success of all his measures to secure the triumph of his party and his own complete personal ascendancy, the cardinal was suddenly surprised by conspirators in his stronghold, and cut off by "a fate as tragical and ignominious" as almost "any that has ever been recorded in the long catalogue of human crimes."[2] Only the deep feeling of relief thus given from merciless oppression could prompt or excuse the lines of Sir David Lindsay—

> "As for the Cardinal, I grant
> He was a man we weill culd want,
> And we'll forget him sune ;
> But yet I think the sooth to say,
> Although the loon is weill away,
> The deed was foully dune."[3]

---

[1] Calderwood's History, i. 155, 156, 160 ; Laing's Knox, i. 95, 96, 105. [Calderwood says that Williams was born "beside Elstone-furde, in East Lothiane."]

[2] Lorimer's Scottish Reformation, pp. 155, 156.

[3] [Though these lines are continually attributed to Lindsay, I do not remember to have ever seen them in any edition of his works, or quoted as his by any earlier writer than Wodrow.]

When it became known that the conspirators who assassinated Betoun meant to hold the castle of St Andrews, they were joined by a considerable number of their friends from among the reforming gentry of Fife, and gradually by others from a greater distance who were friendly to the Reformation and the English alliance, and in consequence were then being subjected to many annoyances at the hands of the regent and his new following. Among these last, about Pasche 1547—in charge of his pupils, the sons of certain lairds in East Lothian—came John Knox, whose life, ever since he had cast in his lot with Wishart, had been made so miserable to him by the regent's bastard brother[1]—the aspirant to the vacant archbishopric — that, but for this refuge unexpectedly opened to him, he would have found it necessary to leave his native land and follow Alesius, Fyfe, and others to Germany or Switzerland. At the time when he arrived in St Andrews there was a truce between the regent and the occupants of the castle, and with the latter the inhabitants of the city had pretty free intercourse. The reforming citizens resorted at times

[1] [According to Knox, though "called bastard brother to the governour," many deemed him to be a son of "the old Bischope of Dunkelden, called Crychtoun" (Laing's Knox, i. 105). Buchanan says he was "first callid *Cuningham*, estemit *Cowane*, and at last Abbot *Hamiltoun*" (Admonition to the trew Lordis). In a transcript used by Ruddiman, *Givane* occurs instead of *Cowane*.]

to the services in the chapel of the castle; and John Rough, the chaplain of the garrison, under the powerful protection he enjoyed, occasionally forced his way into the parish church and preached there to the assembled citizens.

Knox was no sooner settled in St Andrews than he resumed the system he had followed with good effect in East Lothian, causing his pupils to give account of their catechism in public to all who chose to come, and opening up in a plain and colloquial manner the Gospel of St John. His great ability and success as a teacher, and his wonderful gift of persuasive speech, thus became generally known. After private but unsuccessful efforts had been made by Balnaves and others to induce him to become colleague to John Rough, a formal call to the ministry was, with the counsel of Sir David Lindsay,[1] publicly addressed to him from the pulpit by Rough, in the name of the rest, and he was solemnly adjured not to despise the voice of God speaking to him. Thus honourably called to assume the office of a public preacher in that reformed congregation, he at last entered on the work with all his heart, and made full proof of his ministry before the assembled citizens in their parish church, as well as before the rude

---

[1] [Laing's Knox, i. 186. Though the Lyon King was then in St Andrews, he was not one of those who were sheltering in the castle (Laing's Lindsay's Poetical Works, 1879, vol. i. pp. xxxix, xli).]

garrison in the castle chapel. He administered the Sacrament of the Lord's Supper in the simple form he always used, and continued the public catechising of his pupils, which the people of the town heard repeated till they had the substance of his teaching by heart, and thus was spread a knowledge of Gospel truth even among those who could not read. A very graphic account is given in his History of the sermons, catechisings, and disputations he held with the popish champions, by means of which the new doctrines gained a hold on the minds of the citizens of St Andrews which they never wholly lost. But times of trial were to come ere the cause should finally triumph in that city, or in his native land; and the earnest preacher, whose mouth God had opened in that old parish church, was to be taught by sad experience how hard it is to leave all and simply follow Christ, ere he was to be privileged to see the full fruit of his labours.

Those who had presumed to take into their hands "the sword of God" as they called it, and to mete out to the tyrant cardinal the punishment which human justice was too weak to award, were made to feel that they who take the sword must expect to suffer from the sword. They had been able to withstand the power of the regent and the attacks of his unskilful captains; but help and skill at last came to the aid of these from their co-religionists abroad — chief among them being a militant ecclesiastic entitled Prior of Capua—and the succour promised to the garrison by England having been again and again delayed, they were obliged to surrender the castle to the representative of the French king.[1] The occupants of the castle—those who had come to it for shelter, as well as those who were really guilty of the murder—were deprived of liberty, and dealt with as criminals of the worst class. For nineteen months [2] our reformer had to work as a chained slave on board the French galleys, generally at Rouen or Dieppe, though sometimes a cruise was taken to more distant waters. Once, at least, he was brought within sight of the towers of the city where he had begun his ministry; and then he solemnly affirmed that he believed God would once more allow him to proclaim His word there. Even then he maintained unshaken faith in God, and at times indulged in sallies of pleasantry against his popish custodiers; but he would have been more than human if the iron had not entered into his soul, and if traces of the sternness thence arising had not long been visible in his character.

Early in 1549 he was, by English influence, re-

---

[1] [Knox says that the castle was rendered "upone Setterday, the last of Julij" (Laing's Knox, i. 205); Bishop Lesley says "the xxix of Julij" (Lesley's History, 1830, p. 195). In 1547, the last of July fell not on Saturday but on Sabbath.]

[2] Laing's Knox, vi. 104.

leased from his captivity in the French galleys, and
from his exile.[1]   He proceeded first to London,
and thereafter to Berwick, with the approval of
the English Privy Council.   There he was as
near to his persecuted fellow-countrymen as it
was safe for him to go, and there many of them
might resort to him; and in fact so many did
so, that the president of the English Northern
Council became anxious for his transference
farther south.   There also, through the appointment of the Privy Council, a wide field of
usefulness was opened to him among the English.
Into this he entered with his whole soul, preaching the Gospel with great boldness and success
not only to the garrison and citizens of Berwick,
but also in the surrounding districts; and proving
himself a true successor of those early Scottish
missionaries who had originally won over to the
Christian faith the heathen Saxons of Northum-
bria.   At Newcastle, in 1550, he discussed, before
Tonstal, Bishop of Durham, his doctors, and the

---

[1] [The negotiations for the release of the captives seem to have
dragged their weary length along very slowly. So early as the 29th
of March 1548, Huntly wrote thus to Somerset: "The governor
has agreed to exchange the men in the castle of St Andrews with
Scots prisoners conform to your desire, and has sent me commission
therein, as I shall show you at my coming to London: or if you
send your mind to my Lord Warden, I shall appoint with him.
The governor has written to the king of France to send the men
taken in St Andrews to Rouen, to be ready for the exchange"
(Bain's Calendar, 1543-67, p. 104).]

Northern Council, the idolatry of the mass; and in the spring of 1551 he removed his head-quarters to that more central and influential town, extending his labours at times, no doubt, into Yorkshire, as well as into Northumberland and Cumberland.

His fame as an eloquent preacher, and able and ready defender of the doctrines of the Reformation, spread southwards; and at the close of 1551, or early in 1552, he was appointed one of the royal chaplains of Edward VI. In the autumn of 1552 he was summoned to the south, and preached with great power and faithfulness before the king and his court. He persistently advocated, along with the other royal chaplains, those thorough-going Protestant doctrines which, in the north, he had previously held and taught and carried out in practice. In conjunction with the other five royal chaplains, he was called to give his opinion of the Articles then proposed to be adopted as the creed of the English Church, and of the revised Communion Office then prepared to take the place of that of 1549. His objections to the act of kneeling in receiving the elements in the Lord's Supper helped to procure the insertion of that rubric which high-churchmen term "the black rubric." He refused both an English bishopric and a London rectory, and continued to labour on, faithfully and devotedly, as a preacher unat-

tached. He had a presentiment that the time
he would have to do so would be brief, and he
improved it to the uttermost. The Reformation
in England at that date had been forced on by
its courtly patrons and their earnest preachers
beyond what was warranted by the hold it had
as yet gained on the mass of the people. When
the good King Edward[1] was succeeded by the
bigoted Mary, nothing remained for the Protestant bishops and preachers but either to prove
the sincerity of their convictions in prison and at
the stake, or to leave the country and reserve
themselves in exile for happier times. Knox, as
a foreigner, was especially warranted to choose
the latter course; and at the urgent request of
his friends in the north he did so, when it was
only not yet too late to escape.

The five years of the reformer's life which followed were not less eventful for himself nor for
those of whom he now became the chosen leader.
After an unsuccessful attempt to set up a substantially Puritan church among the English
exiles at Frankfort, Whittingham and he obtained at Geneva, through the favour of Calvin,
an asylum for themselves and their like-minded
fellow-exiles, where they might be allowed peace-
fully to carry out their own forms of worship and
discipline. But he had not been long there till,

[1] [Edward died July 6, 1553.]

at the earnest invitation of the reforming party,
he paid a visit to his native land — a visit
which was memorable for its immediate, and
still more for its ultimate, results. For several
years the cause of the Reformation had been
making quiet progress. Those who could read
the Scriptures had been drinking the waters of
life from the fountain-head. Those who could
not, drank from the streams opened by the Reformation poets, whose verses were carefully committed to memory. Then came the voice of the
living preacher, accompanied, as it had never yet
been in Scotland, with the demonstration of the
Spirit and with power from on high. The reformer wrote that he would be content to sing his
nunc dimittis after forty such days as he had had
three of in Edinburgh. He prolonged for six
months a visit which he had intended to complete
in as many weeks; and, when he was at last recalled to Geneva by the urgent letters of the congregation there, he promised to his friends in
Scotland that he would return whenever they saw
meet to summon him and to assure him of protection from persecution.

The few quiet years which Knox and his fellow-
exiles passed at Geneva were to be richly blessed
to themselves and to their fatherland. He, at
least, had not gone there to have his views of
Christian doctrine or church order formed or

materially changed.   He went to see the pure
reformed faith (which he and Calvin in common
believed, and independently had drawn from the
Holy Scriptures and from the writings of the
great doctor of the ancient church) exhibiting its
benign influence in quickening to higher life, and
moulding into a united community the volatile
citizens of Geneva.   He came to have his wearied
spirit revived and refreshed by communion with
devoted Christian brethren; and, by witnessing
the success of their labours, to be nerved for
further achievements in the service of their
common Lord and for the good of his native
land.

It was there that Puritanism was organised as
a distinct school, if not also as a distinct party,
in the church.   If it had done nothing more than
what it was honoured to do in the few peaceful
years our fathers were permitted to spend in that
much loved city by the bright blue waters of the
Leman Lake, it would have done not a little for
which the church and the world would have had
cause to be grateful to it still.   There were first
clearly proclaimed in our native language those
principles of constitutional government, and the
limited authority of the "upper powers," which
are now universally accepted by the Anglo-Saxon
race.   There was first deliberately adopted and
resolutely put in practice among British Christians

a form of church constitution which eliminated
sacerdotalism, and taught the members of the
church their true dignity and responsibility as
priests to God and witnesses for Christ in the
world. There was first used that Book of Common Order which was long to be the directory
for public worship in the fully reformed Church
of Scotland, and whose simple rites Bishop
Grindal was forced to own, in his controversy
with the English Puritans, he could not reprove.
There was nearly completed, after the model of
the French version, the English Metrical Psalter.
There was planned and executed a translation of
the Scriptures into our mother tongue, which for
nearly half a century continued to hold its place
alongside of others executed at greater leisure and
more favoured by authority.[1] That was how our

---

[1] [The first edition of the Genevan version was printed at Geneva
by Rouland Hall in 1560. "The changes made in the Geneva
Bible were the adoption of Roman type instead of the black letter,
in which all English Bibles had previously been printed, and the
division of the chapters into verses. These changes were the
principal cause of the wonderful popularity of this version, of which
about 200 editions are known. From 1560 to 1616 no year passed
without one or more editions issuing from the press, in folio, quarto,
or octavo. In 1599 no less than ten distinct editions were printed,
each of which consisted of a large number of copies. The last
quarto printed in England is dated 1615, and the last folio 1616.
After this time a great many editions were printed at Amsterdam
by Joost Broerss and other Dutch printers ; the last folio bears the
imprint of Thomas Stafford, and the date 1644. . . . 150,000
copies were imported from Holland after this version had ceased
to be printed in England. . . . Owing to the vast number of copies

reformer and his tireless associates occupied themselves when left freely to follow their own bent.
That was how he was ultimately prepared for
the great work he was to accomplish in his native
country when finally invited to return to it.

Immediately after the accession of Elizabeth
to the English throne in the autumn of 1558,[1]
the English exiles on the Continent began to
break up their congregations and return to their
native land.   Those at Geneva were among the
first who commenced to do so; but those of them
who had been occupying themselves in that translation of the Bible into English which was to
prove such a blessing to their countrymen decided to remain where they were until they had
finished that work.[2]   Those who returned were
at first favourably received by the queen and her
advisers, and taken into service in the reconstituted church; but when it was found that they
were generally averse to comply fully with the
ceremonies which she fostered, a change took
place.

Knox, who does not seem to have been one

in circulation during the three-quarters of a century that this version
was the household Bible of England, it is now the most common
of all early printed Bibles. . . . The singular rendering of the 7th
verse of the third chapter of Genesis in every edition of the Genevan
version has caused it to be commonly known as the 'Breeches'
Bible " (Dore's Old Bibles, 1888, pp. 203, 204).]

[1] [Mary Tudor died on the 17th of November 1558.]

[2] Troubles at Frankfort, Petheram's reprint, pp. cxci, cxcii.

of the translators, appears to have left Geneva among the earliest. In February 1558-59 we find that he had gone to Dieppe, whence, while assisting in the French Protestant services, he sent a request to Cecil for leave to pass through England on his way to Scotland, and to converse with him on some matters which deeply concerned the welfare of the Protestants in both realms.[1] But his 'First Blast of the Trumpet' was an insult which Elizabeth could not brook, and so, after waiting in vain for the desired permission for a reasonable time, he set sail from Dieppe for Scotland, and arrived in Edinburgh on the 2nd of May 1559, much to the consternation of the popish council then assembled in the city. It dissolved forthwith; but care was taken to get Knox's name, as that of an already condemned heretic, added to the list of Protestant preachers then under summons to appear before the queen regent and her council to answer for their persistence in preaching.[2] Knox at once

---

[1] [After making two requests by messengers, Knox wrote to Cecil from Dieppe on the 10th of April 1559, and on the 22nd sent from the same town a duplicate of that letter with a postscript added (Laing's Knox, ii. 15-22, vi. 15-21).]

[2] [The Provincial Council is said to have closed on the 10th of April (Robertson's Concilia Scotiæ, ii. 151, 176; Lesley's History, p. 271); but Knox says that it sat until he arrived in Scotland (Laing's Knox, i. 291); and that the date of his arrival was the 2nd of May (Ibid., i. 318, vi. 21); and an anonymous writer alleges that the council broke up when assured that Knox had come (Wodrow Mis-

resolved to throw in his lot with his brethren, and went north to Dundee where the zealous Protestants of Fife, Angus, and Mearns were already assembling, determined to make common cause with their preachers, and to go forward in peaceful form to Stirling in order that they might do so, and leave the queen and her council in no doubt as to the position which they were henceforth to occupy towards her and them. They accordingly marched forward from Dundee to Perth, and sent on Erskine of Dun to Stirling to apprise the queen and council of their attitude and intentions. It is said that she promised Erskine that the prosecution of the preachers would be abandoned, but they were condemned in absence and outlawed, and the breach between the two parties thus became irrevocable. Nothing remained for the queen, from her point of view, but to prosecute the matter to the bitter end, if thereby she might succeed in silencing and repressing the Protestants.

After the regent's falsehood to Erskine and persistence in her fatal policy, the reformers proceeded at once to set about such reform as they desired, and commenced rather roughly at Perth, where they had the majority of the population in

cellany, pp. 56, 57). M'Crie suggests that, although the Acts were concluded on the 10th of April, the council may not have then closed (Life of Knox, 1855, p. 126, n.).]

their favour.   Knox, along with Moray, went to
Fife as soon after as it became apparent that
forcible measures must be taken to secure toleration for the Protestants.   After a few brief
visits to other towns he presented himself at the
public preaching-place in St Andrews.   Modern
historians will not allow us to say that it was
in that city that he had received his university
training, or had first listened to the preaching of
the reformed doctrines, or been brought to a
personal knowledge of the truth ; but they leave
untouched, as previously stated, the more important facts that it was there, when in charge
of his pupils at the university, that he had first
ventured at the hazard of his life openly to make
known to others that which had been blessed of
God to the quickening of his own soul, and
publicly to exert in the cause of the Reformation
those rare gifts of telling argument and persuasive
speech which were destined so signally to contribute to its ultimate and permanent triumph
throughout the land.   It was there, probably in
the old parish church, that he had been first
solemnly called to the ministry of the Word in the
reformed church ; and there, in the chapel of the
old and now ruined castle, that he had first celebrated the Lord's Supper with the same purity
and simplicity with which it was afterwards
observed   in   the   fully   reformed   Church   of

Scotland.[1]   Even in exile and working as a slave in the galleys his heart had turned with special pleasure to the scene of his first labours, and he had cherished the confident expectation that God would again bring him to the place where he had first opened his mouth, and permit him again to preach from its pulpit the precious truths of His Holy Word.[2]

This expectation he believed that God had then fulfilled, and neither the threats of adversaries could make him quail from his purpose, nor the counsels of timid friends move him to let slip the opportunity which he believed God had then given him of bearing full and faithful testimony to the truth of God in that important city.[3]   He therefore boldly proclaimed before the dignitaries of the church, the doctors of the university,[4] and

---

[1] [While it is apparent from Knox's own narrative that his first public sermon was delivered in the parish church of St Andrews (Laing's Knox, i. 189), it is not quite so clear whether Rough addressed the call to him in that church or in the chapel of the castle, though it rather appears to have been in the former (Ibid., i. 186-188); and the precise building in St Andrews in which he first celebrated the Lord's Supper seems to me to be also uncertain (Ibid., i. 201).]

[2] Laing's Knox, i. 228.   [3] Ibid., i. 348, 349; vi. 25.

[4] [Many members of the university became Protestants. The twenty-one men in St Andrews, whom the first General Assembly deemed qualified "for ministreing and teaching," were with few exceptions professors, or regents. For the number of the ecclesiastics who joined the congregation at St Andrews in the early months of the Reformation, see *supra*, p. 13.   In September,

the magistrates of the burgh, as well as before
more humble citizens, that doctrine of the grace
of God which had long been his own solace
and support, and was then being more generally
recognised and embraced by his countrymen.
Having thus seized the opportunity and improved
it to the utmost, his efforts were so abundantly
blessed by God that the cause of truth and right
finally triumphed there. The reformed worship
was by general consent peaceably set up, and the
authority of the archbishop was virtually ended
in the very stronghold of his power. That which,
with the divine blessing, the reformer's preaching
then accomplished in St Andrews, was by the
same or similar means effected in the chief cities
of the kingdom, and throughout the greater part
of the lowlands, almost within the compass of a
single year. In fact, four months after his arrival,
he could write to his friends : " Nothwithstand-
ing the fevers have vexed me, . . . yitt have I
travelled through the most part of this realme
where (all praise be to His blessed Majestie)
men of all sorts and conditiouns embrace the
Truthe. . . . We doe nothing but goe about
Jericho, blowing with trumpets as God giveth
strenth, hoping [for the] victorie by His power

1566, St Andrews was emphatically declared to be "the most
flourishing city as to divine and human learning in all Scotland"
(Laing's Knox, vi. 546).]

G

alone." [1]   The reformer's expectation of victory,
and of victory by the persuasive means which
Bishop Hooper affirmed were alone legitimate
and in accord with Christ's will, was neither
disappointed nor long deferred.   The great body
of the nation, with unexampled rapidity and
unanimity, embraced the truth, and submitted to
the discipline of their teacher, and under its
salutary influence, as Stähelin in his 'Johannes
Calvin' affirms, from being one of the rudest,
most ignorant, indigent, and turbulent peoples,
grew to be one of the most civilised, educated,
prosperous, and upright which our family of
nations can show.

Believing that we have no cause to be ashamed
of the great revolution which was thus effected,
or of aught which has legitimately followed from
it, but that we need to have our pure minds
stirred up by way of remembrance of the great
things the Lord has done for us, I proceed to
direct attention to the distinctive characteristics
of the Scottish Reformation in respect of doctrine,
worship, government, discipline, and church life,
and the lessons which such a review should tend
to rivet on the hearts of those who still hold fast
its principles and long to see them more fully
carried out.

[1] Laing's Knox, vi. 78.

CHAPTER VI.

THE OLD SCOTTISH CONFESSION OF 1560.

KNOX, in his ' History of the Reformation,' has stated that the preparation of this Confession was entrusted to the same six ministers who were commissioned to draw up the Book of Discipline — viz., Wynram, Spottiswoode, Willock, Douglas, Row, and himself.[1] It has been frequently taken for granted that the Confession was prepared and revised within four days after the formal charge to frame it was issued by the Parliament, and that the Book of Discipline was not ordered to be prepared till after the Parliament of 1560 was adjourned. It is evident, however, from the dates specified in the Introduction, and at the conclusion of the copy of the Book of Discipline engrossed by Knox,[2] that the original charge to frame it had been granted on the 29th April 1560, or just two days after the

---

[1] Laing's Knox, ii. 128.   [2] Ibid., ii. 183, 257.

nobles and barons signed one of those "godly
bands" or covenants[1] by which they pledged
themselves to stand by each other in setting
forward the Reformation of religion according
to God's Word ; and it can hardly be supposed
that that book should have been taken in hand
some months before the Parliament met, and that
no attempt should have been made in this interval
to prepare materials for the 'Confession of Faith.'
Besides, Knox has not stated that within four
days after the charge was formally issued the
Confession was *prepared*, but only that it was
presented, so that we may hold with Dr M'Crie
that "the ministers were not unprepared for
this task," which was then formally devolved
on them by the Parliament.   Knox has further
stated that the Confession was accepted by
the Parliament in the form in which it was laid
before them *without change of a single sentence*.[2]
Others supplement his statement by explaining
that before it was publicly presented it was submitted privately to certain lords of Parliament,
and by their direction was handed for revision to
the rather time-serving Wynram and the anon

---

[1] [For this band, see Laing's Knox, ii. 61-64.]

[2] ["Quhilk thay willinglie acceptit and within foure dayis pre-
sentit this Confessioun as it followis, without alteratioun of any
ane sentence" (Laing's Knox, ii. 92).]

time-serving and vacillating Laird of Lethington,
who softened many harsh expressions in it, and
even recommended the omission of a chapter or
part of a chapter from it. This they say was a
chapter bearing the title, "Of the obedience and
disobedience due from subjects to magistrates."[1]
But the chapter on the "Civil Magistrate" still
found in the Confession treats so fully and expressly of the obedience due to magistrates, that
it is difficult to see how place could ever have
been sought for an additional chapter on the
same subject. There may possibly at first have
stood in the chapter still retained some such
clause or sentence regarding the *limits* of obedience as we find in the corresponding chapter of
some of the Genevan symbolical books,[2] and
this may have been the matter deemed unfit to
be "entreated of" at that time, and recommended by the revisers to be omitted; or it may
be that, after all, their recommendation and the
suggestions of the English ambassador on the
subject were not followed in this instance, and

[1] [These statements are based on the information which Randolph
sent to Cecil on 7th September 1560 (Laing's Knox, vi. 120, 121).]

[2] " At vero in praefectorum obedientia unum semper excipiendum
ne ab ejus obedientia nos deducat, cujus decretis regum omnium
jussa cedere par est. . . . Adversus ipsum si quid imperent nullo
sit nec loco nec numero, sed illa potius sententia locum habeat,
obediendum Deo magis quam hominibus."

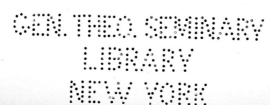

that we have the chapter still as it was originally framed by Knox and his associates.[1]

In endeavouring to form an estimate of the real merits of this Confession, we must make due allowance for the circumstances in which it was composed. Even though we suppose that the materials of it had been collected beforehand, only four days seem to have been allowed to the committee to put them into final shape.

We must not look either on the one hand for an exhaustive and logical elaboration of the several doctrines of the system and nicely balanced statement of complementary truths, or on the other for a careful avoidance of incidental expressions which seem dogmatically to deter-mine points not fully or directly handled in the places where we should have expected them to be so. Yet, if we make such due allowance, look at it from the proper point of view, and peruse the work not only in the now obsolete Scotch, but also in the neat Latin version which often accompanies it, and is said to have been the work of Archbishop Adamson,[2] we shall not

---

[1] This seems to be the opinion of Dr Laing (Knox's Works, vi. 121, n.) Indeed one can hardly read chapter xviii. without having a suspicion induced that Knox may have proved too strong for them in regard to some of what they termed the more harsh expressions in the treatise, as well as in regard to the particular chapter in question.

[2] [The Scotch and Latin versions are printed in parallel columns n Dunlop's 'Collection of Confessions' ii. 13-98.]

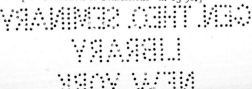

hesitate to own that it holds a distinguished place among the Confessions of that age, and is a credit to our reformer and his associates. Coinciding not infrequently in expression and agreeing generally in its definitions of doctrine with the other Reformed or Calvinistic Confessions (an agreement which its framers explicitly testified by inserting among the subordinate standards of their church, first Calvin's Catechism, and a few years after the Later Helvetic Confession and the Heidelberg Catechism), the Scottish Confession of 1560 had characteristics of its own,—a framework rather historical than dogmatic, and a liberal and manly, yet reverent and cautious spirit. It probably contributed to mould the early Scottish theology into a form somewhat less minute and rigid than the Swiss, yet considerably less vague and indefinite than the earlier English.

The first topic deserving of notice, from the place it holds both in the preface and in the body of this treatise, is the distinct and hearty acknowledgment of the supreme authority of the written Word of God, or "the buiks of the Auld and New Testamentis," which books are briefly but sufficiently defined as those "quhilk of the ancient have been reputed canonicall."[1] In these

---

[1] "Libros, qui ab infantia usque ecclesiae semper habiti sunt canonici" (Latin version, Dunlop, ii. 70).

they affirm " that all thingis necessary to be beleeved for the salvation of mankinde is sufficiently expressed," and to these they desire in all things to conform, protesting that, if any man should note any article or sentence in their Confession contrary to the Scriptures, and should " of his gentleness " admonish them of the same, they " do promise unto him satisfactioun fra the mouth of God, that is, fra His Haly Scriptures, or else reformation of that quhilk he sal prove to be amisse." [1]

In the opening chapter the unity and attributes of God, and the trinity of persons in the Godhead, are briefly but definitely treated of.[2]

[1] Dunlop's Confessions, ii. 17, 18 ; Laing's Knox, ii. 96. A similar protestation is made in the Preface to the First Book of Discipline (Dunlop's Confessions, ii. 518 ; Laing's Knox, ii. 184).

[2] The sources from which this chapter was taken can still be pretty clearly traced. I place in parallel columns its statements and those of the two Confessions from which it was probably taken :—

" We confesse and acknawledge ane only God, to whom only we must cleave, whom onelie we must serve, whom onelie we must worship, and in whom onelie we must put our trust.

" Je confesse qu'il y a un seul Dieu auquel il nous faut tenir, pour le servir, adorer, et y avoir notre fiance et refuge."—Confession subscribed by students in Academy in Geneva.

" Who is eternall, infinit, unmeasurable, incomprehensible, omnipotent, invisible : ane in substance, and zit distinct in thre personnis, the Father, the Sone, and the Holie Gost."— Old Scottish Confession, in Dunlop's Confessions, ii. 21, 22.

" I beleve and confesse my Lorde God eternal, infinite, unmeasurable, incomprehensible, and invisible, one in substance, and three in persone, Father, Sonne, and Holy Ghoste."—Confession of English Congregation at Geneva, in Laing's Knox, iv. 169 ; Dunlop's Confessions, ii. 3.

In subsequent chapters the divinity of our blessed Lord is fully asserted, and the " heresies of Arius, Marcion, Eutyches, Nestorius, and sik uthers as either did denie the eternitie of His Godhead, or the veritie of His humaine nature, or confounded them or zit devided them," are specifically rejected.[1] The second chapter treats of the creation and fall of our first parents, while the third treats of the effects of the fall in language no less explicit than that of the other Protestant Confessions, Lutheran and Reformed ; and as it not only clearly embodies the teaching of our reformers on this subject, but gives a brief summary of their views regarding the application of the Gospel remedy, it may be as well I should quote it at length. It is as follows : " Be quhilk transgressioun, commonlie called original sinne, *wes the image of God utterlie defaced in man*, and he and his posteritie of nature become enimies to God, slaves to Sathan, and servandis unto sin.[2] In samekle that deith everlasting hes had and sall have power and dominioun over all that have

---

[1] This also comes from a Genevan source :—

" We condemne the damnable and pestilent heresies of Arius, Marcion, Eutyches, Nestorius, and sik uthers."—Old Scottish Confession, as above, ii. 31.

" Idcirco detestor omnes haereses huic principio contrarias puta Marcionis, Manetis, Nestorii, Eutychetis, et similium."— Genevan Confession.

[2] Extraneum ab omni benedictione Dei, Satanae mancipium, sub peccati jugo captivum, horribili denique exitio destinatum et jam implicitum.—Calvin,

not been, ar not, or sall not be, regenerate from above : quhilk regeneratioun is wrocht be the power of the Holie Gost, working in the hartes of the elect of God ane assured faith in the promise of God reveiled to us in His Word, be quhilk faith we apprehend Christ Jesus with the graces and benefites promised in Him."[1]

After this follow several chapters on the history of the promises of redemption, the preparation for the coming of the promised Redeemer, the

---

[1] Dunlop's Confessions, ii. 24, 25 ; Laing's Knox, ii. 98. It has been questioned if this description of faith is one which Calvin and his stricter followers would have used. But nothing is more common, even in the earliest edition of his Institutes, than to find him describing faith as the apprehension of Christ with His gifts, or graces, as well as with His righteousness : "Apprehendimus ac obtinemus et . . . Christi *dona* amplectimur, quod ipsum est habere veram, ut decet fidem." "Haec omnia nobis a Deo offeruntur ac dantur in Christo Domino nostro nempe remissio peccatorum gratuita, . . . *dona et gratiae* Spiritus Sancti si certâ fide ea amplectimur." In one of these chapters [of the Scottish Confession] relating to the incarnation of Christ Jesus, He is spoken of not only, as in most of the Protestant Confessions, as the promised Messiah, the just seed of David, the Immanuel, or God in our nature—God and man in one person—but also as the *Angel of the great counsel of God* [Dunlop's Confessions, ii. 31 ; Laing's Knox, ii. 99]. This expression is no doubt a translation of the μεγαλης βουλης αγγελος of the Septuagint, and is the more remarkable, not only as showing familiarity on the part of some of the framers of the Confession with a somewhat unusual rendering of one of the most explicit Messianic prophecies of Isaiah, but also as showing that they had perceived the true significance of an expression which last century gave rise to no little discussion and misconception. So far as I can remember, this remarkable expression does not appear in any other of the Protestant Confessions of that age.

dignity and constitution of His person, His incarnation, sufferings, and death, His resurrection and ascension, and the blessed effects re-
sulting from them to His people. In another
of these chapters distinct reference is made to
" the eternall and immutable decree " from
which the appointment of the God - man as
our Redeemer, and " al our salvatioun springs
and depends ";[1] and in another all that is
good in us is traced up to that decree of the
eternal God who of mere grace elected us in
Christ Jesus His Son before the foundation of
the world was laid. The same mysterious subject is again referred to in the sixteenth chapter, which treats of the church, and, like the
earlier Confession used by Knox's congregation
at Geneva and our later Confession, identifies
that invisible but real church, which is " the
bodie and spouse " of Christ Jesus, with the
elect of all ages, nations, and tongues, so that
" as without Christ Jesus there is nouther life
nor salvation, so sal there nane be participant
therof bot sic as the Father hes given unto His
Sonne," and who in time come unto Him.[2] Many
individual expressions occurring in these chapters
can be clearly traced to one or other of Calvin's
Confessions, or to the earliest edition of his

[1] Dunlop's Confessions, ii. 32 ; Laing's Knox, ii. 100.
[2] Dunlop's Confessions, ii. 60, 61 ; Laing's Knox, ii. 108.

Institutes;[1] but the only Confession I can remember in which a similar, though shorter, history
of the preparation for the coming Redeemer is

[1] The following are a few specimens of close verbal coincidence
between the Scottish Confession and the first edition of Calvin's
Institutes :—

1. "It behooved that the
Sonne of God suld descend unto
us, and tak himself a bodie of
our bodie, flesh of our flesh, and
bone of our bones, and so become the Mediator betwixt God
and man, giving power to so
many as beleeve in Him to be
the sonnes of God."—Dunlop,
ii. 33, 34.

Filii Dei sumus quod naturalis
Dei Filius sibi corpus ex corpore
nostro, carnem ex carne nostra
ossa ex ossibus nostris composuit
ut idem nobiscum esset.

2. "Quhatsaever wee have
tynt in Adam is restored unto us
agayne."—Dunlop, ii. 34.

Ut quod in Adamo perdidimus
Christus restitueret.

3. "It behooved farther the
Messias and Redemer to be very
God and very man, because He
was to underlie the punischment
due for our transgressionus, and
to present himselfe in the presence of His Father's judgment
as in our persone to suffer for our
transgression and inobedience,
be death to overcome him that
was author of death. Bot because the onely Godhead culd
not suffer death, neither zit culd
the onlie manhead overcome the
samin, He joyned both togither
in one persone that the imbecil-
litie of the ane suld suffer and
be subject to death quhilk we
had deserved : and the infinit
and invincible power of the

Praeterea sic nostra referebat,
verum esse Deum et hominem
qui Redemptor noster futurus
esset. . . . Prodiit ergo verus
homo, Dominus noster, Adae
personam induit . . . ut Patri
se obedientem pro eo exhiberet
ut carnem nostram in satisfac-
tionem justo Dei judicio statueret
ac sisteret, ut in eâdem carne
peccati   poenam   persolveret.
Quum denique mortem nec solus
Deus sentire, nec solus homo
superare   posset,   humanitatem
cum divinitate sociavit ut alterius
imbecillitatem morti in poenam
persolveret, alterius virtute adversus mortem in victoriam luc-
taretur.

given, is the 'Summa Doctrinæ' of John Alasco,[1] which may be regarded as the Confession of Faith, not only of the ministers but also of the members of the church of the foreigners in London. Knox was brought into contact with them both in London and in Frankfort, agreed with them generally in opinion, and largely adopted their forms and arrangements in matters of worship and discipline.

A group of chapters[2] treats of the nature and work of the Holy Spirit, the cause of good works, the works which are reputed good, the perfection

uther, to wit, of the God-head, suld triumph and purchesse to us life, libertie, and perpetuall victory."—Dunlop, ii. 35, 36.

4. "That Hee being the cleane, innocent Lambe of God, was damned in the presence of an earthlie judge, that we suld be absolved befoir the *tribunal* seat of our God."—Dunlop, ii. 37, 38.

Judicis scilicet sententia damnatus pro nocente et malefico ut apud summi judicis *tribunal* ejus damnatione absolveremur.

5. "Suffered . . . the cruell death of the Crosse, quhilk was accursed be the sentence of God." —Dunlop, ii. 38.

Crucifixus in cruce quae Dei lege maledicta fuerat.

6. "Suffered for a season the wrath of His Father quhilk sinners had deserved. Bot zit we avow that He remained the only wel-beloved and blessed Sonne of His Father, even in the middest of His anguish and torent."—Dunlop, ii. 38.

Divini judicii horrorem et severitatem sensisse . . . luens poenas non suae . . . sed nostrae iniquitati. Neque tamen intelligendum est patrem illi unquam iratum fuisse. Quomodo enim dilecto filio, in quo illi complacitum est, irasceretur.

[1] Alasco's Works, ii. 296, 298. [2] Chapters xii.-xv.

of the Law of God, and the imperfection of man. Those who have overlooked the explicit statement in the third chapter concerning the depravity of man have generally overlooked or failed to perceive the full significance of the emphatic statements in the twelfth chapter regarding our entire dependence for spiritual renovation, and all good, on the Holy Spirit. The words are: "Of nature we are so dead, so blind, and so perverse, that nether can we feill when we ar pricked, see the licht when it shines, nor assent to the will of God when it is reveiled, unles the Spirit of the Lord Jesus quicken that quhilk is dead, remove the darknesse from our myndes, and bowe our stubburne hearts to the obedience of His blessed will;"[1] and again, "As we willingly spoyle ourselves of all honour and gloir of our awin creation and redemption, so do we also of our regeneration and sanctification."[2] These statements, however they may be viewed by others, seem to me no less explicit than those of the later Confession, which have been sometimes contrasted with them. "This effectual call is of God's free and special Grace alone, not from anything at all foreseen in man, who is

---

[1] Dunlop's Confessions, ii. 46. "Sunt autem dona Spiritus Sancti, per quem regeneramur, e diaboli potestate et vinculis explicamur, in filios Dei gratuito adoptamur, ad omne opus bonum sanctificamur."—Calvin.

[2] Dunlop's Confessions, ii. 47.

altogether passive therein *until*, being quickened and renewed by the Holy Spirit, he is thereby enabled to answer this call, and to embrace the Grace offered and conveyed in it." [1] The last of this group of chapters contains the fullest and most direct exposition the Confession embodies of the views of its framers in the article of Justification. It is as follows: " It behovis us to apprehend Christ Jesus with His justice and satisfaction, quha is the end and accomplishment of the Law, be quhome we ar set at this liberty that the curse and malediction of God fall not upon us, albeit we fulfill not the same in al pointes. For God the Father, beholding us in the body of His Sonne Christ Jesus, acceptis our imperfite obedience as it were perfite, and covers our warks, quhilk ar defyled with mony spots, with the justice of His Sonne." [2] To the same

---

[1] Westminster Confession, chap. x.

[2] Dunlop's Confessions, ii. 58. There is hardly one of these expressions that may not be found in Calvin's Institutes :—

It behoves us to apprehend Christ Jesus with His justice and satisfaction.	Confiteor nos justificari per fidem quâtenus per eam apprehendimus Jesum Christum.
We are set at this liberty that the curse and malediction of the law fall not upon us.	Omni execratione quae nobis incumbebat eximeremur dum in eum traduceret. Fides, in Christi damnatione absolutionem, benedictionem in maledictione, apprehendit.
God the Father, beholding us in the body of His Son Christ	Ubi nos in filii sui communionem semel recepit, opera

effect it is said in chapter xxv. that "albeit sinne remaine and continuallie abyde in thir our mortall bodies, zit it is not imputed unto us, bot is remitted and covered with Christ's justice."[1] It has been questioned, however, whether we have in these statements the doctrine taught generally in the reformed churches regarding the *articulus stantis vel cadentis ecclesiæ.* This can be a question only with those who forget that the church which received this Confession, and required her adult members to assent to the heads of it, appointed for the instruction of her youth the Catechism in which this doctrine of Calvin is stated in his own words ; and that the very men[2] who in 1560 drew it up, in 1566, along with their brethren of the General Assembly,

Jesus, accepts our imperfect obedience as it were perfect.

Covers our works, which are defiled with many spots, with the justice of His Son.

nostra grata acceptaque habet, non quod ita promereantur sed quia condonatâ eorum imperfectione, nil in illis intuetur, nisi quod a Spiritu suo profectum, purum ac sanctum est.

Nullae nostrae sordes aut immunditiae imperfectionis imputantur, sed illa puritate Christi ac perfectione velut sepultae *conteguntur.* Cujus perfectione tegatur nostra imperfectio. See also Calvin's Catechism in Dunlop's Confessions, ii. 175.

[1] Dunlop's Confessions, ii. 95 ; Laing's Knox, ii. 119.

[2] [Of the six, all save Willock sign the letter to Beza on 4th September 1566 (Laing's Knox, vi. 548-550).]

declared of the *Later Helvetic Confession*—which is admitted to contain what has been termed "the Lutherano-Calvinian view" of justification—that therein was "most faithfully, holily, piously, and indeed divinely explained" what they themselves had for eight years been constantly teaching, and still by the grace of God continued to teach, and that in consequence they felt constrained not only to express their approval, but their "exceed-ing commendation of every chapter and of every sentence," save the one relating to holidays.[1] It may be taken for granted that they knew their own meaning, and that of their Swiss brethren;[2]

[1] Laing's Knox, vi. 546-548.

[2] Considerable ingenuity has been expended in the attempt to show that the words "who is the end and accomplishment of the law" are to be understood in some other than their most obvious and commonly received meaning. Without questioning the com-petency of such ingenious rather than ingenuous exposition, were a case raised before the judicial committee of a modern privy council to have the expounder tried and condemned as a heretic, I venture to think that when the matter to be determined is rather what, in point of fact, did Knox and his associates hold and teach, the fol-lowing brief quotation from the "godly and perfect" treatise of Balnaves on Justification must go pretty near to settle it : "Christ is the end of the law (unto righteousnes) to all that beleeve—that is, Christ is the consummation and fulfilling of the lawe, and that justice whiche the lawe requireth ; and all they which beleeve in Him are just by imputation through faith, and for His sake are repute and accepted as just " (Laing's Knox, iii. 492). If more than this has been taught in recent times, I should be greatly inclined with Principal Lee to trace it to Jonathan Edwards, or perhaps even to the great Independent, Dr Owen, rather than to the Westminster divines, or the earlier Scottish.

H

the more especially as in our day Stähelin, whose impartiality and historical reputation will not be challenged, has adduced the statement in chapter xv. as one of his proofs that Calvin himself could not have framed the Scotch Confession otherwise than Knox has done.[1]

The nature of the church, and the notes by which the true church is to be discerned, are explained in chapters xvi. and xviii. As in most of the other Reformed or Calvinistic Confessions, greater prominence is assigned to the Invisible Church, consisting of the elect of all times and nations, than to the general visible church subsisting at any particular time in the world and embracing all who profess faith in Christ and submit to the godly discipline He has prescribed. The notes by which it may be discerned whether any branch of the professing church is indeed part of the true Kirk of Christ are stated *negatively*—not to be " antiquitie, title usurpit, lineal descente, place appointed, nor multitude of men approving," as Roman Catholics were wont to allege; and *positively* to be " the trew preaching of the Worde of God," " the right administration of the Sacraments," and " ecclesiastical discipline uprightlie ministred as Goddis Worde prescribes." [2]   " These articles," as Principal

---

[1] Stähelin's Johannes Calvin, ii. 88.
[2] Dunlop's Confessions, ii. 66-68 ; Laing's Knox, ii. 110.

Lee has so pithily expressed it, "have been almost as disagreeable to some Episcopalian writers as they were to the most servile adherents of the pope. It is thought a most dangerous omission to make no mention of uninterrupted succession and conveyance of authority from the apostles. This omission has been somewhat incorrectly charged against the reformers of our church. They do certainly mention *lineal succession*, but they mention it only to disown it. They say that though the Jewish priests in our Saviour's time 'lineally descended from Aaron,' yet no 'man of sound judgment will grant that they were the Church of God.'"[1] They further assert that wherever the three notes given above are found and continue for any time (be the number never so few above two or three), there without all doubt is the true Kirk of Christ, who according to His promise is in the midst of them; and in this they are borne out not only by Calvin but by Luther, who boldly affirmed: "Were I the only man on earth that held by the Word, *I alone would be the church*, and I would be justified in pronouncing of all the rest of the world that it was not the church."

The only other parts of the Confession I deem

[1] Lee's Lectures on the History of the Church of Scotland, i. 124, 125.

it necessary to refer to in this review of it are the chapters relating to the sacraments and the right use of them.   It was asserted some years ago by a leader of modern thought in Scotland that Knox did not go beyond the Zwinglian doctrine regarding the Sacrament of the Lord's Supper ; and that his Order for the administration of it was a bold protest against the " mystical jargon " which Luther employed, and from which Calvin was not free.   When he made this assertion he seems to have forgot that the address in Knox's Order for the administration of the Lord's Supper was little else than a translation of that in Calvin's Liturgy, and teaches exactly the same mystical doctrine. This doctrine is no less explicitly taught in the Confession ; and Stähelin, whose competence to judge in the matter cannot be questioned, maintains that the Zwinglian doctrine is as explicitly rejected as the Romano-Lutheran ; and that the language as well as the doctrine closely resembles Calvin's.   The text of the common editions of the Confession speaks of two *chief* sacraments only as being appointed under the New Testament as well as under the Old.   From this expression, some, who are more familiar with Anglican than with Calvinistic formularies, have concluded that Knox, like several of the earlier English reformers, attributed a *quasi*-sacramental character to some of the other rites regarded as sacraments by the Romanists. But in the copy of the Confession reprinted in Dr Laing's edition of Knox's History the word *chief* is omitted in the second instance, and the clause runs *two sacraments only*.[1] Perhaps it will be accepted as some confirmation of the correctness of this reading that it is identical with that found in Alasco's 'Epitome Doctrinæ Ecclesiarum Frisiæ Orientalis,' from which treatise the opening sentence of chapter xxi. of the Scottish Confession may possibly have been taken,[2] though the verbal coincidence with the early edition of Calvin's Institutes is in some respects more marked.

Such are the main contents and general bearing of this ancient Scottish Confession. Notwithstanding the confident assertions to the contrary made of late both within and without the Presbyterian churches, I venture to think that no one who, with a good conscience and

---

[1] Laing's Knox, ii. 113. [In the Confession, as printed in the Acts of the Parliaments of 1560 and 1567 ratifying it, the word *chief* is retained (Acts of Parliament, ii. 532; iii. 20). The Confession of 1616 bears that: "We believe that there be only two sacraments appointed by Christ under the New Testament, Baptisme and the Lord's Supper" ('Booke of the Universall Kirk,' iii. 1137). Concerning the sacraments the First Book of Discipline says: "They be two, to wit, Baptism and the Holy Supper of the Lord Jesus" (Dunlop's Confessions, ii. 520; Laing's Knox, ii. 186).]

[2] Hujus generis *duo praecipua* in vetere ecclesiâ fuerunt circumcisio et agnus paschalis. Nos illorum loco *duo* etiam habemus baptismum et caenam domini.

honest intent, could sign that Confession, and answer in the affirmative the questions regarding election put to candidates for the ministry at their ordination, need hesitate to put his name to that which in 1647 was received as "in nothing contrary" to the former, and held its place alongside of it even after the restoration of Charles II., and under the episcopal *régime*.[1] Most assuredly at least no one need hesitate to do so who would have put his name to that Confession which was drawn up in the time of the first episcopacy,[2] and which is quite as distinctively Calvinistic as the Westminster Confession, while it ventures incidentally to determine some points the Westminster divines have wisely left undetermined.[3] The old Confession can advance no claim to the terse English style, the logical accuracy, the

---

[1] "The Confession of Faith made by Mr Knox, and ratified in Parliament by King James VI., together with the Westminster Confession (both agreed on by the General Assembly of Presbyters), are owned next to the Word of God, by both parties, as the Standard of the doctrine of our Church" (Case of Suffering Church of Scotland).

[2] It is printed at length in Calderwood's History, vii. 233-242; and also in the 'Booke of the Universall Kirk,' iii. 1132-1139; and is supposed to have been mainly the work of Howie, Melville's successor at St Andrews.

[3] [In speaking of this Confession of 1616, Dr Grub says that it "agrees with the old one in all important points, the chief difference being in its more marked enunciation of the doctrine of Calvin in regard to election and predestination" (Grub's History, ii. 306).]

judicial calmness, and intimate acquaintance with early patristic theology which characterise that mature product of the faith and thought of the more learned Puritans of the south. I am not ashamed to avow that it has long appeared to me that there is somewhat to be said in favour of the opinion that Scottish presbyterianism gained quite as much as, nay, more than, it lost, by being brought into contact with the broader, richer, and decidedly more catholic spirit of the south, and adding to its earlier symbolical books those which it still holds in common with almost all the orthodox presbyterians of the Anglo-Saxon race. No one who will take the trouble to read the report of the discussion on Arminianism in the Scottish General Assembly of 1638 [1] will, I am sure, be so bold as to affirm that the type of theology then prevalent among Scottish ministers was in any material respect different from that which was set forth in the Confession of 1647, and which has never since, either under episcopal or presbyterian *régime*, been set aside in the National Church. The teaching of the latest of our symbolical books imposes nothing in regard to the doctrines known as Calvinistic [2] but what is explicitly contained or fairly deducible

---

[1] Printed in Peterkin's Records of the Kirk, pp. 155-160.
[2] Generally so designated, but really as old as the days of Paul and Augustine.

from the earliest Confession drawn up for the
English church at Geneva, of which Knox was
pastor, and adopted (along with the larger one
on which I have been commenting) at the beginning of the Reformation in Scotland, and printed
in Scotch psalm-books[1] as late as 1638, in which
it is asserted " which church is not seene to man's
eye but only knowne to God, who of the lost
sonnes of Adam hath ordained some as vessels
of wrath to damnation, and hath chosen others
as vessels of His mercy to bee saved, the which
also in due time He calleth to integritie of life and
godly conversation to make them a glorious
church to Himselfe."[2]

Probably, however, the main argument against
recurring to the old Scottish Confession of 1560
is that derived from the unmeasured language of
vituperation in which it, as well as the contemporary forms of recantation[3] required of priests at

---

[1] [After 1564-65, the Book of Common Order was usually printed
with a complete metrical version of the Psalms (Laing's Knox, vi.
279, 280, 284); and was comprehended under the name ' Psalm
Book' (*infra*, p. 128). Mr Cowan, of 47 Braid Avenue, Edinburgh,
informs me that the Confession, drawn up for the English congregation at Geneva, appears in every edition of the Book of Common
Order which he has examined, from the Geneva edition of 1556
down to the edition printed by Evan Tyler in 1644.]

[2] Dunlop's Confessions, ii. 8 ; Laing's Knox, iv. 171, 172.

[These forms of recantation may be seen in the Maitland Miscellany, iii. 215-221 ; and in the Register of St Andrews Kirk-
session, Scot. Hist. Soc., i. 11-18.]

that date, indulges when referring to the teaching
of the members of the pre-Reformation church.
No doubt it might be deemed sufficient proof of
this to subjoin the examples furnished in chapter
xviii. on the "Notis" or marks by which "the
trewe Kirk is decernit fra the false," where the old
church is designated the "pestilent synagoge,"
"the filthie synagogue," and "the horrible harlot,
the kirk malignant"[1]—the last words no doubt
meant as a translation of the Vulgate rendering
of Psalm xxvi. 5, *ecclesiam malignantium*,[2] translated "the congregation of evil doers" in our
authorised English version. But I may add, in
corroboration, that in chapter xxi. on the true
uses of the sacraments, the papists are charged
with having "perniciouslie taucht and damnablie
beleeved" the transubstantiation of the bread into
Christ's natural body and of wine into his natural
blood,[3] and that in the last chapter the language
of Rev. xiv. 11 ("the smoke of their torment

---

[1] Dunlop's Confessions, ii. 65, 66 ; Laing's Knox, ii. 109, 110.

[2] The designation is undoubtedly Knoxian, as it occurs in his
dispute with Friar Arbuckill in 1547. To the reformer's assertion
"that the spous of Christ had nether power nor authoritie against
the Word of God," the Friar replied, "Yf so be, ye will leave us
na kirk ;" and to that the reformer rejoined, "In David I read
that thare is a church of the malignantis, for he sayis, *Odi ecclesiam
malignantium*. That church ye may have without the Word, . . .
of that church yf ye wilbe, I can not impead yow" (Laing's Knox,
i. 200).

[3] Dunlop's Confessions, ii. 80 ; Laing's Knox, ii. 114.

ascendeth up for ever and ever : and they have no rest day nor night, who worship the beast and his image ") is adduced in proof of the ultimate fate of those who delight in superstition or idolatry.[1]

The same unrestrained spirit is shown in some contemporary Confessions, notably in the earliest Danish one, the framers of which seem to have kept closer to Luther than to the more gentle Melanchthon : but however excusable it may have been in the fierce battle then forced on them, there can be no doubt that the calmer and more measured language of the later Confession is a decided improvement on the statements of the earlier one ; and I do not hesitate to say that, with the simpler formula of 1693-94 recently restored, and the explanatory act which accompanies it—emphasising the distinction between matters of minor importance and the great doctrines of the faith—the position of the ministers of our church in these respects is as nearly what it should be as is that of the ministers in any of the allied Presbyterian churches.

[1] Dunlop's Confessions, ii. 96, 97.

CHAPTER VII.

THE BOOK OF COMMON ORDER.

THIS, though in point of time the first composed of the symbolical books of the Scottish
Reformation, was the last to be formally assigned
its honoured place. The title it commonly bore
in that age was the Book of Common Order.
In the First Book of Discipline it is called "the
Order of Geneva" and "the Book of our Common Order."[1] In recent times it has been more
generally designated as Knox's Liturgy. It has
usually been deemed sufficient to say that it
was drawn up and first privately and then publicly printed at Geneva, and was directly taken
from the liturgy then used there, as well as

[1] Dunlop's Confessions, ii. 520, 583; Laing's Knox, ii. 186, 239.
[In another passage it is spoken of as "the Booke of the Common
Order, called the Order of Geneva" (Dunlop's Confessions, ii. 548;
Laing's Knox, ii. 210).] The Book of Common Order, which has
been frequently reprinted, is included in vols. iv. and vi. of Dr
Laing's edition of Knox's Works.

approved by Calvin. But this is only partially
true. The first English congregation on the
Continent which invited Knox to be one of its
pastors was that formed at Frankfort in 1554,
and admitted to hold its services in the same
church as the congregation of French-speaking
exiles on condition of using the same ceremonies and Confession of Faith as the French.[1]
The minister and other office-bearers accordingly signed the Confession of Faith along with
those of the French congregation, and it was
ultimately incorporated into the Book of Common Order as the exposition of the Apostles'
Creed in the baptismal service. The first draft
of the Book of Common Order was drawn up
before the end of 1554, and privately printed,[2]

[1] The extract from the minutes of the city council embodying
these conditions, which I found in Withof's 'Vertheidigung' and
communicated to Dr Hume Brown, was printed by him in the
Appendix to his 'John Knox,' and is also reprinted here in
Appendix D.

[2] "At lenght it was agreed that the Order of Geneua (whiche
then was alreadie printed in Englishe and some copies there amonge
them) shulde take place as an Order moste godly and fardeste off
from superstition. But Maister Knox beinge spoken unto, aswell
to put that Order in practise, as to minister the communion, refused
to do ether the one or the other, affirminge, that for manie con-
siderations he coulde not consente that the same Order shulde be
practised, till the lerned men off Strausbrough, Zurik, Emden,
&c., were made privy" (Brief Discourse of the Troubles begun at
Frankfort in the year 1554, Petheram's reprint, p. xxvii). We
have the following additional entry : "After longe debatinge to
and fro, it was concluded that Maister Knox, Maister Whittingham,

to implement the stipulation for conformity with the French in ceremonies as well as in Confession of Faith, and it seems to have been mainly owing to Knox that it was not adopted at once, but that time was given for circulating and examining it. Unfortunately the ambitious plan was taken of inviting the English exiles at Strassburg and Zurich to join with them in their proposed action, which led to those unfortunate disputes, chronicled at length in the 'Troubles at Frankfort,' and to the departure of a large number of the English exiles to Geneva, where through the kindness of Calvin a hospitable reception was promised them, and the Church of Marie la Neuve was assigned for their services and those of the Italian exiles, but without any hampering clause about identity of ceremonies or Confession of Faith. The congregation which shared with the English exiles the church of "the white ladies," or Cistercian nuns, at Frankfort, consisted chiefly of the company of French-speaking exiles which had been originally gathered at Strassburg by Farel, tended for several years by Calvin, and then

Maister Gilby, Maister Fox and Maister T. Cole shulde drawe forthe some Order meete for their state and time : whiche thinge was by them accomplished and offred to the congregation (beinge the same Order off Geneua whiche is nowe in print). This Order was verie well liked off many, but suche as were bent to the Booke of Englande coulde not abide it" (Ibid., pp. xxxvi, xxxvii).

by Poullain, or Pollanus, under whom, when
the Interim was imposed on the city, they had
to seek a new home. This they ultimately
found in England, to which Bucer and Martyr
from the same city had already been invited
and had gone. Glastonbury Abbey was assigned for their residence by the king and
council, and there they lived in peace and
quiet till the close of the reign of Edward VI.
In 1551 Pollanus published the first edition
of his 'Liturgia Sacra seu Ritus ministerii in
ecclesia peregrinorum profugorum propter Evangelium Christi Argentinæ.' No doubt he had
heard that the favour shown to Alasco and
his congregations of French and Flemings in
London was intended to help on further reformation in the Church of England also, and so
in a lengthy dedication to the king he bespeaks
his favour not only to his congregation but also
to their book, affirming "ut in cultu Dei ex-
terno ita etiam in disciplina morum nullam
esse puriorem aut quæ propius accedat ad illam
quæ fuit temporibus Apostolorum." No doubt
it was in a similar spirit and in similar terms
that he pressed the forms of his book on the
acceptance of the English exiles at Frankfort,
and to a great extent with success. Their Book
of Common Order is founded on Farel's and
Calvin's services, but is so after these services

have passed through the alembic of Pollanus and been modified and supplemented by him. This will appear from several of the notes subjoined, and will be more fully shown in the Appendix.[1]

The exclusive authority of this book—previously drafted but first used in Knox's congregation at Geneva—was not asserted by the General Assembly till 1564: nevertheless, even in 1560, the Book of Discipline indicated a very marked preference for its regulations, speaking not only of it as the book of *our* Common Order, already used in some churches, but specially commended its form for administration of the Lord's Supper; and in giving directions for the celebration of the sacraments and marriage, and for the burial of the dead, it followed closely the regulations of this book. In 1561 Quintine Kennedy, Abbot of Crossraguel, in his oration against the Protestants, alluded to it in such a way as implied that it was already well known and in general use in Scotland.[2] In 1562 the General Assembly enjoined the observance of a uniform Order in the adminis-

---

[1] [It is greatly to be regretted that Dr Mitchell does not seem to have been able to prepare the Appendix to which he here refers; but after this lecture had left his hands he expressed his "strong conviction that the words and matter of Knox's Latin Prayer Book of 1556 were derived directly from the Liturgia Sacra of Pollanus." On this point he entertained "no doubt whatever."]

[2] Laing's Knox, vi. 162.

tration of the sacraments and the celebration of
marriage according to the " Booke of Geneva "—
i.e., the Order used by Knox's congregation there ;[1]
and in 1564 it further ordained that " everie
minister, exhorter, and reader sall have one of
the Psalme Bookes latelie printed in Edinburgh,
and use the Order contained therein [that is,
the Order in Knox's Book] in prayers, marriage,
and ministration of the sacraments." [2]

There seems sufficient reason to believe that
for some years before the establishment of the Reformed Church, the morning and evening prayers,
along with the lessons from Holy Scripture, as
contained in the Second Prayer Book of Edward
VI., were used at least in part of the assemblies
held by the reformed for worship and mutual
edification ;[3] and perhaps they may have con-

---

[1] Booke of the Universall Kirk, i. 30.   [2] Ibid., i. 54.

[3] [The grounds on which this opinion is usually based are given
in Laing's Knox, vi. 277, 278. To these may be added the terms
of the summons raised by Sir James Archebald, Vicar of Lintrathin,
against his parishioners, on the 27th of May 1560, for payment of
his teinds, &c., on the plea that he "is lauchfullie providit be the
lawis and practik of oure realme, observit in tymes past, of the said
vicarage, and hes bene in possessioun of the samyn thir divers yeris
bigane, and hes causit *the commone prayeris and homilies* be red
owlklie to the parrochinaris of the said parrochin, and uther wyiss
is content to abyde sik reformatioun as the Lordis of our Secreit
Counsale plesis mak thairintill, and als is adjonit to Goddis congregatioun, and takis part with the saidis Lordis in setting fordwart
the commone caus, to the gloir of God and commone weill of our
realme " (Spalding Miscellany, iv. 120).

tinued to be so used for a year or two afterwards, though no formal sanction was ever given
by the General Assembly even to those parts of
that book, still less to the other parts to which
Knox's party had always objected.   But it is
now ascertained that as early as 1556, or at least
1557, Knox had recommended, and that soon
after some of the more fully organised congregations adopted, a form of service more simple, and
more nearly resembling the Genevan than the
Anglican.[1]   It is known that when the treaty of
peace between France, England, and Scotland
was being negotiated in July 1560, the ministers
and congregation of Scotland, thinking their own
profession after the order and discipline of Geneva
to be more pure than the Anglican, as containing
no other ceremonies than are expressly mentioned
in the Scriptures, " wald not ressave or admitt any
uther." [2]

Randolph, the English ambassador, in his letters to his Government, not only admits that they
were "lothe to remytte anie thing of that that
thei *have receaved*," [3] but also leads us to conclude
that the practice of their leading ministers in
public worship at this early date was not very

[1] Laing's Knox, iv. 137-139. [Laing gives the 7th of July 1556
as the correct date of this letter, and says that it is by some oversight that M'Crie in the later editions of his ' Life of Knox ' has
dated it 7th July 1557 (Ibid., iv. 140).]

[2] Lesley's History, p. 292.   [3] Laing's Knox, vi. 119.

I

dissimilar to that of their successors in the next century. "The Byshop of Athens," he says, "preacheth earnestly, and prayethe hartely for the Queene's Majestie our Soveraigne, and greatly extollethe her benefyttes; Mr Wyllocke specially by name prayethe both for France and Englande; Mr Knox, universally for all Prynces lyvinge in the feare of God, desyring Him to turne the hartes of other, and to sende them in the rycht way."[1] About the same period, in one of his letters to Mrs Lock, Knox links together "Mr Parson's *pattering of his* CONSTRAINED *prayers*" and "the masse-munging of Mr Vicar and of his wicked companions," in such a way as shows that he was no great admirer of the one or the other.[2] In tolerating for a little the use of the morning and evening services of the Prayer Book of Edward VI., our reformers can be judged inconsistent only by those who do not know that in the time of the good King Edward considerably greater latitude was allowed in the celebration of those services than has ever since been suffered in the sister church. The minister, for instance, was expressly permitted to shorten them *according*

---

[1] Laing's Knox, vi. 118. This evidently shows that they used not the *ipsissima verba* of the prayer for all estates, but variant words, "like in effect." [Randolph's letter is dated 25th August 1560. Alexander Gordon, Bishop of Galloway, was titular Archbishop of Athens.]

[2] Laing's Knox, vi. 13. [This letter is dated 6th April 1559.]

to his *discretion* when a sermon or other divine ordinance was to follow. He had a sort of sanction for any neglect of minuter directions as to kneeling, crossing, &c., from a general rubric which intimated that these things were to be left free "as every man's devotion serveth." He had also a pretty full indulgence practically conceded for deviating from the strict injunctions of the book in regard to surplices and other ecclesiastical vestments,[1] which were never adopted or tolerated by Knox and his associates, the rigid enforcement of which in the days of Queen Elizabeth produced great misery and discontent at the time, and paved the way for more and greater in the days of James and Charles, her successors. It is by no means so clear as some have recently asserted it to be, that Knox used this liturgy habitually when he was in England, acting as one of the court chaplains and special preachers in the time of Edward VI. The observance of the liturgy was not enforced in the northern part of the kingdom when Knox began his labours there. And even at the time when he removed to the southern province it was not necessary that he should use the liturgy in the office he held, as the special preachers of that day, and even the lecturers for long after, often delivered

---

[1] Liturgies of Edward VI., Parker Society, pp. 157, 158. [The "certain notes" thus referred to pertain to Edward's First Liturgy.]

their discourses in the open air, and used before
them only free prayer or a short prayer similar
to that which is still employed by the university
preachers at Oxford and Cambridge. It was not
till a considerably later period that "to gall
tender consciences" it was required of all *lecturers*
and *special preachers* that they should also personally read the liturgy so many times every year.
Dr Lorimer has proved that Knox used at Berwick a simpler form of communion service,
moulded so far as yet traced on Swiss and German offices.[1]   And it can be established on the
best of all authority — Knox's own testimony
—that he neither approved of nor was willing
to conform to the communion office. Then no
sooner was he beyond the restraint of English law
than he proposed for adoption in his congregation, first at Frankfort and then at Geneva, the
form ultimately adopted in Scotland after his
return thither.

As has been already mentioned, the exclusive
authority of the Book of Common Order, as a
guide and aid to ministers in conducting public
worship and administering the sacraments, was
asserted by the General Assembly in 1564. It
continued to hold the place thus given to it down
to 1637, when it was superseded, in so far as the
king and his council were concerned, first, by

[1] Lorimer's Knox and the Church of England, 1875, pp. 29-32.

what is known as Archbishop Laud's Liturgy, and then by an injunction of the disappointed prelates, which required that, till further order should be taken, neither the new nor the old liturgy should be used in the public services, in Edinburgh, but only those prayers which the ministers had been accustomed to make before and after their sermons.[1] Thus the bishops themselves were the unwitting instruments of first setting aside a partially liturgic, and introducing instead a wholly extemporary, form of worship into Scotland. There is no reason, however, for maintaining that the Book of Common Order, while it continued in authority, was regarded as more than a guide or model, at least to the ordained ministers, or can be so regarded by any one who studies with care its rubrics and general

[1] [On the 29th of July 1637—six days after the riot in St Giles—it was reported to the Privy Council by Archbishop Spottiswoode, for himself and in name of the remanent bishops, that it seemed expedient to them "that there should be a surcease of the service-booke" till the king signified his pleasure as to the punishment of "that disorderlie tumult"; and "that a course be sett down for the peaceable exercise thereof." He also reported that "the saids bishops had appointed and given order that, in the whole churches of this citie [*i.e.*, Edinburgh], sermon sall be made at the accustomed times, by regular and obedient ministers, and that a prayer sall be made before and after sermon, and that neither the old service nor the new established service be used in this interim." The Council remitted to the bishops "to doe therein according to the power incumbent unto thame in the dewtie of thair office" (Peterkin's Records of the Kirk, p. 52).]

contents, far less was observed as a rigid liturgy, every word of which must be repeated unvaryingly by the officiating minister. It has indeed been maintained, even in recent times, and by ministers of the National Church, that " the idea of extemporaneous prayer as an appropriate vehicle of public devotion was one quite unknown to the Reformation." But this cannot be made good with respect to any of the Reformed or Calvinistic churches, and certainly least of all with respect to the National Church of Scotland at any period of its history.

Our reformers laid it down in their First Book of Discipline as a fixed principle that " it is neither the clipping of their crownes, the greasing of their fingers,[1] nor the blowing of the dumb dogges called the bishops, neither the laying on of their hands, that maketh true ministers of Christ Jesus. But the Spirit of God, inwardly first moving the heart to seeke to enter in the holy calling for Christ's glory and the profite of His Kirk, and thereafter the nomination of the people, the examination of the learned, and publick admission, . . . make men lawfull ministers." [2] They distinctly taught that no one was to be regarded as a lawful minister of Christ into whose mouth

---

[1] [In Knox's version—" the crossing of thair fingaris " (Laing's Knox, ii. 255).]

[2] Dunlop's Confessions, ii. 603.

Christ had not put *some word of exhortation* or vouchsafed some gift of expounding and preaching the Word of God,[1] and they expressly encouraged their ministers to look for their Master's aid and guidance in praying as well as in preaching. Hence throughout their Book of Common Order they carefully abstained from imposing the *ipsissima verba* of particular forms as rigidly binding, or even from encouraging their ministers to rest contented with the stated repetition of them.

"When the congregation is assembled," run its tolerant rubrics, "the minister useth one of these two confessions, or *like in effect*."[2] "This done, the people sing a psalme altogether in a plain tune, which ended, the minister prayeth for the assistance of God's Holie Spirit *as the same shall move his heart*, and so proceedeth to the sermon. The minister, after the sermon, useth this prayer following, or *such like*."[3] "Then the people sing a psalme, which ended, the minister pronounceth one of these blessings, and so the congregation departeth."[4] Such are its few and simple directions for the ordinary form of public worship; and as if even these might fail to beget in the minds of some of the old priests a sense

[1] Dunlop's Confessions, ii. 526, 530, 532, 536, 603; Laing's Knox, ii. 191, 194, 196, 199, 255.

[2] Dunlop's Confessions, ii. 417; Laing's Knox, iv. 179; vi. 294.

[3] Dunlop's Confessions, ii. 421; Laing's Knox, iv. 182; vi. 297.

[4] Dunlop's Confessions, ii. 425; Laing's Knox, iv. 185; vi. 298.

of their freedom from minute restrictions and a burdensome ritual, it is added: "It shall not be necessarie for the minister daylie to repeat all these things before mentioned; but, beginning with *some maner of confession,* to proceede to the sermon, which ended, he either useth the prayer for all estates before mentioned, or else *prayeth as the Spirit of God shall move his heart,* framing the same according to the time and matter which he hath entreated of." [1]   To the same effect, in the First Book of Discipline, after recommending that in all the large towns there should every day be either sermon or common prayers with reading of Scriptures, it is said: "What day [2] the publick sermon is, we can neither require *nor greatly approve* that the common prayers be publickly used, lest that we should either foster the people in superstition, who come to the prayers as they come to the masse; or else give them occasion, that they think them no prayers which be made before and after sermons." [3]   Even in the most solemn of its

[1] Dunlop's Confessions, ii. 426.   There is a similar rubric in the Liturgy of Pollanus: "Minister, nomine Domini invocato, ut Spiritu Sancto adjutus, possit digna Deo atque salutaria ecclesiae eloqui recitat textum."

[2] The Liturgy of Pollanus appoints sermons to be preached on the mornings of Tuesday and Thursday.   The service is to begin with a psalm, which being sung, the minister having invoked the Holy Spirit recites his text and proceeds with his sermon.   He concludes with some shorter prayer "prout animus tulerit."

[3] Dunlop's Confessions, ii. 583; Laing's Knox, ii. 238.

special services and in the most solemn part of it, the prayer of thanksgiving and consecration in the communion, the rubric is : " The minister . . . giveth thanks either in these words following *or like in effect.*"[1] The same thing is confirmed by many of the rubrics of the other occasional services in the Book of Common Order,[2] and by the express testimony of Calderwood, Row, and others who officiated as ministers of the church while the book was in use. The first named of these, though entertaining so strong a regard for its venerable forms that even on the approval of the Westminster Directory in 1645 he is said to have opposed the adoption of any Act expressly abrogating the Book of Common Order, had not hesitated when contrasting it with the English Liturgy thus to speak of the nature and extent of the submission expected to be given to it : " Habemus quidem nos etiam in Ecclesiâ nostra

[1] Dunlop's Confessions, ii. 450 ; Laing's Knox, iv. 194.

[2] In the Order of the General Fast it is stated : " The exhortation and prayers of everie several exercise we have remitted to be gathered by the discrete ministers, for time preased us so that we culd not frame them in such order as wes convenient, nether yit thought we it so expedient to pen prayers unto men, as to teach them with what hart and affection and for what causes we shuld pray, in this great calamitie " (Dunlop's Confessions, ii. 695 ; Laing's Knox, vi. 421). See also Dunlop's Confessions, ii. 698 ; Laing's Knox, vi. 470. Even the Order of Excommunication might be " enlarged or contracted as the wisedome of the discreit minister shall thinke expedient " (Dunlop's Confessions, ii. 746 ; Laing's Knox, vi. 470).

Agendas, et ordinem in sacris celebrandis ser-vandum, *sed nemo alligatur precibus aut exhorta-tionibus liturgiae nostrae*, proponuntur tantum ut peradigmata, quibus precum aut exhortationum materia et forma quoad substantialia indicantur, non ut eisdem verbis adstringantur ministri. Totos ego tredecim annos, quibus functus sum ministerio, sive in sacramentis, sive in aliis sacris celebrandis, exhortationibus aut precibus quae extant in Agendâ nostrâ, *nunquam usus sum*. Sic etiam alii complures ; et omnibus etiam liberum est idem facere." [1]   While in regard to the Liturgy by which it was attempted in 1637 to supplant the Book of Common Order, Row thus expresses himself: " Though they amend all those errours, and that in all the Service Book there were no materiall errour at all, neither masse nor popish ceremonie ; and though they should read nothing but Canonicall Scripture, yea say that all their prayers and exhortations were merelie

---

[1] Calderwood's Altare Damascenum, 1623, p. 613. In this and the preceding pages I have made use of materials contributed by me to a Report anent Innovations in Public Worship, presented to the General Assembly in 1864. [Elsewhere, Calderwood says : " None are tyed to the prayers of that book ; but the prayers are set down as samplers " (Calderwood's History, 1678 ed., p. 25). Principal Baillie's evidence is to the same 'effect : " The Warner is here also mistaken in his beliefe that ever the Church of Scotland had any liturgy ; they had and have still some formes for helpe and direction but no tie ever in any of them by law or practise " (Review of Bramhall's Faire Warning against the Scots Discipline, 1649, p. 57).]

words of Holie Scripture, yit it is not lawfull to introduce a reading ministrie, and to stint men (gifted of God, who has the spirit of their calling, able ministers of the gospell who hes the Spirit of adoption teaching them to pray, Gal. iv. 6; Rom. viii. 26; and to whom God hes opened a doore of utterance, to speak the gospell with boldness, haveing touched their lips with a coall from His awin altar) to such a Liturgie as is to be made the onlie forme of God's publict worship. For though I confess good use may be made of a formed Liturgie and publict service, to serve for a rule to other kirks to fall on the like way, finding it warranted by the Word, and to be as a monument to the posteritie, who thence may learn what forms have been, are, and ought to be used; and that it may lead the way, and be a directorie to those that are beginning in the ministrie; yit certainlie reading of prayers and exhortations is not the way whereby the Lord in His Word has appoynted His servants of the ministrie to worship Him, or to convert, edifie, and comfort, or strengthen soulls; but seing they have receaved gifts for praying and preaching, they ought to stirre up the gift of God, and putt the talent to use; and though in their privat studies they may borrow some help from other men's gifts and labours, yit *neither is it lawfull for a man to tye himself, or for bishops to tye all ministers, to a prescript and stinted forme of words in prayer and exhortation.*"[1] Henderson says that while they had their Directory and prescribed Order, they were "not tyed to set formes and words."[2]

It is plain, therefore, that the General Assembly, by the sanction it gave to the Book of Common Order, did not mean to restrict its ordained ministers to the use of a certain unvarying form of words, but to provide such a Directory or model as would guide them in "the substance and right ordering of all the parts of divine worship," as well as guide the readers and others not fully admitted to the ministry of the Word, through whose special aid alone they were able, in a time of so great dearth of qualified ministers, to supply in part the spiritual destitution of their countrymen. Nor in granting such an amount of liberty, at least to their ordained ministers, did they follow a course which was, as has been so confidently asserted, altogether novel, but rather, as in several other things, carried out more thoroughly and consistently[3] what others of the

[1] Row's History, Wodrow Society, pp. 403, 404.

[2] Order and Government of the Church of Scotland, 1641 : Address to the reader.

[3] Certainly not more consistently than Pollanus in the following rubric : "Hae sunt precationum in liturgiis certae formulae, *quae tamen sequitur minister* SUO ARBITRIO ut tempus fert et res

Reformed churches had adopted at least partially. In almost all the Reformed or Calvinistic
liturgies the prayers are left partly free, and in
several of them no form is furnished even as a
guide or model for the prayer immediately preceding the sermon (and the same might be said of
some of the earlier Lutheran *Agend-bücher*). In the
churches of Basle, which probably in this respect
only followed the general practice of the churches
of East Switzerland, Hagenbach informs us that
there was for fifty years after the Reformation no
form of prayer, before or after sermon, imposed
by public authority, and for fifty years longer
only the prayer after sermon for all estates
and conditions of men.[1] What, therefore, dis-

postulat. Neque enim ullâ praescriptione formularum alligandus
est Spiritus Dei ad eum verborum numerum, cui non liceat subjicere
vel supponere si meliora suggerat. . . . Hae formulae *serviunt
tantum rudioribus. Nullius libertati praescribitur,* tantum ne ab
eâ ratione discedatur quam nobis Jesus Christus praescripsit. . . .
Cumque is (*scilicet* Spiritus Sanctus) apud tribunalia subministret
quae dicenda sint, non deerit nobis [si] cum vera fide coram Deo nos
sistemus sensu orationis excitati."

[1] "Von vorgeschriebenen Kirchengebeten vor und nach der
Predigt finden wir keine Spur, vielmehr das sichere Gegentheil.
. . . Ums Jahr 1589 finden wir zuerst das sogenannte Lob und
Dankopfer und die daran gehängten Fürbitten für die Obrigkeit,
und die übrigen christlichen Stände. . . . Erst nach der Mitte des
siebzehnten Jahrhunderts . . . suchte man auch im Liturgischen
die Willkür der einzelnen in engere Schränken zuruckzuführen"
(Geschichte der ersten Basler-konfession, S. 249-251).

tinguished our reformers from their successors, and from the English Puritans of the seventeenth century, was not that the former disapproved of or curtailed free prayer while the latter advocated and encouraged it, but that the former retained in their Book of Common Order a variety of forms, not only as models, but also as aids to the officiating minister, while the latter put their Directory into such a shape that even the "help and furniture" it provided required the exercise of thought and care on the part of the minister to adapt it for use. This certainly was no great divergence, considering how thoroughly both parties were agreed, on the one hand, as to the liberty which should be left to ordained ministers, and, on the other, as to the limitations within which it should be confined.

From the notices given in his 'Order and Government of the Church of Scotland,' and from the specimens of Henderson's prayers which accompany his printed discourses, it is further evident that he, like Calderwood, habitually used free prayer both before and after sermon. There seems reason to suppose that in not a few cases the readers also before 1638 took the liberty of varying from the forms in Knox's Book and exercising their own gifts. The charges made against the character of their prayers, in what is called the King's Declaration, but what was in reality the declaration of some of his prelates, is only intelligible on this supposition.[1] And the Assembly, as I read their deliverance, rather deny that the prayers of the readers were of the particular character charged than affirm they were the identical prayers contained in Knox's Book.[2]

[1] [The charges are in the alleged causes which led James VI., immediately after his accession to the English throne, to endeavour to bring about uniformity in the services of the church throughout the whole kingdom, and run thus: "That diversitie, nay deformitie, which was used in Scotland, where no set or publike forme of prayer was used, but preachers or readers and ignorant schoolmasters prayed in the church, sometimes so ignorantly as it was a shame to all religion to have the Majestie of God so barbarously spoken unto, sometimes so seditiously that their prayers were plaine libels, girding at soveraigntie and authoritie; or lyes, being stuffed with all the false reports in the kingdome" (Large Declaration, 1639, p. 16).]

[2] [The committee appointed by the General Assembly to examine the Large Declaration describe it as dishonourable to God, to the king, and to the kirk; and as "stuffed full of lies and calumnies." Concerning this part in particular they say: "To the great dishonour of this kirk [it] is affirmed in this Declaration that there is a great deformitie in our service—no forme of publict prayer, but preachers, readers, and ignorant schoollemasters, praying in the church, sometymes so ignorantlie," &c. (Peterkin's Records of the Kirk, pp. 265, 266).]

CHAPTER VIII.

THE FIRST BOOK OF DISCIPLINE; OR,
THE BOOKE OF THE POLICIE OF THE CHURCH.

I REGARD the First Book of Discipline as, in several respects, the most thoughtful, judicious, practical, and comprehensive of the documents connected with the organisation of the Reformed Church of Scotland. It was drawn up by the same six men[1] who were subsequently entrusted with the preparation of the Confession of Faith; and it has been said that they first settled the titles of the several chapters, and then apportioned the preparation of so many of them to each. But this is matter of pure conjecture. The portion on the universities, from the multitude of its practical details, we cannot but assign mainly to Douglas, the Principal of St Mary's College, and Wynram, the sub-prior of

[1] [The six were John Wynram, John Spottiswoode, John Willock, John Douglas, John Row, and John Knox (*supra*, p. 99).]

the Augustinian Monastery at St Andrews. One can hardly doubt that the rest, if not actually drafted by Knox, was carefully remoulded by him; and it bears evidence of acquaintance with books which were far more likely to have been known to him than to any of the others — as Herman of Cologne's Book of the Reformation, Latin versions of some of the earlier Kirchen-bücher or Kirchenordnungen of the German Protestants, and probably of the famous Ordonnances of Calvin, as drafted at Geneva after his return from exile.

I. *The Government of the Church.*

The opinions of our reformer and his associates respecting the government and discipline of the church are gathered partly from the opening chapters of the Book of Common Order, but mainly from the treatise ultimately entitled the First Book of Discipline. I believe that a careful study of these will lead to a pretty definite conclusion as to what these opinions actually were, and to a pretty decided conviction that, like their opinions respecting matters of doctrine and ritual, they were substantially in harmony with those to which the Scottish nation has been so long and firmly attached. It may be admitted that there were some of Knox's associates who, whatever

K

may have been their own private sentiments,
would, on grounds of expediency, have been contented to retain the former hierarchical government of the church ; and if on such a point any
weight is to be allowed to the assertions of Spottiswoode,[1] the popish Archbishop of St Andrews
might possibly in that case not have refused to
follow the course taken for a time by his relatives
in St Mary's College, and to remain at his post
at the head of the reformed church.   But from
the disastrous issue of the compromise in their
case, as well as from what is known and indis-
putable of his own history and character, there
is no reason to suppose that anything was lost,
but on the contrary that incalculable gain ac-
crued to the reformed church from this temptation not being put in his way.   It was long
maintained by the leaders of the Scottish episcopalians that Knox himself, to a certain extent,
yielded to the wishes of his less thoroughgoing
associates, and was implicated with them in
certain attempts to continue or restore the sem-
blance of a hierarchy in the new church.   In
fact, some of them went so far as to assert
that it was not till after his death that controversy arose as to whether the episcopal or
presbyterian form of government was the more
primitive and scriptural.   These views, if I

[1] Spottiswoode's History, Spot. Soc. ed., i. 371, 372.

understand rightly, are now abandoned by their
ablest men; and it was full time that they
should be so. The works of Whitgift, which
have been republished in our own day and made
more generally accessible, clearly show that the
controversy about the presbyterian government
of the church had been formally raised even in
England at least as early as 1568; while the
Later Helvetic Confession, approved by the
Church of Scotland in 1566 at the request of
Knox himself,[1] as clearly shows that the principles on which the controversy fell to be
decided had been generally adopted by the followers of Calvin even at an earlier date. These
principles were: First, that the names of bishop
and presbyter are in Scripture used indiscrimin-
ately to denote the holder of the same office;
second, that the only office-bearers of permanent
divine appointment in the church are the pastor,
the doctor, the elder, and the deacon. In fact,
at the head of Calvin's Ordonnances Ecclesias-
tiques, drawn up, if not printed, as early as
1541, we find the following: "Il y a quatre
ordres d'offices que notre Seigneur a institue
pour le gouvernment de son eglise, premierement
les pasteurs, puis les docteurs, apres les ancients,
quatrement les diacres," which passed substantially into the Book of Common Order in 1556.

[1] *Supra*, pp. 112, 113.

This being the case, we are not guilty of any anachronism in attributing substantially presbyterian opinions to our reformer, even if we have to grant that the particular church court first known as the greater eldership or presbytery, and now exclusively enjoying the title of presbytery, existed at that time only in a rudimentary form.

The Book of Common Order of 1556 is the earliest authentic document casting light on the opinions of our reformers respecting the government and discipline of the church. The introductory part of the book treats at length of the permanent office-bearers of the church, the manner of their election, the duties of their respective offices, and the assemblies they were to hold in common for government and discipline. The enumeration of the office-bearers and the description of their duties is quite in harmony with what the Books of Discipline subsequently laid down. The office-bearers recognised are the minister, the elder, the deacon, and the doctor; and the duties assigned to each are such as have generally been allotted to these functionaries in the presbyterian churches. The terms in which the last-named of them is referred to are specially deserving of notice. They effectually close a loophole, that might otherwise have been imagined to be left,

for the introduction of either bishop or superintendent as an essential and ordinary office-bearer
in the church on the pretext that, even if he
were so, he could be of little use in the single
English congregation at Geneva.[1]   " Wee are
not ignorant," it is said, "that the Scriptures
make mention of a fourth kind of ministers left
to the church of Christ, which also are verie
profitable where time and place doth permit ;
but for lack of opportunity in this our dispersion
and exile we cannot well have the use thereof,
and would to God it were not neglected where
better occasion serveth. These ministers are
called teachers or doctors, whose office is to
instruct and teach the faithfull in sounde doctrine, providing with all diligence that the puritie
of the Gospel be not corrupt either through
ignorance or evill opinions."[2]   Now, can it be
supposed that Knox would have said all this of
the doctor and not a word of the superintendent,
if he had deemed both to be of like permanence
and necessity in the church of Christ ; or that
he would have devoted several pages to explain
the duties of the office-bearers, and their assem-

---

[1] The appointment of such an official as chief minister of the
English congregation of Frankfort had, however, been urged by
Knox's opponents there, but was refused by his party (Discourse
of Troubles at Frankfort, pp. xiv, xlvii, cxvii, cxxxv-cxxxviii, cxlvi,
cxlvii).

[2] Dunlop's Confessions, ii. 409, 410 ; Laing's Knox, iv. 177.

blies for the interpretation of the Scriptures and the administration of discipline, and not have uttered one word about the bishop, had he believed that that official was the chief or even an essential minister of the church? Can it be supposed likely that he would have been so silent, even if there had been no bishop, as confessedly there was no doctor, among the English in Geneva; or possible that he could have been so with Miles Coverdale,[1] a regularly consecrated bishop attending on his ministrations and acting as an elder in his congregation, unless he had regarded (and wished it to be known that he regarded) the simple presbyter as *jure divino* on a level with the diocesan bishop, to say nothing of the fact that his party at Frankfort had refused to have a bishop or superintendent over their congregation?

This examination of the introductory chapters of the Book of Common Order will enable us the better to understand and explain the parts of the Book of Discipline drawn up in 1560 re-

---

[1] The great services Coverdale had rendered to the cause of Protestantism by his translation of the Scriptures did not suffice to blot out from the minds of Elizabeth and her ministers the remembrance of his connection with Knox and Goodman. He was welcomed at the consecration of Archbishop Parker, though he came in his black gown, for they could not well do that without him; but all Grindal's efforts failed to secure for him a Welsh bishopric, or even to get him left unmolested in the parochial benefice he conferred on him.

specting the ministers and office-bearers of the
church. Even the ordinary ministers of the
church must all be well qualified to preach the
gospel of salvation, as many of the common people
were unable to read,[1] and could only be saturated
with its teaching by the living voice of the
preacher who, by sermons and catechising on the
Lord's day, and in the towns also by the sermon
during the week, was to his utmost to carry home
the truth to their hearts. Our reformers judged it
necessary " that His Gospell be truely and openly
preached in every church and assembly of this
realme ";[2] that no one " unable to edifie the
church by wholesome doctrine" should be promoted to or retained in ecclesiastic administration;[3] and held that the sacraments cannot be
" rightlie ministred by him in whose mouth God
hath put no sermon of exhortation."[4] Instead
of entrusting parishes, as was so often done in
England, to men able only to read homilies prepared by others, they affirmed that it was alike
to have no minister at all and to have an idol in
place of a true minister, yea, in some cases it was

[1] Even in St Andrews, with all its equipment of schools and
colleges, the common people are represented in 1547 as welcoming
Knox's offer of a public disputation, because though they could not
all read his papers they could understand what he addressed to
them *vivâ voce* (Laing's Knox, i. 189).

[2] Dunlop's Confessions, ii. 518 ; Laing's Knox, ii. 185.

[3] Dunlop's Confessions, ii. 526 ; Laing's Knox, ii. 191.

[4] Dunlop's Confessions, ii. 530; Laing's Knox, ii. 194.

worse.[1]   Men of best knowledge of God's Word
and cleanest life were to be nominated annually
for election as elders and deacons.[2]   The former
were to assist the minister in all affairs of the
kirk, to hold meetings with him for judging
of causes, admonishing evil livers, yea, to take
heed to the life, manners, diligence, and study of
the ministers, as well as of the flock.[3]   The
deacons were to assist in judgment, but chiefly
to collect and distribute what was provided for
the poor.   They might also, as in the French
Church, be admitted to read the Scriptures and
common prayers in the congregation if required
and qualified to do so.[4]   Besides ministers,
elders, and deacons, generally recognised in the
reformed churches as holding offices of divine
institution, and being of "the ministry" or consistory of the church, certain other functionaries
are mentioned in this Book of Discipline, to
whom special duties are assigned, at least for a
time.   These are the readers, or exhorters, and
the superintendents, and both classes appear to be
spoken of in such a way as to make it clear that
they were not to be permanently retained as
orders of office - bearers in the church distinct
from those above named.

[1] Dunlop's Confessions, ii. 530 ; Laing's Knox, ii. 194.
[2] Dunlop's Confessions, ii. 577 ; Laing's Knox, ii. 233.
[3] Dunlop's Confessions, ii. 578 ; Laing's Knox, ii. 234, 235.
[4] Dunlop's Confessions, ii. 581 ; Laing's Knox, ii. 236, 237.

Readers, or exhorters, were to be provided for those churches which could not presently be supplied with ministers. These readers were to be men judged most apt distinctly to read the common prayers and the Scriptures, but they were to be encouraged and urged so to exercise their gifts that they might grow in knowledge and utterance, and in time might come to be entrusted with the power of preaching the Word, administering the sacraments, and discharging all the functions of the ordinary pastor.[1] Special provision was made for the spiritual improvement of these readers or exhorters in those weekly meetings for the interpretation of Scripture which, originally introduced among the exiles at Frankfort and Geneva, were after their return set up by them in England under the name of prophesying, and in Scotland under the name of the exercise.[2]

The portion of the book relating to the superintendents opens with a statement of the reasons which had led its framers "to make difference betwixt preachers *at this time*."[3] These last

[1] Dunlop's Confessions, ii. 532 ; Laing's Knox, ii. 195, 196. [Readers who were able to *exhort* and explain the Scriptures were to have their stipends augmented until they attained the honour of a minister (Dunlop's Confessions, ii. 536, 537 ; Laing's Knox, ii. 199, 200).]

[2] [The readers who had "any gift of interpretation" were to take part in these meetings (Dunlop's Confessions, ii. 590 ; Laing's Knox, ii. 244).]

[3] Dunlop's Confessions, ii. 539 ; Laing's Knox, ii. 202.

words, as has often been remarked, would have
been unmeaning had they regarded the superintendent's office as by divine institution permanent in the church and superior to that of
the ordinary minister.   Accordingly, when they
proceed to state in detail the reasons which induced them to sanction such a difference, these
are found to be—not, as in the Anglican Ordinal,
that there have always been in the church of
Christ distinct orders of bishops and presbyters,[1]
nor even as in Alasco's book that such offices
were in some sort necessary, though, save in
matters executive, in no way superior to their
brethren the ordinary ministers of the church,
but—that the dearth of qualified preachers or
ministers at that time in Scotland was so great,
that if each were to be settled in a single town
or parish, and allowed to make continual residence
therein, the larger part of the realm would be left
altogether destitute of that efficient spiritual instruction, oversight, and training which the people
themselves eagerly longed for, and the reformed
leaders earnestly desired to provide for them.   To
meet this emergency, without being obliged to
avail themselves so generally and unrestrictedly

---

[1] ["It is evident unto all men, diligently reading Holy Scripture
and ancient authors, that from the apostles' time there hath been
these orders of ministers in Christ's church : bishops, priests, and
deacons" (Liturgies of Edward VI., Parker Society, p. 331).]

as the English had done of the former popish incumbents, they deemed it most expedient that these should, for a time at least, be restricted to the humbler duties of readers; and that from the whole number of godly and learned men then in the realm ten or twelve should be selected, and one of them assigned to each of the proposed provinces, which he should visit annually through its whole extent, preaching from time to time in every parish not provided with an ordained and preaching minister, seeing to the administration of the sacraments and of church discipline in such parishes, and presiding at the meetings of the provincial synod, and at the examination and admission of ministers and readers appointed to serve at the churches.

It used to be maintained by Scottish episcopalians, and has been reiterated even in our own day, that there is hardly any difference to be discerned between these superintendents and the old bishops save the substitution of a name which is bad Latin for one which is good Greek. This is more smart than true. The following very material differences will at once occur to any one acquainted with the First Book of Discipline, and with the constitution and practice of episcopal churches. (1) The bishop in the latter must be consecrated to his office by three, or at least two, bishops who have derived their office in the like lineal succession from their predecessors; while the superintendent, according to the practice of the Church of Scotland, and the constitution of the Church of the Foreigners in London, might be set apart to his office by a simple presbyter or ordinary minister of the church.   (2) The distinctive duties of the bishop are such as, according to the practice of the churches recognising the necessity of his office, cannot be delegated save to one of his own order, while there was no duty entrusted to the superintendent in the Church of Scotland which might not be devolved on a mere presbyter; and it was the custom of the General Assembly to delegate to ordinary ministers the whole functions of visitation and superintendence in provinces not provided with a permanent superintendent, and to do so at times even in the case where the former popish bishop of the diocese had joined himself to the Reformed Church.   (3) It is not generally recognised in episcopal churches as a duty specially incumbent on the bishop to preach regularly in the several churches of his diocese (certainly it was not expected of the English bishops who were contemporary with the Scottish superintendents);[1] but it was one of the main duties expected of these superintendents, and one of the chief

---

[1] The jest attributed to Queen Elizabeth that she had *made* a bishop but *marred* a good preacher shows this.

reasons assigned for the institution of their office, that the Gospel might be preached from time to time in all those parishes not provided with a more stated ministry, and that thus men in every corner of the land might attain some knowledge of the truths of our holy religion, as well as some feeling of godliness. (4) Finally, the bishop in all episcopal churches, so far as my knowledge extends, is allowed to claim a negative voice in synods of his clergy, and can in no case be taken under discipline and judged by them, but only by a synod of his own order; while the superintendent in the Scottish Church was merely the permanent Moderator of Synod, and was bound to give effect to the decision of the majority, or to carry it by appeal before a higher court; and he was not only liable to be judged and punished for neglect of duty and for personal misconduct by the General Assembly, but was also liable to be charged with such offences before his own synod, and to be judged and punished by it. On these grounds I am so far from admitting that the superintendent was in all respects identical with the bishop, that I am inclined to hold that it was just because he was so completely stripped of all real episcopal power that, when the hierarchy was revived, even the most moderate of the bishops found they could not contain themselves within the limits prescribed to the superintendents in

the First Book of Discipline; and that one of the
main obstacles in the way of their success in
the struggle with their refractory presbyters was
occasioned by their own hasty promise to observe
the caveats founded on the previous practice in
the case of superintendents, and especially by
their promise to be subject to the judgment and
censure of the General Assembly.

The form of church government in Scotland
was still further connected with that of the
Calvinistic churches on the Continent (particularly that of France) by the establishment
and gradation of church courts — the General
Assembly having jurisdiction over the whole
church, the provincial synod over the ministers
and congregations within a particular province,
and the session or lesser eldership or consistory
over one or more neighbouring congregations.[1]
What afterwards came to be known as the greater
eldership, or presbytery, or classical consistory,[2]
does not appear at first under that distinctive

[1] In the chief towns, just as in Geneva, there seems from early
times to have been a common or "general session," although there
were several congregations in each, as in Edinburgh, Glasgow,
Dundee, and Perth.

[2] Even the Second Book of Discipline does not sharply dis-
tinguish between the lesser and greater eldership or presbytery;
and Gillespie admits they were not distinguished in the primitive
church, though he holds that both were needed in Scotland to do
the work which the one presbytery did in the primitive church
(*infra*, pp. 230-233).

name; but even the germ of this was implanted in that weekly meeting of ministers and elders for the interpretation of Scripture termed the exercise, which was authorised both by the Book of Common Order and the First Book of Discipline.[1] It was soon established in all the considerable towns in Scotland where there was a fully constituted reformed church, and though at first it may possibly have confined itself to the object it was immediately intended to serve, and may have intervened only by advice in matters of discipline, yet it was not in the nature of things that such a gathering of ministers and elders from neighbouring churches should take place from week to week without such cases as occupied the attention of parochial consistories being discussed and advised on, as well as the doctrinal and critical questions arising out of their exercises, which they were expressly empowered to dispose of. The tendencies of the institution were so manifest, and the powers it speedily assumed so undisguised, that Queen Elizabeth became alarmed, and insisted on the suppression of it throughout the province of

[1] [The Book of Common Order distinguishes between the weekly meeting of the ministers and elders in their assembly or consistory, and the weekly meeting of the congregation for the interpretation of the Scriptures (Dunlop's Confessions, ii. 411-413 ; Laing's Knox, iv. 177-179). For the nature and object of the exercise see *infra*, pp. 170-173.]

Canterbury, notwithstanding the remonstrances and entreaties of the good Archbishop Grindal, and his repeated and urgent petitions that she would rather endeavour to confine it to the original purpose, in which it had been of great service, than suppress it altogether. In the province of York, where the institution had taken firmer root, and where the contentions between Papists and Protestants had gained more prominence than those between Puritans and anti-Puritans, it was tolerated for a considerably longer period. When in 1581 Scotland was regularly divided into presbyteries, the exercises previously existing in particular towns were merged in, and their work devolved on, these; and in the beginning of the seventeenth century, when episcopacy was restored, the name of presbytery was again frequently exchanged for that of exercise.

Of these several church courts perhaps the most distinctive as well as the most important was the General Assembly, which was originally held to represent the whole church; and which may still, after the lapse of ages, be held substantially to do so — having representatives not only from each of the presbyteries but also from each of the universities and royal burghs in the kingdom. It has been wont to meet not (as such national synods have generally done elsewhere) occasion-

ally and chiefly for legislative purposes, that is,
authoritatively to explain the church's creed and
enact canons to regulate the administration of
discipline, but frequently and at short stated
intervals to review the proceedings of the inferior
judicatories of the church, as well as to legislate
regarding matters of doctrine and discipline.
Whether its peculiar vitality in the Scottish
Church is to be ascribed to its popular constitution, or to the fact that it has in general faithfully
represented the national sentiments in those controversies which in successive generations have
been agitated in our country; or whether the
groundwork of it had not been laid long before in
those national councils of the church which the
popish ecclesiastics had, under the bull of Pope
Honorius III.,[1] deemed themselves warranted to
hold every year, and at which the king and his
nobles appear often to have been present, and
whether, therefore, in the maintenance of this
quasi-Gallican liberty, as well as in some minor
matters enumerated by Lord Hailes, there may
not have been a closer and more real connection
between the pre- and post - Reformation church
in Scotland than has been commonly admitted,
it would now, perhaps, be very difficult to deter-

---

[1] [The bull, which is printed in Concilia Scotiæ, ii. 3, is dated
"xiiij kalendas Junij pontificatus nostri anno nono," *i.e.*, the 19th
of May 1225.]

mine.   But it will be allowed on all hands that this venerable court—which was so early established and has subsisted almost uninterruptedly since the Reformation, and has exercised such extensive legislative and judicial powers—is the most distinctive characteristic of the Scottish Church, and has had great influence in the development of Scottish opinion and religious life.

II. *The Discipline of the Church.*

The opinions of our reformer and his associates regarding the discipline and practical organisation of the church have hardly ever been made a subject of serious controversy, even by those who have so long called in question the generally received ideas regarding his opinions on the government of the church.   That which marked out the early Reformed Church of Scotland most distinctively among the churches of the Reformation was the fact that she advocated, and resolutely carried into practical operation, that "godly discipline" which they all admitted had been used in the primitive church in her best and purest days, and the restoration of which, they perhaps ventured to hint, was much to be desired, but which yet they had not the courage to demand from the civil power as of essential concern to the wellbeing of their churches.

Even Luther, who began so well, hesitated and quailed before the claims of the civil powers, and left it to Calvin to carry out his own earlier conceptions, and those of the Hessian Synod of 1528.[1] Our reformers, however, boldly laid down the absolute necessity of it in their Book of Common Order, and named in their Confession as one of the three distinctive marks of a true church of Christ, "ecclesiastical discipline up-rightlie ministred as Goddis Worde prescribes, whereby vice is repressed and vertew nurished." [2] Not content to exercise such a discipline merely under this clause of their State-ratified Confession, they sought and obtained an explicit acknowledg-ment of the church's privileges in special Acts of Parliament, which continue in force at the present day, and have enabled the Church of Scotland to maintain a stricter and more efficient discipline than any other established church has ventured to aim at.

The nature and ends of this discipline are pretty fully explained in the introductory chapters of the Book of Common Order, in the Book of Discipline, and the Order of Excommunication and Public Repentance. "As no citie, towne, house, or family," it is affirmed in the first of

---

[1] See Schenkel's article, "Kirche," in Herzog's Real-Encyklo-pädie.

[2] Dunlop's Confessions, ii. 68 ; Laing's Knox, ii. 110.

these treatises, "can maintain their estate and
prosper without policy and governance, even so
the Church of God, which requireth more purely
to be governed than any citie or family, cannot
without spirituall policy and ecclesiastical discipline continue, increase, and flourish;[1] and as
the Word of God is the life and soule of this
church, so this godly order and discipline is, as
it were, sinews in the body, which knit and joine
the members together with decent order and
comelinesse; it is a bridle to stay the wicked from
their mischiefs, it is a spurre to pricke forward
such as be slow and negligent; yea, and for all
men it is the father's rod, ever in a readiness
to chastise gently the faults committed, and
to cause them afterward to live in more godly
feare and reverence."[2]   Three causes are assigned
why such discipline should be retained and
practised in the church—viz., that evil men may
not be numbered among God's children, that the
good may not be infected by association with the
ungodly, and that the individual taken under discipline may be made ashamed of his fault, and so

[1] See Calvin's Institutes, book iv. chap. ii.—"As no city or
village can exist without a magistrate and government, so the
Church of God stands in need of a spiritual polity of its own.   This
is altogether distinct from the civil government, and is so far from
hindering or impairing it, that it rather does much to aid and
promote it."

[2] Dunlop's Confessions, ii. 413; Laing's Knox, iv. 203.

may be induced to repent and amend. This is
said to be the object even of excommunication—
the highest censure the church can inflict on an
offending brother—that he, being brought to a
due sense of his sin and misery, may be saved
in the day of the Lord. It is expressly provided
that, in regard to this last and highest censure,
nothing is to be attempted without the determination of the whole church—*i.e.*, of the ordinary
members of the church—and they are affection-
ately reminded that it is their duty to take good
heed " that they seeme not more ready to expell
from the congregation than to receave againe
those, in whom they perceave worthy fruits of
repentance to appeare," and " that all punishments, corrections, censures, and admonitions
stretch no farther than God's Word with mercy
may lawfully beare." [1]

The Order of Excommunication and Public
Repentance, sanctioned by the General Assembly
in 1569, long continued to be used as a directory
in the administration of discipline. It was compiled by Knox, or rather abridged by him from
Alasco's ' Modus ac Ritus Excommunicatïonis '
and his ' Forma ac Ratio Publicæ Penitentiæ,'

[1] Dunlop's Confessions, ii. 414-417 ; Laing's Knox, iv. 204-206.
If this humanity is not observed in private as well as in public,
there is danger lest instead of discipline we fall into a kind of
Gehenna, and instead of correctors and educators become execu-
tioners of the brethren (Calvin).

used with the approbation of Edward VI. in the Church of the Foreigners in London. It breathes throughout a spirit of tender regard for erring brethren and earnest longing for their recovery, quite as strongly as it manifests a spirit of holy zeal for the glory of God and the purity of His church. In all save the most notorious and urgent cases, the offender was to be dealt with repeatedly both in private and in public to confess his aggravated offence before the extreme penalty was inflicted on him. If these dealings and admonitions proved in-effectual, the minister was once more to explain the nature of his offence, and the frequency of the public and private admonitions addressed to him, was then to appeal to the elders and deacons to confirm the truth of what he said, and finally was to ask of the whole church if they thought such a contempt should be suffered amongst them, and only in the event of no man making further intercession for the erring and obstinate was the minister to pro-ceed to pronounce the fearful sentence.[1]

In the times of declension which arose after James VI. took the government into his own

[1] The form of absolution then appointed to be used was, with consent of Henderson, modified by the Westminster divines into the shape in which it appears in their Directory for Church Gov-ernment and Excommunication, and as modified was afterwards inserted in our Form of Process of 1707.

hands, the strict exercise of such discipline became specially odious to the king and his gay courtiers, and incessant efforts were made to relax its rigour. These, however, were in general directed to effect this object rather by means of than in spite of the church, by securing that cases involving the sentence of excommunication should be reserved for the determination of the higher courts of the church, on which the king and his friends could bring their influence to bear with most effect. Even during the domination of the Second Episcopacy it is well known, from records still extant, that kirk-sessions and presbyteries were continued, and were allowed, with the sanction of the bishop, to maintain a discipline which in the present day would not be generally accounted lax. The grotesque penances so often resorted to in the times immediately succeeding the Reformation, and for the use of which our forefathers have been subjected to so much abuse and ridicule, were by no means confined to them, and probably had been suggested by similar grotesque ones in use before, and were employed by the Court of High Commission, by the Church of England, and by other churches too, in so far as they ever ventured to exercise discipline on notorious offenders. Even those melancholy trials of witches, for which they have been so severely blamed, were not originated by them, and were countenanced quite as much by their opponents, and by no one more than by the pope and his entourage, as well as by James VI., the great patron of the bishops, and for long were clamoured for by the people.

To us, living in the light and glorying in the toleration of the nineteenth century, some of these disciplinary provisions may seem harsh, several of the details frivolous, others inquisitorial; and the very principle of such a close identification of the ecclesiastical and civil, as that all offences against morality and church discipline were to be also dealt with and punished by the state, more than questionable. But to men living in the sixteenth century and just emerging out of the ignorance and licence which the old church had tolerated, and longing to be moulded into a community really holy and self-denying and quickened to a higher life — enthused with a longing to reach loftier heights in it—the iron discipline of Calvin and Knox was welcome as requiring only what they felt to be their duty and their true interest. We may extend to the disciple what the historian of French Protestantism has said of the master, and so far varying the words of Haag affirm: "The institutions of Calvin [and Knox] accomplished what was proposed. In less than three generations the Genevese [and Lowland Scots] were entirely remoulded. To frivolity and licentiousness succeeded that somewhat austere strictness of morals which in earlier days distinguished the disciples of the reformer[s]. History tells of only two [three] men who have been able permanently to impress their stamp on an entire people—Lycurgus and Calvin [and Knox], whose characters in fact have much in common." [1] The Athenians made merry over the black broth of the Spartans; but Sparta conquered Athens. How many accusations and witticisms have been launched against the Calvinistic spirit, and yet Calvinistic countries led the way in Christian activity and civil freedom, and to them even those who abuse them are largely indebted for their blessings.

III. *The Prerogatives and Duties of Church Members.*

The thorough agreement of our reformers' ideas respecting the nature of the church with those of the apostles and primitive Christians comes out even more emphatically in the statements they make in the First Book of Discipline and the

[1] La France protestant, deuxième édition, iii. 530.

Book of Common Order about the ordinary
members of the congregation, and the arrangements there recommended for promoting their
spiritual welfare, and calling forth all their gifts.
Not only are they to be allowed a voice in the
choice of their ministers, elders, and deacons, in
the exclusion of members from the church and
their readmission into it, and through their representatives in the government of the church
generally; not only are they to have week-day
and Sabbath services, and frequent communions
for their edification and growth in grace,—but in
the principal congregations there are to be weekly
meetings for the study and interpretation of the
Scriptures. At these meetings every man was
to be allowed to speak his mind and propose
his doubts, to exercise his gifts for the edification of the brethren, or to " inquire as God shall
move his heart and the text minister occasion." [1]
The opening paragraph of chapter xii. of the
First Book of Discipline shows us whence this
remarkable institution was derived, and proves
clearly that Neander was not the first in post-
Reformation times who discovered the full significance of certain well-known passages in St Paul's
First Epistle to the Corinthians, but only a restorer of the long-forgotten teaching of Calvin,

[1] Book of Common Order, in Dunlop's Confessions, ii. 412;
Laing's Knox, iv. 179.

Alasco, and Knox. The paragraph is as follows : " To the end that the kirk of God may
have a tryall of men's knowledge, judgements,
graces, and utterances ; as also, such that have
somewhat profited in God's Word may from time
to time grow in more full perfection to serve the
kirk as necessity shall require ; it is most expedient
that in every towne where schooles and repaire
of learned men are, there be a time in one certain
day every week appointed to that exercise which
S. Paul calls prophecying ; the order whereof is
expressed by him in thir words : ' Let the
prophets speak two or three and let the other
judge, but if anything be revealed to another that
sitteth by, let the former keep silence ; for ye
may one by one all prophesie that all may learne,
and all may receive consolation.' . . . By which
words of the apostle, it is evident that in the
Kirk of Corinth when they did assemble for that
purpose, some place of Scripture was read, upon
the which one first gave his judgement to the
instruction and consolation of the auditors ; after
whom did another either confirme what the
former had said, or added what he had omitted,
or did gently correct or explaine more properly
where the whole verity was not revealled to the
former ; and in case things were hid from the
one and from the other, liberty was given for a
third to speak his judgement to the edification

of the kirk." The exercise or practice here authorised by the apostle, it is next affirmed, is a thing most necessary for the kirk of God this day in Scotland, "for thereby, as said is, shall the kirk have judgement and knowledge of the graces, gifts, and utterances of *every man within their bodie*, the simple and such as have somewhat profited shall be encouraged daily to studie and to proceed in knowledge, and the whole kirk shall be edified ; for this exercise must be patent to such as list to hear and learne, and *every man shall have liberty to utter and declare his minde and knowledge to the comfort and consolation of the Kirk.*" [1] Then after appointing some prudent regulations to prevent this liberty of prophesying from encroaching on the province of the regular ministry of the church, or degenerating into a school for the encouragement of rash speculation instead of ministering to the comfort and godly edifying of the brethren, directions are given that the ministers of the landward parishes adjacent to every important town, together with the readers within six miles, should assist those that prophesy within the towns, that they themselves may learn or others may learn from them. "And moreover," it is again repeated, "men in whom is supposed to be any gifts which might edifie the church if they were well imployed must be charged . . . to

[1] Dunlop's Confessions. ii. 587-589 ; Laing's Knox, ii. 242, 243.

joyn themselves with the session and company of interpreters. . . . For no man *may be permitted as best pleaseth him to live within the kirk of God,* but every man must be constrained by fraternall admonition and correction to bestow his labours, when of the kirk he is required, to the edification of others."[1] Such was the remarkable provision made by our reformers, that every adult member of the church should enjoy such means of grace as were fitted to promote his growth in Christian knowledge as well as in spiritual life, and should have reasonable opportunity of using for the glory of God and the good of his brethren the gifts with which the Spirit of God had furnished him. It may be questioned whether some such institution is not as much needed in the present day, if the members of the church are to be preserved from the temptations to doubt with which they are surrounded, and if they are to be encouraged to supplement the labours of their ministers and elders in winning back those who have been seduced into the paths of error or sin; and whether its influence, if it were only set about with earnestness, would be less powerful to preserve and reclaim than it was in those earlier times.

Dunlop's Confessions, ii. 590, 591 ; Laing's Knox, ii. 244, 245.

IV. *Education of the Young and University Reform.*

The care and anxiety of our reformers were not confined to the adult members of the church. They were extended in a special manner to the young, and were manifested towards them, if possible, with more intense earnestness and loving tenderness. Though parish schools, in the later sense, were not yet devised, detailed arrangements were made that the readers at the several kirks should impart religious knowledge and the elements of primary education to the young of the flock, and that those who showed an aptitude for learning and capability of being trained to be of service to kirk or common-weal should have access at various centres to higher training. "Seeing," they say in their importunate pleading with the nobles on their behalf, "that God hath determined that His kirke here in earth shall be taught not by angels but by men, and seeing that men are borne ignorant of God and of all godlinesse, . . . of necessity it is that your honours be most careful for the vertuous education and godly upbringing of the youth of this realm, if either ye now thirst unfainedly [for] the advancement of Christ's glorie or yet desire the continuance of His benefits to the generation following; for as the youth must succeed to us,

so we ought to be carefull that they have knowledge and erudition to profit and comfort that
which ought to be most deare to us, to wit, the
kirk and spouse of our Lord Jesus."[1] To secure
this noble end it was deemed necessary that,
besides the readers' schools, every considerable
town should have at least one schoolmaster
appointed who was competent to teach grammar
and the Latin tongue; and that in the more
notable towns, especially the old cathedral cities,
where the revenues of the prebendaries or of
the monks might be made available, there should
be a college in which at least logic, rhetoric,
and the languages—*i.e.*, Latin and Greek—should
be taught by competent masters, for whom and
for the poorer scholars attending them suitable
stipends and bursaries should be provided out of
the aforesaid revenues. The fruit of such an
organisation, it is affirmed, would soon appear.
" For first, the youthhead and tender children
shall be nourished and brought up in vertue *in
presence of their friends*, by whose good attendance
many inconveniences may be avoyded in which
the youth commonly fall either by overmuch
libertie which they have in strange and un-
knowne places while they cannot rule themselves, or else for lack of good attendance and
of such necessaries as their tender age requires.

[1] Dunlop's Confessions, ii. 547 ; Laing's Knox, ii. 209.

Secondly, the exercise of children in every kirke shall be great instruction to the aged and un-learned," who had never been taught to read, and in whose presence in the Sunday afternoon service they were examined. Lastly, "the great Schooles called the Universities shall be replenished with these that shall be apt to learning; for this must be carefully provided that no father, of what estate or condition that ever he be, use his children at his own fantasie especially in their youthhead; but *all must be compelled* to bring up their children in learning and vertue." Thus boldly did our reformers lay down the principle of compulsory education, which men in our own day have only hesitatingly adopted, but with greater consistency or daring than our contemporaries have yet evinced, for they proposed to apply the principle to the children of the rich and potent, as well as to those of the poor and vicious. Those higher classes, they say, "may not be permitted to suffer their children to spend their youth in vaine idleness as heretofore they have done, but they must be exhorted, and by the censure of the kirk compelled, to dedicate their sonnes by training them up in good exercises to the profite of the kirk and commonwealth." This they expect the rich to do at their own expense, while they desire the children of the poor to be supported at the charge of the kirk. The sons neither of rich nor poor are to be permitted to reject learning if they develop any aptitude for it, but are to be "charged to continue their studie that the commonwealth may have some comfort by them." To secure this object, discreet and learned men are to visit the schools every quarter, and examine what proficiency the pupils have attained.[1]

To these suggestions regarding primary and secondary schools succeeds a very detailed statement of the changes desired in the universities to adapt them to the new order of things. And then they conclude as follows: "All other things touching the books to be read in ilk classe, and all such like particular affaires, we referre to the discretion of the masters, principals, and regents, with their well-advised counsel; not doubting but if God shall grant quietnesse, and give your wisedomes grace to set forward letters in the sort prescribed, ye shall leave wisdome and learning to your posterity—a treasure more to be esteemed than any earthly treasure ye are able to amasse for them, which without wisdome are more able to be their ruin and confusion than their help and comfort. And as this is most true, so we leave it with the rest of the commodities to be weighed by your honours' wisedome, and set forwards by

[1] Dunlop's Confessions, ii. 548-550; Laing's Knox, ii. 209-211.

your authority to the most high advancement of this commonwealth committed to your charge." [1]

These touching appeals were not made altogether in vain. Though neither quietness nor a large measure of grace was granted to the rough barons so earnestly and tenderly addressed, yet the goodly fabric of our church and commonwealth was reared up in those troublous times. The full and liberal adoption of the plan of national education sketched by our reformer and his associates still remains in part to be desiderated, and is worthy to be striven for by the churches which claim to represent them. The partial carrying out of their views, more than any other influence that can be named, has conduced to elevate our people and raise Scotland to the rank it now holds among the nations; and we can hardly doubt that the more complete realisation of them in the careful Christian training of the young and the adult members of the church, and the extension of the blessings of education and religion to the masses so long left to grow up in ignorance and vice, would tend greatly to bring back the disaffected to the paths of peace and life, to raise the members of the church in the scale of intelligence and virtue, to make the nobles more than ever heretofore the *decus et tutamen patriæ*, and to bind all, both classes and

[1] Dunlop's Confessions, ii. 561 ; Laing's Knox, ii. 220, 221.

masses, closely together in the bonds of mutual Christian affection and true patriotism.

V. *Care of the Poor.*

I must still add that the same enlightened principles which guided them to make careful provision for these important objects, led them also to take a kindly interest in the humbler poor and aged, and to urge both on the state and on the members of the church the duty they owed to this long despised and neglected class of the population. First, for the poor peasantry who were not paupers, but who, they allege, had been grievously oppressed by the exactions of the clergy in the times immediately preceding, they present the following earnest plea : " With the griefe of our hearts we heare that some gentle-men are now as cruell over their tenants as ever were the Papists, requiring of them (the tiends and) whatsoever they afore payed to the kirk, so that the Papistical tyrannie shall onely be changed into the tyrannie of the lord and laird. We dare not flatter your honours, neither yet is it profitable for you that we so doe : (for neither shall we,) if we permit cruelty to be used ; neither shall ye, who by your authoritie ought to gaine-stand such oppression, nor yet they that use the same, escape God's heavie and fearfull judgements.   The gentlemen, barones, earles, lords, and others must be content to live upon their just rents, and suffer the kirk to be restored to her (*right and*) *liberty ;* that by her restitution, the poore, who heretofore, by the cruell Papists, have been spoiled and oppressed, may now receive some comfort and relaxation, and their tiends and other exactions *be cleane discharged* and no more taken in time comming.   The uppermost claith, corps-present, clerk-maile, the pasche-offering, tiend-ale, and all handlings[1] upaland can neither be required nor recieved of good conscience." [2]

The history of the world, the history of the Christian church, has few passages more noble than this, where these poor ministers, not yet assured of decent provision for their own main-tenance, boldly undertake the patronage of the peasantry, and say they would rather suffer them-selves than ask that teinds should be exacted from those who had been so long ground down, not only by the exaction of these from their crofts and even from their gardens, but also by a multi-

[1] [Dr Mitchell seems to have thought that *handlings* should be read *haldings.*]

[2] Dunlop's Confessions, ii. 562, 563.   [The words which in this quotation are enclosed in parentheses are not in the copy of the Book of Discipline preserved by Knox (Laing's Knox, ii. 221, 222). Instead of the words, "if *we* permit cruelty to be used," that copy reads, "if *you* permit suche creualtie to be used"; and after the words, "comfort and relaxation," is the clause, "Concludit be the Lordis."]

tude of other imposts, which, although their very
names are now almost forgotten in Scotland, had
been long felt to be a grievous oppression. Was
it any wonder that those crushed and down-
trodden classes should rally round their pro-
tectors, and under their kindly and godly training
should grow up to be a strength to the church
and a power in the state? Charming fancy
pictures are still sometimes drawn of the stately
monastery—with its handsome church and kindly
and cultured monks—as a centre of civilising and
Christianising influences to the district in which
it was erected. These influences no doubt had
a certain reality in the early ages of the church,
and even in the days of the good Queen Margaret; but in Scotland, at least, these days had
long passed away before the sixteenth century;
and the monasteries, as a whole, had become a
source of weakness and scandal, rather than of
strength and honour to the dominant church.
In fact, their wealth, being to a large extent
derived from the teinds of parishes, should have
been devoted to the spiritual interests of these
parishes, whereas the vicars appointed by them
being generally put off with a miserable pittance
and left largely dependent on these hated and
oppressive exactions—corpse presents, uppermost
cloth, Pasche-offerings—could not fail to alienate the peasantry from the monasteries and their

rural representatives. Such charges of oppression could never have been so publicly made against them had they not been notoriously true. And if further evidence were needed, it may be found in abundance in the poems of Sir David Lindsay and the Wedderburns. The picture the former has drawn of the poor peasant driven out of house and holding [1] by these oppressive exac-

---

[1] The pauper comes on the stage with the words—

> "Of your almis, gude folks, for God's luife of heavin,
> For I have motherles bairns either sax or seavin;"

and proceeds in piteous strain—

> "Gude man, will ye gif me of your charitie,
> And I sall declair yow the black veritie.
> My father was ane auld man, and a hoir,
> And was of age four scoir of yeirs and moir.
> And Mald, my mother, was four scoir and fyfteine,
> And with my labour I did thame baith susteine.
> Wee had ane meir, that caryit salt and coill,
> And everie ilk yeir scho brocht us hame ane foill.
> Wee had thrie ky, that was baith fat and fair,
> Nane tydier into the toun of Air.
> My father was sa waik of blude, and bane,
> That he deit, quhairfoir my mother maid gret maine :
> Then scho deit, within ane day or two ;
> And thair began my povertie and wo.
> Our gude gray meir was baittand on the feild,
> And our Land's laird tuik hir for his hyreild,
> The vickar tuik the best cow be the heid,
> Incontinent, quhen my father was deid.
> And quhen the vickar hard tel how that my mother
> Was deid, fra hand he tuke to him ane uther :
> Then Meg, my wife, did murne baith evin and morow,
> Till at the last scho deit for verie sorow :
> And quhen the vickar hard tell my wyfe was dead,
> The thrid cow he cleikit be the heid.
> Thair umest clayis, that was of rapploch gray,
> The vickar gart his clark bear them away.
> Quhen all was gane, I micht mak na debeat,
> Bot with my bairns past for till beg my meat.
>   Now, haif I tald yow the blak veritie,
>   How I am brocht into this miserie."
>   —Laing's Lindsay's Poetical Works, 1879, ii. 99, 102, 103.

tions is known to be true to the life; and contributed greatly to the overthrow of the merciless
oppressors who, until the very eve of the triumph
of the Reformation, could not be persuaded either
to abolish or abate their dues.[1]

[1] [In the Articles addressed by some of the temporal lords and
barons to the queen regent, and sent by her to the Provincial
Council convened in Edinburgh a few weeks before the Reformation burst like a tempest upon the country, it was requested that
"the corps presentes, kow, and [um]est claith, and the silvir commonlie callit the kirk richts, and Pasch offrands quhilk is takin at
Pasch fra men and women for distribution of the sacrament of the
blessit body and blood of Jesus Christ," should no longer be ex-
torted under pain of excommunication or debarring from the sacraments, but left to the free will of the givers (Concilia Scotiæ, ii. 148,
149). The Council met this demand for reformation by enacting
that in future the poor should be freed from mortuary dues, while
those not quite so poor were only to pay them in a modified form ;
and the small tithes and oblations were to be taken up before Lent
so as to avoid the appearance of selling the sacrament (Ibid., ii. 167,
168, 174). When, on the 27th of May 1560, the reforming vicar of
Lintrathin raised a summons against his parishioners for payment of
his teinds, "the cors present and umest clayth of all yeris and termes
bigane restand unpayit" were specially excepted from his claim
(Spalding Miscellany, iv. 121).]

CHAPTER IX.

THE LAST DAYS OF JOHN KNOX.

THE eighth decade of the sixteenth century was memorable in the history of Protestantism in its Presbyterian or Calvinistic form, and the year 1572 has been termed its *annus mirabilis*. It marked a crisis in the long and bloody struggle of the Protestants in the Netherlands with their Spanish oppressors,—a struggle which issued in securing the independence of the Dutch people, and settling on a Calvinistic basis the Reformed Church of Holland. It formed the turning-point in the tragic fortunes of the Reformed Church of France, at which, from being able to claim as adherents a majority of the landed gentry and a large minority of the more intelligent and wealthy *bourgeois* in the provincial towns, and being only weak among the citizens of the capital and the peasantry of northern and central France, she was, by an act of base treachery and fiendish cruelty, hurled from her promising position, sadly crippled in numbers and influence, permanently weakened and cast down, though not crushed or driven to despair.[1] This decade was especially memorable in the history of the Reformed Church of Scotland as having witnessed the removal of the ablest and best of the lay defenders of the Reformation, the death of our great reformer himself, and the return to Scotland of the intrepid and devoted man who was to take up and complete the work, from which failing health and a grieved spirit had obliged Knox to withdraw. The assassination of the Good Regent (as the Earl of Moray was deservedly surnamed) was unquestionably the most disgraceful of all the murders perpetrated in Scotland in the interests of faction during those years of confusion and strife.[2] It brought no permanent advantage to the party of reaction. It wrought much woe to the country, which under his firm yet kindly rule had begun to settle into order and to recover its prosperity.

This great national calamity preyed on the spirit and broke the already waning strength of Knox. In the month of October in that year[3]

[1] Dr Lorimer in British and Foreign Evangelical Review for 1872, p. 758.

[2] [The Good Regent was assassinated on the 23rd of January 1569-70.]

[3] [1570.]

he had a stroke of paralysis or of apoplexy, which for a time laid him aside altogether from work, and permanently enfeebled his constitution. As in the case of Wycliffe in the fourteenth century, his opponents exulted over his misfortune, and circulated maliciously exaggerated accounts of his condition, on which probably their more malicious and notoriously fictitious accounts of his last illness were founded. But this first seizure was not so severe as to put a final arrest on his activities. Before many weeks were over he had so far recovered as to be able, in part at least, to resume his labours. He was able in a measure to continue them through the anxious and unquiet months of the succeeding winter and spring — bearing faithful testimony to the principles, religious and political, which he had long professed; standing up resolutely in defence of the authority of the young prince, when many, who had formerly sworn allegiance to him, led by the intriguing laird of Lethington and the "fause" house of Hamilton, went over to the party of his popish mother. He exposed their sophistries, and fearlessly rebuked their defection, even after they had gained for the time the supremacy in Edinburgh. Others might truckle to them or quail before them, but that palsied old man, with all his former plainness and much of his former fire, persevered in denouncing their treachery and discrediting their proposals. Threatenings were uttered against his life if he persisted in his course; protection seems to have been refused him by the party against the violence of their lawless followers; and one evening (as had often happened to Calvin in his years of conflict) a musket-ball was fired in at the window of his house, and lodged in the roof of the apartment in which he was sitting. Again and again faithful citizens, an attached kirk-session, and John Craig, then his colleague in the ministry, entreated him to remove for a time to some place where his life would be safe from violence, and whence he could return to his loving and beloved flock as soon as the prevailing faction should be put down, or should vacate the city. But he heard them all unmoved, until at last they were constrained to tell him plainly that if he was attacked they had made up their minds to peril their lives in his defence, and if they were compelled to shed blood in the contest it must lie on his head. Thus "sore against his will,"[1] as one of the earliest historians of his declining years tells us, and "almost thrust out by the authority of the church court,"[2] as another of them has it, he, on the 5th May 1571, took farewell of Edinburgh for a time, and crossing the Firth of Forth

---

[1] Bannatyne's Memoriales, Ban. Club, p. 118.
[2] See Laing's Knox, vi. 651.

at Leith moved on by short and easy stages through Fife to the city in which " God had first opened his mouth" to proclaim His truth, and for which to the last he, as well as the Good Regent, cherished a special affection. As Mr John Davidson, then a teacher in one of the colleges, has expressed it in homely Scotch :—

> " Thou knawis he lude the by the lave,
>   For *first* in the he gave the rout
>   Till Antechrist that Romische slave,
>   Preicheing that Christ did only save.
>   Bot *last* of Edinburgh exprest,
>   Quhen he was not far fra his grave
>   He came to the by all the rest." [1]

In St Andrews the reformer was sure to be free from personal danger, and on the whole to have the sympathy of the citizens; though it was not to be supposed that—in the city and university where the late Archbishop Hamilton had been long supreme, and had recently been claiming to exercise the authority of Chancellor of the University, and new founder of St Mary's College,[2] and where he had left behind several relations and dependents more compliant with the new order of things than himself — there were not to be found in this crisis several in-

---

[1] M'Crie's Knox, 1855, p. 459; Rogers' Three Scottish Reformers, p. 97.

[2] [Archbishop Hamilton was hanged at the market cross of Stirling on the 7th of April 1571.]

fluential persons who had more sympathy with
their late chief and with the selfish and crooked
policy of the Hamiltons than with the straight-
forward course and steadfast fidelity of the
dauntless reformer, and who would have little
relish for his earnest warnings and stern reproofs. The notices preserved to us regarding
this last and, so far as is yet known, longest
visit of Knox to St Andrews are both detailed
and interesting. From the simple and loving
Memorials of his attendant, Richard Bannatyne,
we learn that all the time he was there—*i.e.*,
from the beginning of July 1571 to the 17th
of August 1572—he preached every Sunday, and
expounded the prophecies of Daniel to the
middle of the ninth chapter, applying the words
of the prophet to the circumstances of Scotland
at the time, and inveighing in the strongest
terms against "the bloody house of Hamilton"
and its abettors for their deceit, treachery,
and turbulence, their base murder of the Good
Regent, and cunning plot to restore a popish
queen.[1] These themes, to which in the appli-
cations of his sermons he ever and anon returned, woke up all the fire and fervour of the
old man eloquent; and if it might not be said,
as in earlier days, that every sermon was of
more value to the cause he defended than five

[1] Bannatyne's Memoriales, Ban. Club, p. 255.

hundred armed men, yet the report of his un-
tiring zeal and unswerving fidelity would still
contribute greatly to animate and cheer the
adherents of the young prince and of the new
regent in all parts of the land.

As I have hinted, there were some in the
city to whom such discourses could not fail to
be distasteful—some who refused to attend on
his ministry, and were perhaps so stung by
what was reported of his sharp but not undeserved reproofs that they were compelled to
throw off the mask they had hitherto worn,
and soon after openly to apostatise from the
faith which for several years they had professed
and taught. But the effect on many of the
young men in attendance on the university, or
acting as regents in its colleges, was salutary
and enduring ; and perhaps it was not without special intention that, when the door was
shut against him in Edinburgh and the ears of
the men in power there were closed against his
counsels, he betook himself to what was still
the principal university in the realm, and made
his last appeals to the rising hopes of the
church and country there. Such discourses as
he then delivered, coming from one they had
already learned to venerate, could not fail to
form or foster in their ingenuous minds that
fidelity to the reformed faith, that jealousy of

popery, and that hatred of its cruelty and
tyranny, which distinguished them to the last.

James Melville, whose plastic nature and
gentle spirit retained through life the impressions then made, supplements in his Diary the
notices in Bannatyne's Memorials, and, in a
passage which has been often quoted, gives a
very fresh and vivid sketch of the old reformer.
" Bot of all the benefites I haid that yeir"—
the first year he was a student in St Andrews,
and had " drunk of St Leonard's well "—" the
greatest," he tells us, "was the coming of that
maist notable profet and apostle of our nation,
Mr Jhone Knox, to St Androis ; wha be the
faction of the Quein occupeing the castell and
town of Edinbruche was compellit to remove
thairfra with a number of the best, and chusit
to com to St Androis. I hard him teatche ther
the prophecie of Daniel that simmer and the
wintar following. I haid my pen and my litle
book, and tuk away sic things as I could com-
prehend. In the opening upe of his text he
was moderat the space of an halff hourc ; bot
when he enterit to application he maid me sa
to grew and tremble that I could nocht hald a
pen to wryt. I hard him oftymes utter these
thretenings [against the faction then] in the
hicht of their pryde, quhilk the eis [*i.e.,* eyes]
of monie saw cleirlie brought to pass within

few yeirs upon the captean of that castle, the Hamiltones, and the Quein hirselff. He ludgit down in the Abbay besyde our Collage."[1] So far was it from being true, as is commonly asserted, that he had caused the destruction of the abbey and of the abbey church or cathedral in 1559, that in 1571 he found a habitable building there, in which he, a frail old man, with his wife and children, could pass the winter in comfort. It, we know from a letter of his antagonist, Archibald Hamilton, was "the new ludgene of the abbey,"[2] or *novum hospitium,* built for the reception of Mary of Guise, the queen of James V.[3] It was in the immediate vicinity of St Leonard's College, and our diarist further tells us: "Our regents, Mr Nicol Dalgleise, Mr Wilyeam Colace, and Mr Jhone Davidsone, went in ordinarilie to his grace [or devotional

[1] Melville's Diary, Wodrow Society, p. 26.

[2] [Archibald Hamilton's letter or protestation is in Bannatyne's Memoriales, pp. 262, 263.]

[3] [According to Martine, it was built, not for the reception of Mary of Guise, but when James V. was married to Magdalene, the fair daughter of Francis I., in 1537, the tradition being that the physicians chose this place as peculiarly suitable for such a delicate creature ; and that "so many artificers were conveened and employed, and the materials so quicklie prepared, that the house was begun and finished in a month" (Reliquiæ Divi Andreæ, p. 190). There is better evidence to show that Mary of Guise spent her honeymoon within its substantial walls in the summer of 1538 (Lesley's History, pp. 155, 156 ; Pitscottie's History, 1778, pp. 250, 251).]

exercises] efter denner and soupper. . . . Mr
Knox wald sum tymes com in and repose him
in our Collage yeard [that is the gardens immediately to the west of the *novum hospitium*,
adjoining St Leonard's College], and call us
schollars unto him and bless us, and exhort
us to knaw God and His wark in our contrey,
and stand be the guid cause, to use our tyme
weill, and lern the guid instructiones, and follow the guid exemple of our maisters." [1] No
wonder, in these circumstances, that he is able
to add, "Our haill collage, maisters and schollars, war sound and zelus for the guid cause,"
or that we can now still further add that
thence proceeded several of the men who were
to uphold it most resolutely in the evil days
which followed.

In the New College we are told, "whowbeit
Mr Jhone Dowglass, then Rector [and Principal]
was guid aneuche," yet the "uther maisters and
sum of the regentes war evill‑myndit," and
"hated Mr Knox and the guid cause"; [2] and two
of them, Archibald and John Hamilton, soon
after apostatised, betook themselves to the Continent, and rose to high office in the Universities
of Louvain and Paris, where the one in not
inelegant Latin, and the other in courtly Scotch,
sought to vindicate their conduct, and to traduce

[1] Melville's Diary, p. 26.   [2] Ibid.

N

and refute their former co-religionists. Some of
the masters of the Old College also, as Bannatyne
has recorded, hated the plain-speaking reformer,
though "be outward gesture and befoir his face
thei wald seime and apeir to favore and love
him above the rest."[1]   The Hamiltons especially
seem to have given him considerable occasion to
complain of their bitter and unguarded criticisms,
and one of them, stung by his denunciations,
challenged him to defend his doctrine in the
schools of the university.   This he at first
refused, maintaining that the pulpit was not to
be controlled by the university schools, nor the
church put into subjection to the academy.

St Andrews at that time was the *rendezvous* of
others of the adherents of the young prince, who
did not feel themselves safe under the faction
then in possession of the castle and city of
Edinburgh.   One of these, Mr John Durie of
Leith, was "for stoutness and zeall in the guid
cause mikle renouned and talked of."   He was an
enthusiastic leader of the volunteers of his day.
"The gown was na sooner af and the Byble out
of hand fra the kirk, when on ged the corslet,
and fangit was the hagbot, and to the fields."[2]
Another was Robert Leckprevick, the famous
printer, who brought his types and printing-press
with him, and so did notable service to the cause.

[1] Bannatyne's Memoriales, p. 256.   [2] Melville's Diary, p. 32.

" He haid then in hand," Melville tells us, " Mr
Patrik Constant's [or Adamson's[1]] Catechisme
of Calvin, converted in Latin heroic vers, quhilk
with the author was mikle estimed of ";[2] and
deservedly so, for Adamson was an accomplished
scholar, was using his scholarship for the church's
good, was eulogised by Lawson, Knox's colleague
and successor, and had not yet developed that
spirit of subserviency to the powers that be which
afterwards proved his ruin.

The printer had also the honour of publishing
in St Andrews the last work which engaged the
thoughts of the reformer. This was his ' Answer
to a letter of a Jesuit named Tyrie.' It had been
drawn up some years before, but was now carefully revised and enlarged, and exhibited his
matured views respecting several of the most
notable subjects of controversy between the
reformed and unreformed churches. Possibly it

---

[1] [In the rather scurrilous Legend of the Bischop of St Androis,
it is said :—

> " Ane baxters sone, ane beggar borne,
> That twyse his surnaime hes mensworne ;
> To be called Constene he thocht shame,
> He tuke up Constantine to name.
>
> .   .   .   .   .   .
>
> Thinking that poore professione vaine,
> He changed his surname ower agane ;
> Now Doctor Adamsone at last,
> Whairthrow he ower to Paris past."
> —Dalyell's Scotish Poems, 1801, ii. 309, 310.

He inherited both names from his ancestors, who were called
Constantine or Adamson (M'Crie's Melville, 1856, p. 461).]

[2] Melville's Diary, p. 32.

may have been because he had detected through all their disguises the secret leaning of the two Hamiltons to Romanist or semi-Romanist views regarding the apostolical succession, the nature of the sacraments, and the unfailing visibility and perpetuity of the church, that he now so fully entered into a controversy which previously he had been inclined to shun. Perhaps this is what is hinted at in the preface, in which he says: "Wonder not, gentill reidar, that sic ane argument suld proceid fra me in thir dolorous days after that I have taken gude-night at the warld and at all the fasherie of the same. . . . There ar sevin yeares past sen a scrole send from a Jesuite to his brother was presented unto me be a faithfull brother requyring sum answer to be maid to the same. . . . Amongs my other caires I scriblit that which followis, and that in few dayis; which being finished I repented of my laubour, and purposed fullie to have suppressed it. Which, na dout I had done, if that the devil had not steirit up the Jesuites of purpois to trouble godlie harts, with the same argumentis which Tyrie usis, amplifyed and set furth with all the dog eloquence that Sathan can devyse for suppressing of the free progres of the Evangell of Jesus Christ." Then, after a touching reference to the hard lot of his dispersed flock "suffering lytill les calamitie than did the faithfull efter

the persecutioun of Steaphen," and an earnest
petition that God would grant them one day to
meet in glory, he entreats the brethren to pray for
him, that God " in His mercy will pleis to put end
to my long and panefull battell," as he was unable
to fight as erewhile he had done, and longed for
release, though still resigned to bear patiently
whatsoever God saw meet to lay upon this, his
" wicked carkase." [1]

In March 1572 the General Assembly was held
at St Andrews in the schools of St Leonard's
College.[2] This place was no doubt chosen in
part at least for the convenience of the aged
reformer, whose counsel in that time of trouble
was specially needed. It was the last Assembly
at which he was able to be present, and probably
the first witnessed by Davidson and Melville.
" Thair," the latter narrates, " was motioned
the making of bischopes, to the quhilk Mr
Knox opponit himselff directlie and zealuslie ";[3]
and thus probably were implanted in the
youthful student's mind the germs of those
presbyterian principles which were nurtured
by intercourse with his uncle Andrew Melville,
and were retained by him to the last with
heroic tenacity.

[1] Laing's Knox, vi. 481, 482.
[2] [This Assembly met on the 6th of March 1571-72.]
[3] Melville's Diary, p. 31.

Two months before this a convention at Leith had given its sanction to a sort of mongrel episcopacy, nominally to secure the tithes more completely to the church, but really to secure the bulk of them by a more regular title to certain covetous noblemen who sought in this way to reimburse themselves for their services in the cause of the Reformation.[1] Chief among these noblemen was the Earl of Morton, then one of the chief supporters of the young prince, and soon after regent of the kingdom. Having secured a presentation to the Archbishopric of St Andrews for Mr John Douglas before mentioned, he came over to the city, had him elected by the chapter in terms of the convention, and on the 10th of February inaugurated into his office. This function was performed by Wynram, Superintendent of Fife, according to the Order followed in the admission of Superintendents, save that the Bishop of Caithness, the Superintendent of Lothian, and Mr David Lindsay, who sat beside Douglas, laid their hands on his head. Knox had preached that day as usual; but, as Bannatyne is careful to tell us, had "refuised to inaugurat the said bischope";[2] and as others add had "denounced anathema

---

[1] [This convention was held in January 1571-72. See Booke of the Universall Kirk, i. 203-236 ; Calderwood's History, iii. 168-196.]

[2] Bannatyne's Memorials, p. 223.

to the giver, anathema to the receaver," [1] who as rector and principal had already far more to do than such an aged man could hope to overtake.[2] It was in reference to the same appointment that Adamson, as yet uncorrupted by Court influences, had a few days before in a sermon from the same pulpit given utterance to his famous distinction of three kinds of bishops, my lord bishop, my lord's bishop, and the Lord's bishop, the first of whom had been in time of popery, the second was now brought in merely to enable my lord to draw the kirk rents, and the third was the evangelical pastor as he should be in times of thorough reformation.[3]

---

[1] Calderwood's History, iii. 206.

[2] [Dr Laing has not only indicated that there has long been much uncertainty and speculation as to the parentage and social status of John Douglas, but has stated that he "was descended from the Douglasses of Pettendreich" (Laing's Knox, i. 286 n.) Principal Lee has said : " All the accounts of Douglas which I have ever seen in modern books abound with errors. He is represented as having been an obscure Carmelite friar whom the Earl of Argyle chose to employ as his chaplain, and for whom the Archbishop of St Andrews expressed the strongest aversion. He was quite a different man—a man of family undoubtedly, and most probably related to James Douglas the Earl of Morton, son of Sir George Douglas of Pinky, and, like him, a branch of the great family of Angus " (Lee's Lectures, ii. 3). When working in the Register House, I found unimpeachable evidence concerning his parentage. On the 2nd of January 1563-64, letters of legitimation were granted in favour of Mr John Douglas, Rector of the University of St Andrews, bastard son natural of quondam Robert Douglas in Langnewtoune (Register of Privy Seal, xxxii. 23).]

[3] Melville's Diary, p. 32 ; Calderwood's History, iii. 206.

One more brief sketch from the Diary of the quaint but graphic chronicler on whom I have repeatedly drawn may conclude our notice of these last labours of the reformer, and bring us to his last illness and death. "The town of Edinbruche recovered againe [out of the hands of the queen's faction] and the guid and honest men therof retourned to thair housses,[1] Mr Knox with his familie past hame to Edinbruche." During the time of his residence in St Andrews he was very weak. "I saw him everie day of his doctrine," says Melville, "go hulie and fear with a furring of martriks about his neck, a staff in the an hand, and guid godlie Richart Bal-landen, his servand, halding upe the uther oxtar, from the abbey to the paroche kirk; and be the said Richart and another servant lifted upe to the pulpit, whar he behovit to lean at his first entrie; bot or he haid done with his sermont he was sa active and vigorus that he was lyk to ding that pulpit in blads, and fly out of it."[2]

Soon after his return to Edinburgh he found himself quite unable to preach in the large church which he had formerly occupied, and a smaller one was fitted up for him in the western

---

[1] These honest men earnestly implored their pastor to return also to Edinburgh, if he could do so without serious injury to his health.

[2] Melville's Diary, p. 33.

part of the nave of St Giles.[1] But not even so were his services to be long available. On one occasion only after his return may it be said that the old fire burst out with all its former fierceness and brilliancy. This was in September, when tidings reached him of the bloody massacre of St Bartholomew's day in France. "Being conveyed to the pulpit," Dr M'Crie tells us, "and summoning up his remaining strength, he thundered the vengeance of God against 'that cruel murderer and false traitor, the King of France,' and [borrowing the language of the Old Testament prophets] desired Le Croc, the French ambassador, to tell his master that sentence was pronounced against him in Scotland, that the divine vengeance would never depart from him nor from his house, if repentance did not ensue; but his name would remain an execration to posterity, and none proceeding from his loins should enjoy his kingdom in peace."[2] The only further notice of his work is by Melville, who simply informs us that after "instituting in his roum, be the ordinar calling of the kirk and congregation, Mr James Lawsone, a man of singular

---

[1] [Dr Cameron Lees says that the Tolbooth, in which Knox preached for some little time and where he delivered his last sermon, was "the portion of St Giles which had been cut off the western part of the nave, and was used for meetings of the Council" (St Giles', 1889, p. 157).]

[2] M'Crie's Knox, 1855, p. 269.

learning, zeal, and eloquence, . . . he tuk him to his chamber and most happelie and comfortablie departed this lyff." [1]

With this kindly notice by his youthful admirer this lecture would have ended, had I not promised to the late Dean Stanley several years ago that, when a suitable opportunity occurred, I would not fail publicly to advert to a shameless misrepresentation of the closing scene to which he had directed my attention. This originated with Archibald Hamilton, already referred to as one of the two masters of the New College, who apostatised from the Protestant faith, and after his flight to the Continent published the most barefaced lies of his old antagonist and the noble men who were associated with him in his hard battle and well-earned triumph. These lies were exposed and refuted at the time by Principal Smeton of Glasgow, himself a convert from that Society of Jesus which Hamilton ultimately joined. But as they have been revived in our own day, and distributed in the form of a tract by Popish emissaries at the doors of Protestant churches in London, and as one of a series bearing the sensational title of "Death-bed Scenes," I shall, in fulfilment of my promise, subjoin a brief account of the reformer's last illness and death, taken almost exclusively from the contemporary narra-

[1] Melville's Diary, p. 33.

tives of Bannatyne and Smeton, the former of whom was an eye-witness, and the latter of whom had full information from Lawson,[1] who also was an eye-witness of all. This, I feel assured, is all that is required to set matters in their true light.

The vague charges of immorality brought against the reformer by those calumniators, ancient and modern, may be dismissed at once as nothing more than the stock-in-trade of hard-pressed controversialists in the sixteenth century. Had there been the slightest foundation for them, some of Knox's many opponents in Scotland— Ninian Winzet, or the Abbot of Crossraguel, or Tyrie the Jesuit, or Hamilton himself before he left the country—would not have scrupled openly to upbraid him with them. Neither would the culprits among the Protestant clergy and laity, whom at various times he subjected to so rigorous a discipline, have borne this patiently at his hands had he himself been a known offender. It was his character which gave him his influence both at home and abroad, both with friends and with foes, and could it have been successfully assailed, it would not have been left to two Jesuits in a

---

[1] [In the opinion of Dr David Laing, Lawson was the author of the Vera Historia extremae vitae et obitus eximii viri Joannis Knoxii, appended to Smeton's Responsio ad Hamiltonii Dialogum, in 1579 (Laing's Knox, vi. 646).]

foreign land to lead the assault after he was silenced in death.

Such, however, I hardly need to assure you was not the end of the restorer of a really holy church in Scotland, if aught of credit is to be given to the unanimous testimony of those who attended him during his last illness and witnessed its closing scene, though it may have been the end which Popish controversialists in the sixteenth century deemed meet for him—as well as for Luther and Calvin and many more of whom the world was not worthy—as it is in one of the foulest legends with which their successors in the nineteenth century think it fair to supplement the legends of their predecessors in the sixteenth. According to them Luther was the child of a demon, not figuratively but literally; Calvin was eaten up of worms, like Herod who slew the children of Bethlehem and was smitten by the judgment of God, because (though apparently in this they confound him with a later Herod) he affected divine honours. To mention such slanders, as the sceptical Bayle has said with special reference to the case of Knox, is all that is needed to refute them. They are the product of malignity so evident that it defeats itself. I know but one parallel to them in our literature, and it has the excuse that it has come down to us from the dark ages.[1] Some would persuade us that the time has come when we might afford to forget old controversies and to shake hands with our former antagonists, but such occurrences as these tend to show that such forgetfulness and affectation of cordiality is likely to be all on one side.

And now let me simply set over against these fables, in as abridged form as I can, the unvarnished statements of Bannatyne and Smeton, the latter of which was published in reply to Hamilton who first gave shape to these charges, and which hitherto has been deemed a conclusive refutation of them.[2]

On the 10th of November, the day after he inducted Lawson as his colleague, he was seized with a violent cough and began to breathe with difficulty. Many, who desired ardently, if it were possible, to detain him a little longer here, advised

[1] Walsingham's abuse of Wycliffe. [Thomae Walsingham, Historia Anglicana, ii. 119, 120; and Ypodigma Neustriae a Thoma Walsingham, p. 340; Rolls series. Translations will be found in Vaughan's John de Wycliffe, 1853, pp. 468, 469; and in Lechler's Wycliffe, Relig. Tract Soc., p. 423.]

[2] [For the substance of Archibald Hamilton's account, see M'Crie's Knox, 1855, p. 405. Bannatyne's account is in both editions of his work (Journal of Transactions, 1806, and Memoriales of Transactions, 1836). It is likewise in Laing's Knox, vi. 634-645; and there (pp. 649-660) is also given a translation of Smeton's (or Lawson's) account. The accounts of Bannatyne and Smeton do not always agree as to the exact day on which certain events happened.]

him to call in the assistance of skilful physicians. He readily complied with their advice, though he felt that the end of his warfare was now nigh at hand. Next day he caused the wages of all his servants to be paid, and earnestly exhorted them all to be careful to lead holy and Christian lives. On the 13th, being obliged by the increase of his malady to leave off his ordinary course of reading in the Scriptures (for every day he had been wont to read some chapters of the Old and New Testaments, especially some of the Psalms and Gospels), he directed his wife and servant to read to him each day the 17th chapter of St John's Gospel, one or other of the chapters of St Paul's Epistle to the Ephesians, and the 53rd chapter of Isaiah. On the 14th he rose early, apparently supposing it had been the Lord's day, and being asked why he did so when he was so ill, he replied that he had been meditating all night on the resurrection of the Lord (the subject which would have fallen to be treated next in order by him in his ministry), and that he was now prepared to ascend the pulpit to communicate to his brethren the consolation he had enjoyed in his own soul. Next day, though very sick, he prevailed on Durie, already mentioned, and another friend, Steward by name, to remain to dinner with him, ordered a hogshead of wine in his cellar to be pierced for them, and desired

Steward to send for some of it as long as it lasted, for he should not tarry till it was done. Little is recorded of him for several days after this, but it was probably in this interval that he was visited by many of the chief of the nobility, including the Earl of Morton, so soon to be created regent,[1] and by many members of his congregation. All of these he " solidly exhorted " and comforted. On the 20th or 21st he gave orders that his coffin should be prepared. On the 22nd he sent for the ministers, elders, and deacons of the church, that he might give them his last counsels and take final farewell of them. In the brief but solemn address which he delivered to them he called God to witness, whom he served in the Gospel of His Son, that he had taught nothing but the pure and solid doctrine of the Gospel of the Son of God, and had never indulged his own private passions, or spoken from any hatred of the persons of those against whom he had denounced the heavy judgments of God. He exhorted them to persevere in the truth of the Gospel and in their allegiance to their young sovereign, and dismissed them with his solemn blessing. To Lawson and Lindsay, whom he

---

[1] [Morton was elected regent on the 24th of November 1572, the day on which Knox died (Acts of Parliament, iii. 78 ; Bannatyne's Memoriales, p. 280). Bannatyne places Morton's visit on the 19th ; Smeton leaves the day uncertain.]

asked to remain behind, he gave a last earnest message for his old friend Kirkaldy of Grange, the commandant of the castle, who had gone over to the party of the queen,[1] and whose soul, notwithstanding, he said, was dear to him—as being one of his congregation in the castle of St Andrews, and a sharer in his hard lot in France —so that he would not have it perish if by any means he could save it. "Go and tell him," he said, "that neither the craggy rock in which he miserably trusts, nor the carnal prudence of that man whom he regards as a demigod, nor the assistance of foreigners, as he falsely flatters himself, shall deliver them, but he shall be disgracefully dragged from his nest to punishment and hung on a gallows in the face of the sun, unless he speedily amend his life and betake himself to the mercy of God."

On the 23rd the difficulty of his breathing had greatly increased, and he seems to have thought that his end was near at hand. To one of his most intimate friends who asked him if he felt great pain, he replied that that was not reckoned as pain by him which would be the end of many miseries and the beginning of perpetual joy. And soon after, apparently supposing his end was come, he repeated the Lord's Prayer and the

[1] For a defence of Kirkaldy see Barbé's Kirkaldy of Grange, Famous Scots Series, pp. 108-124.

Apostles' Creed, adding certain paraphrases of his own on each petition of the prayer and article of the creed to the great comfort of those who stood by; and then lifting up his hands to heaven he once more said, " Lord, into Thy hands I commend my spirit." During the succeeding night he caused the 15th chapter of 1st Corinthians to be read and re-read to him, and repeatedly said to himself, " O! how sweet and salutary consolation does the Lord provide for me in this chapter." The following day, about noon, he once more sat up in bed, but owing to his extreme weakness was not able to remain long in that posture. About three in the afternoon one of his eyes failed, and his tongue performed its office less readily than before. About six in the evening he again said to his wife, " Go, read where I cast my first anchor," referring to the instructions he had given on the 13th.[1]

When this had been done, he continued for some hours in troubled slumber. It is in this occurrence alone that there can be got the slightest foundation for the slanders which his traducers have circulated. And it is only necessary to quote the account given of it by those who witnessed it to show that it was as honourable to the dying confessor as the gross mis-

[1] For a different interpretation see Taylor Innes's John Knox, Famous Scots Series, pp. 30, 31.

representation of it was dishonourable to his
opponents. During these hours he uttered frequent sighs and groans, so that those who stood
by could not doubt that he was contending with
some grievous temptation. When he awoke they
asked him what was the cause of his distress.
He answered that in the course of his life he had
had many contests with his spiritual adversary.
Often he had been tempted to despair of God's
mercy because of the greatness of his sins, often
also tempted by the allurements of the world to
forget his calling to endure hardness as a good
soldier of Christ Jesus. But now the cunning
adversary had assailed him in another form, and
endeavoured to persuade him that he had merited
heaven itself and a blessed immortality by the
faithful discharge of the duties of his high office.
"But blessed be God," exclaimed the dying reformer, "who hath brought seasonably to my
mind those passages of Scripture by which I was
enabled to quench the fiery dart, 'What hast
thou, that thou hast not received?' 'By the grace
of God I am what I am,' and 'Not I, but the
grace of God in me' . . . wherefore I give thanks
to my God by Jesus Christ who has been pleased
to grant me the victory. And I am firmly persuaded that . . . in a short time, without any
great bodily pain, and without any distress of
mind, I shall exchange this mortal and miserable

life for an immortal and blessed life through Jesus Christ."

This persuasion of his speedy and happy departure was soon to be justified by the event. After evening prayers Dr Preston, his physician, asked him whether he had heard them, when he replied, "I would to God that ye and all men heard them as I have heard them, and I praise God for that heavenly sound." Shortly after the signs of immediate dissolution appeared, his friends gathered round his bed, and his faithful servant addressed him: "Now, sir, the time that you have long called to God for, to wit an end of your battle, is come. And seeing all natural power now fails, remember those comfortable promises, which often times ye have shown to us, of our Saviour Jesus Christ. And that we may understand and know that ye hear us, make us some sign." And so he lifted up one of his hands, and incontinent thereafter rendered up his spirit apparently without pain or movement, so that he seemed rather to fall asleep than to die.

Such was the account of his last illness and death transmitted by those who attended on him and witnessed it, a death worthy of his noble life, and fully justifying the brief comment of Smeton, "Surely, whatever opprobrious things profane men may utter, God hath in him given us an

example of the right way as well of dying as of
living." It is true, as his heartless traducer takes
care to remind us, no dirge was chanted over his
remains, no mass of requiem was celebrated for
his soul. He and his countrymen had long ceased
to believe in the worth of such priestly ceremonies, or to imagine that their eternal state
could be affected by them, or by aught save
Christ's finished work and their own faith and
repentance while God's day of grace was prolonged to them here. The brief eulogy pronounced over his grave by the stern and reserved
regent[1] was a truer and more impressive testimony
to his worth than the most gorgeous celebration
of Romish rites which he could but have shared
with a Borgia or a Betoun. The stern simplicity
of his grave, which, like his master Calvin's, was
till lately preserved in the memory of men without stone or bronze to mark it out, tells a tale
very different from that his traducer hints at;
and if his bitter taunts shall lead the reformer's
countrymen now to erect a material monument
to him in some measure corresponding to the

---

[1] [Morton's testimony to Knox, as recorded by Melville, was :
" That he nather fearit nor flatterit anie fleche" (Diary, p. 60).
As recorded by Calderwood : " Here lyeth a man who in his life
never feared the face of man ; who hath beene often threatned with
dag and dager, but yitt hath ended his dayes in peace and honour.
For he had God's providence watching over him in a speciall maner,
when his verie life was sought" (History, iii. 242).]

benefits he has been honoured to confer on them, this attack on his fair fame will have been over-ruled for good.

But his real monument will never be one graven by art or man's device. It is one more noble, more lasting far. It is to be found in the life God enabled him to live, and the work God honoured him to do. It is to be seen in the plans he devised, in the institutions he founded, in the people he moulded anew, when the old church had confessedly failed in its mission. And while the Scottish nation continues to retain these institutions, and to bear this impress, it will continue the grandest, as it is the most telling, monument to the memory of its noble-hearted and single-minded reformer.

CHAPTER X.

THE SECOND BOOK OF DISCIPLINE.

IN a previous lecture I have endeavoured to give a pretty full account of the First Book of Discipline. It remains yet to say a few words about the Second Book of Discipline.

Principal John Cunningham has said : " The First Book exhibited a system of polity sagaciously suited to the circumstances of the country and the church : it seemed to grow out of the times." [1] I will add that it was not only suited to the times, but to many of the practical needs of the church of all times. I therefore hold that even yet it is worthy of a higher place than to be deemed merely a " collection of parchments and coins deposited beneath it [*i.e.*, the Second Book] by which future generations may read the story of the times in which the building was begun." [2] The

---

[1] Cunningham's Church History of Scotland, 1859, i. 444.
[2] Ibid., i. 445.

Second Book is more a book of constitutional law; and aims, as the Principal says, at elaborating a system from the New Testament without reference to circumstances, and bears far more resemblance to the Ordonnances of Calvin than to the less ambitious and more comprehensive Church Order Books of Germany. But the Second Book of Discipline has even fewer practical details than the ordinances of Geneva. Of course, so far as it actually abolished or modified the regulations of the First Book, these fell to be disused; but in so far as it did not actually do so, they still had a certain validity: and even in the Covenanting times it is generally the Books, not the Book of Discipline, to which reference is made in Acts of Assembly.

No one in our times, perhaps, has shown a more thorough appreciation of the real merits of the First Book than the Duke of Argyll in his well - known essay on " Presbytery." Mr Hill Burton, who depreciates it in comparison with the Second, makes far more than is warranted of the strong language in which it occasionally indulges against the old church, with which he contrasts the more restrained and balanced utterances of the Second Book.[1] I do not yield to many in my admiration of the

[1] Hill Burton's History of Scotland, 1876, v. 203.

courage and calmness of Melville; but I could no more think of placing him, scholarly and bold, yet calm, as he generally was, nor the Book attributed to him, more logical and unimpassionately didactic though it be, before the eager, impetuous, yet sagacious Knox, with his wealth of rude eloquence and thrilling tenderness, and his Book in which these qualities of head and heart are so clearly mirrored, than I would think of placing Calvin, highly as I honour him, before Luther, or his Catechism before the Wittenberg hymn-books.

I do not believe that the principles of the two Books are so widely different as they have sometimes been represented to be, or that the grand ideas of Knox concerning the place of the laity in the church, the education of the young, and the support and kindly treatment of the aged poor, were meant to be rejected or ignored by his great successor; but I do think these matters fall considerably into the background. Some of the noblest conceptions of the earlier Book are narrowed, and the whole system stiffened; and in the contests in which the church had then to engage with the young monarch, in vindication of her independence in her own province, positions were laid down which were soon pressed to consequences from which Knox and his associates would have shrunk.

They, who had been obliged long to contend with a corrupt and obstinate clergy which would grant no real reform in doctrine, no substantial concessions for the alleviation of practical grievances, boldly laid down the principle that "to kings, princes, rulers, and magistrates . . . chieflie and most principallie the conservation and purgation of the religioun apperteinis; so that not onlie they are appointed for civill policie, but also for maintenance of the trew religioun, and for suppressing of idolatrie and superstitioun whatsoever. . . . And therefore wee confesse and avow that sik as resist the supreme power doing that thing quhilk appertains to his charge, do resist Goddis ordinance, and therefore cannot be guiltles."[1]   Melville, who was called to contend with a king bent on securing autocratic power in the church as well as in the state, laid down, with the utmost precision, the principle in chapter x., "Although kings and princes that be godlie, sumtymes be their awin authority whan the kirk is corruptit and all things out of ordor, place ministers and restore the trew service of the Lord efter the examples of sum godly kings of Juda and divers godly emperours and kings also in the light of the

---

[1] Confession of 1560, in Dunlop's Confessions, ii. 92, 93.   [In Laing's Knox, ii. 118, it is *reformatioun and purgatioun* instead of *conservation and purgation.*]

New Testament; yit quhair the ministrie of the
kirk is anes lawfullie constitute and they that
are placeit do thair office faithfullie, all godlie
princes and magistratis aucht to heir and obey
thair voice, and reverence the majestie of the
Son of God speiking be them "; [1] or, as in
chapter i., where it is laid down, " As ministeris
are subject to the judgement and punishment
of the magistrat in externall things if they offend,
so aucht the magistratis to submit themselfis to
the discipline of the kirk gif they transgresse in
matteris of conscience and religioun." [2]

Hill Burton sarcastically remarks that " if we
grant that those who prepared it were what they
called themselves—the Church of God, presided

---

[1] Dunlop's Confessions, ii. 788, 789. [The Second Book of
Discipline has been frequently printed.   It is in Calderwood's
History, Wodrow Society ed., iii. 529-555; Spottiswoode's History,
1655, pp. 289-302; Spottiswoode Society ed., ii. 233-256; Booke
of the Universall Kirk, Bannatyne Club ed., ii. 488-512; Peterkin's
ed., pp. 537-563; Dunlop's Confessions, ii. 757-805.   The quotations in the text are from Dunlop.]

[2] Ibid., ii. 764.   Melville afterwards more pithily expressed the
same principle in his sovereign's presence : " Thair is twa kings
and twa kingdomes in Scotland.   Thair is Chryst Jesus the King,
and His kingdome the kirk, whase subject King James the Saxt is,
and of whase kingdome nocht a king, nor a lord, nor a heid, bot
a member !   And they whome Chryst hes callit and commandit to
watch over His kirk, and governe His spirituall kingdome, hes
sufficient powar of Him and authoritie sa to do, bathe togidder and
severalie; the quhilk na Christian king nor prince sould controll
and discharge, but fortifie and assist, utherwayes nocht fathfull
subjects nor members of Chryst " (Melville's Diary, p. 370).

over by the Lord Jesus Christ as the representative
of the Godhead on earth—it would be difficult
to refuse assent to what follows. Nothing can
be more perfect than the analysis by which the
two ruling powers are separated from each other,
and the ecclesiastical set above the secular." [1]   If
this is not quite borne out, one can hardly help
feeling that more care should have been taken
to mark out the limits of ecclesiastical authority,
and to show that the power of ministers and
elders was as distinctly limited by the laws of
Christ as that of kings and magistrates ought to
be by the laws of the land; or, in other words,
that ministers and elders may err in interpreting
the laws of Christ, just as civil rulers may err
in interpreting the laws of the land. No doubt
the limitation contended for is in words admitted,
"the magistrat neither aucht to preich, minister
the sacraments, nor execute the censuris of the
kirk, nor yit prescrive any rewll how it sould be
done; bot command the ministeris to observe
the rewll commandit in the Word, and punish
the transgressours be civill means. The ministeris exerce not the civill jurisdictioun, bot
teich the magistrat how it sould be exercit
according to the Word." [2]   "It is proper to
kings, princes, and magistrates to be callit lordis

---

[1] Hill Burton's History of Scotland, v. 203.
[2] Dunlop's Confessions, ii. 763.

and dominators over their subjectis, whom they govern civilly; bot it is proper to Christ onlie to be callit Lord and Master in the spirituall government of the kirk, and all utheris that beiris office therein aucht not to usurp dominion therein, nor be callit lordis, bot onlie ministeris, disciples, and servantis. For it is Christis proper office to command and rewll His kirk universall, and every particular kirk, throw His Spirit and Word, be the ministrie of men." [1] But it is not made sufficiently prominent anywhere in the Book that these men are only entitled to unreserved obedience when they truly speak Christ's mind and truly follow His Word. Those who have made most of the Book have neither clearly perceived this nor have they realised the full meaning of the lucid and explicit statement made by Rutherfurd when he was contending against the Erastians and Independents of England. Had they done so, I cannot but think that the bitter divisions among Scottish Presbyterians would have been fewer, and that there would have been far less occasion for the reproach often cast on them, that new presbyter is but old priest writ large.

"That the magistrate is not obliged," Rutherfurd affirms, "to execute the decrees of the church without further examination, whether they be

[1] Dunlop's Confessions, ii. 762.

right or wrong, as Papists teach that the magistrate is to execute the decrees of their Popish
councels with blind obedience, and submit his
faith to them, because he is a layman and may
not dare to examine whether the church doth
erre or not, is clear. 1. Because, if in hearing
the Word all should follow the example of the
men of Berea, not relying on the testimony of
Paul or any preacher, [and] try whether that
which concerneth their conscience and faith be
agreeable to the Scriptures or no, and accordingly
receive or reject; so in all things of discipline
the magistrate is to try by the Word whether
he ought to adde his sanction to these decrees
which the church gives out for edification, and
whether he should draw the sword against such
a one as a heretick and a perverter of souls. But
the former is true; the magistrate's practise in
adding his civill sanction and in punishing here-
ticks concerneth his conscience, knowing that he
must do it in faith as he doth all his moral
actions; *ergo*, the magistrate must examine what
he practiseth in his office according to the Word,
and must not take it upon the meer authority
of the church, else his faith in these moral acts
of his office should be resolved *ultimate* on the
authority of the church, not on the Word of God,
which, no doubt, is Popery, for so the warrant
of the magistrate's conscience should not be 'thus

saith the Lord,' but 'thus saith the church in their decrees.'   2. The magistrate and all men have a command to try all things, *ergo*, to try the decrees of the church, and to retain what is good (1 Thes. v. 21); to try the spirits even of the church in their decrees (1 John iii. 1).   3. We behooved [in that case] to lay down this Popish ground that . . . the church cannot erre in their decrees. . . . Its against Scripture and reason that magistrates, and by the like reason all others, should obey the decrees of the church with a blinde faith, without inquiring in the warrants and grounds of their decrees, which is as good Popery as, Magistrates and all men are to beleeve as the church be-leeveth, with an implicite faith, so ignorance shall be the mother of devotion.   Whoever impute this to us—who have suffered for nonconformity, and upon this ground, that synods can erre, re-fused the ceremonies—are to consult with their own conscience whether this be not to make us appear disloyall and odious to magistracy in that which we never thought, far lesse [presumed] to teache and professe it to the world." [1]

Even more notable are the utterances of George Gillespie, when vindicating against the Erastians of the south that more free government of the church by its own courts from which they feared

[1] Rutherfurd's Divine Right of Church Government, 1646, pp. 596, 597. [1 John iii. 1 is a misprint in the original for 1 John iv. 1.]

so many evils. " I dare confidently say," he
affirms, "that, if comparisons be rightly made,
presbyterial government is the most limited and
the least arbitrary government of any other in
the world."[1]   And, after entering into details to
make good this affirmation in regard to the papal
and prelatical forms of government, he proceeds
to maintain that Independents "must needs be
supposed to exercise a much more unlimited or
arbitrary power than the presbyterial churches
do," because they exempt individual congregations from all control and correction by superior
courts, and because it is "one of their three
grand principles which disclaimeth the binding
of themselves for the future unto their present
judgement and practice, and avoucheth the keeping of this reserve to alter and retract."[2]   Some
who think that, after all recent changes, they
more truly hold the opinions of Gillespie than
we do, have laid it down very dogmatically that
even although the constitution of a national
church were in all other respects scriptural, yet
if it did not reserve this power to alter and
retract without let or hindrance, it would still
be at variance with the tenets of the Covenanting
times; but you see here that Gillespie affirms
that that was a principle of the Independents, not

[1] Aaron's Rod Blossoming, 1646, p. 177.
[2] Ibid., pp. 180, 181.

of the Presbyterians, and claims [1] it as a special
merit of the latter that they were willing to explain their doctrine and discipline to the civil
authorities, and, getting these sanctioned, to abide
by them till they were again altered by consent
of church and state. He denies that in claiming
a distinct government for the church the Presbyterians meant to deprive the Christian magistrate
of that power and authority in matters of religion
which the Word of God and the earlier Confessions of the Reformed churches recognised as
belonging to his office. On the contrary, he
maintains that not only in extraordinary cases
when church government doth degenerate into
tyranny, or those who manage it make defection
from the truth, "the Christian magistrate may
and ought to do diverse things in and for religion,
and interpose his authority diverse wayes so as
doth not properly belong to his cognisance, decision and administration ordinarily, and in a
reformed and well constituted church"; [2] but

---

[1] [Dr Mitchell may have found such a claim elsewhere in Gillespie's works ; but it is not distinctly made in that chapter of
'Aaron's Rod Blossoming' from which the quotations in this paragraph are taken, although perhaps it may be held to be implied
in the words : "By which it appeareth that their [*i.e.*, the Independents'] way will not suffer them to be so far moulded into an
uniformity, or bounded within certain particular rules (I say not
with others, but even among themselves) as the Presbyterian way
will admit of" (Aaron's Rod Blossoming, p. 181).]

[2] Aaron's Rod Blossoming, p. 182.

also that, in ordinary cases, he is free to act as his own conscience directs in giving or refusing his sanction to the government and discipline of the church; and that if he is offended with any sentence of its courts, "they ought to be ready, in all humility and respect, to give him an account and reason of such their proceedings, and by all means to endeavour the satisfaction of the magistrate his conscience, or otherwise to be warned and rectified if themselves have erred." [1]

Had the principles thus laid down been more clearly kept in view by the framers of the Second Book of Discipline, its influence for good on Scottish Christianity would have been more unmixed than it has been. Had they been more consistently acted on by Rutherfurd and his associates, who consented to their formal insertion in our later standards, many sad troubles which then and afterwards befel the church, for which they lived and laboured, would have been altogether avoided, or more easily provided against; but as it is, great misunderstandings have certainly arisen. The two Books of Discipline have been too much read apart, instead of being regarded as complementary each of the other; and while all that is liberal and progressive tends, I think, more and more to rally round the one, I believe that much that is nar-

[1] Aaron's Rod Blossoming, p. 183.

rower, but still earnest and resolutely Christian, will continue to draw its inspiration from the other.

The Second Book of Discipline, as well as the First, failed to commend itself to the ruling powers, and to obtain a place in its full form on the statute book. Those of its clauses relating to the functions of the several church courts were inserted almost word for word in the Act of the Scottish Parliament of 1592, reckoned the charter of the presbyterian church. It was, however, several times ratified by the General Assembly, and was partially carried out by its authority from the time of its ratification; and to this extent it, as well as the First Book of Discipline, appears to have been fully recognised. The question of its authority was very fully argued in the famous Auchterarder case. The counsel for the presbytery and the minority of the judges did not venture to argue, however, that as a whole the Second Book of Discipline had received the sanction of the state save in irregular times; but they contended that the notes, contained in Spottiswoode's History, of the clauses respecting which the king and the commissioners of Parliament had come to agreement with the ministers, should be accepted as determining the extent to which it was law. It was affirmed, however, by the majority of the judges that only the clauses actually inserted in the Act of Parliament could be so regarded, and it has since been maintained by Mr Peterkin that the alleged notes of agreement between the king and the church's commissioners are not actually found in the manuscript copy of the History which is preserved in the Advocate's Library.[1] The general theory of the church, however, which may be said to underlie the most important statement of the Second Book of Discipline, is not materially different from that which finds expression in the First. "The kirk of God," it is said, "is sumtymes largelie takin for all them that professe the Evangill of Jesus Christ, and so it is a company and fellowship, not onely of the godly, but also of hypocrites professing alwayis outwardly ane true religion. Uther tymes it is takin for the godlie and elect onlie, and sumtymes for them that exercise spiritual function

---

[1] Peterkin's Booke of the Universall Kirk, 1839, p. 549 n. [The late Bishop Russell, after examining the four MS. copies of Spottiswoode's History, came to the conclusion that the one in the Advocates' Library is only the first and incompleted draft of the work, and that the one in Trinity College, Dublin, is the one which Spottiswoode himself prepared for the press. Bishop Russell accordingly followed the Dublin MS. in his edition of the History printed for the Spottiswoode Society, and that edition (as well as the old folio edition) contains the notes of agreement and disagreement. Peterkin has printed the Second Book of Discipline, from an attested copy publicly read on the 29th of September 1591 "in the elderschip of Haddingtoun," and "subscryvit be the brethren thairof." Of the ten subscribers, nine write *minister* after their names; the other simply signs, "Mr L. Hay, Bass."]

amongis the congregation of them that professe the truth." [1]   These last, ministers, doctors, elders, and deacons, are taken to represent the church in its wider sense, and must have a lawful calling from it.   This lawful calling is said to consist of two parts—viz., election and ordination. Election is defined to be the choosing out of a person or persons most able for the office that is vacant, by the judgment of the eldership and consent of the congregation to which the person or persons are appointed.   Ordination is defined as the separation and sanctifying of the person appointed of God and His kirk after he be well tried and found qualified.   The ceremonies of ordination are declared to be fasting, earnest prayer, and imposition of the hands of the elder-ship.   Then follow two of the most important paragraphs in the Book, which come nearest to supplying that which I deem defective in it, a clear and distinct admission that human rulers in the church as well as in the state have but limited powers.   " All thir [*i.e.*, those various kinds of office-bearers], as they must be raisit up be God and be Him made able for the wark quhairto they ar callit, so aught they [to] knaw their message to be limitit within God's Word, without the quhilk bounds they aught not to passe.   All thir sould tak these titils and names

1 Dunlop's Confessions, ii. 759, 760.

onlie . . . quhilk the Scriptures gevis unto them,
as these quhilks import labour, travell and wark;
and ar names of offices and service, and not of
idlenes, dignitie, warldlie honour or preheminence,
quhilk be Christ our Maister is expresslie reprovit
and forbidden. . . . And generallie thir twa
things aught they all to respect, the glorie of
God, and edifieing of His kirk, in discharging
their dewties in their callings." [1]

It is generally supposed that it is in this Second
Book of Discipline that we have the first clear
institution of that church court which we now
call the presbytery, and it admits of no dispute
that it was in the year 1581, after the final adoption of the Book by the Assembly, that an attempt
was made, with consent of the crown, regularly
to divide the country into presbyteries. These,
however, though marked out on paper in that
year, were in point of fact only gradually set up,
and in general they arose out of, and absorbed
into themselves, the previously existing *exercise*,
which the First Book of Discipline had sanctioned and recommended to meet weekly for the
study and interpretation of the Scriptures.[2] The
introduction of what are called, but erroneously,
lay elders [3] to the place they have so long worthily

---

[1] Dunlop's Confessions, ii. 769.   [2] *Supra*, pp. 170-173.

[3] [" Some reproachfully and others ignorantly call them *lay
elders*. But the distinction of the clergie and laity is popish and

filled in the presbyteries was a still more gradual process. The presbytery of St Andrews, even down to the close of the sixteenth century, appears to have contained no elders save the *doctors*, under which name were comprehended the masters of the university, both professors of divinity and professors of philosophy, and even the doctor or master of the grammar-school. The question, however, has been raised whether it is really the presbytery or the kirk-session which is meant by the word *eldership*, which is generally applied in the Second Book of Discipline to that court to which it asserts that it belongs to see that the Word of God is purely preached within its bounds, the sacraments rightly administered, the discipline maintained, and the ecclesiastical goods rightly distributed; to take care that the ordinances made by provincial, national, and general assemblies are duly executed; and also to make constitutions which concern τὸ πρέπον in the kirk,[1]—all which duties by the Act of Parliament are expressly

anti-christian; and they who have narrowly considered the records of ancient times have noted this distinction as one of the grounds whence the mystery of iniquity had the beginning of it. The name of *clergie* appropriate to ministers is full of pride and vaine-glory, and hath made the holy people of God to be despised, as if they were prophane and uncleane in comparison of their ministers" (Gillespie's Assertion of the Government, 1641, p. 3).]

[1] Dunlop's Confessions, ii. 779, 780.

assigned to the presbytery.[1] This question has
been keenly debated down to our own day. The
weight of authority is certainly very decidedly in
favour of the opinion which identifies this eldership with the presbytery. Among recent authorities we have Dr David Laing and Dr Cook of
Haddington on this side, in opposition to the
late Principal Cunningham of St Andrews; and
among those of a somewhat earlier time we have
Principal Lee, Dr M'Crie, and the late Dr George
Cook of St Andrews pronouncing in favour of the
same view. If we go to older authorities again,
we have Spottiswoode, the episcopal historian,
and Calderwood, the presbyterian, at one in supporting it. I know of no considerable authority
in the seventeenth century which has been
adduced on the other side, save that of Henderson, whose statement, however, is rather
inferential than direct. In fact, the eldership is
used in the Second Book of Discipline itself as a
convertible term with presbytery, and is often so
used in the acts of contemporary assemblies.
When presbyteries came to be set up, they are
sometimes designated by the name of eldership,
and sometimes by that of presbytery; and where
our present authorised version of Scripture reads
"with the laying on of the hands of the presbytery," the Genevan version reads, "with the

[1] Acts of the Parliaments of Scotland, iii. 542.

laying on of the hands of the companie of the eldership." [1]

The only other alternative is that suggested by the late Procurator Cook, that in the Second Book of Discipline the functions of the two courts were as yet undistributed; and that when they came to be legally distributed by the Act of Parliament of 1592, those which the framers of the Second Book assigned to the eldership were in nearly its very words appropriated to the presbytery, and a much more limited province assigned to the kirk-session—the court called by the Puritans of the south by the name of the Lesser Presbytery. Perhaps it may be regarded as a rather curious confirmation of this theory of Procurator Cook's, that what he supposes to have been first intended by the framers of the Book as a common court is asserted by Gillespie, the ablest of their successors in the following century, to have been really characteristic of the presbytery of the primitive church. Whatever may be thought of his argument in vindication of what he calls the two presbyteries, the fact remains that he explicitly admits there was but one in the primitive church; [2] and this will be all the more

[1] [In some editions of the Genevan version the word "eldership" is thus explained in the margin : "Under this name he containeth the whole ministerie of the church which was at Ephesus."]

[2] Assertion of the Government of the Church of Scotland, 1641, pp. 128-130, 136-147.

remarkable if, with Mr Cook, we hold that what the framers of the Second Book of Discipline really designed was one presbytery or eldership governing a larger or smaller number of churches in common; and that we owe the distribution of the power between the two courts rather to the Act of Parliament than to the Second Book of Discipline. I agree with Gillespie, however, that in the circumstances of the church in a thoroughly Christianised country it would have been a matter to be regretted if every congregation had not had its session or lesser presbytery, with such definitely limited powers as by the Act of Parliament, and by the later acts of the church, are entrusted to it; and I am not sure that we do not owe this arrangement to the episcopal rather than to the presbyterian party, and that it was a concession made by them as the only presbytery they could well acknowledge, if they were to leave any function for the bishop at all in this court. At least the rough draft of the clause of the subsequent Act of Parliament in regard to the kirk-session appears first in the conference held between the two parties, and is then noted as having had the express approval of the king and commissioners of Parliament,[1] which

[1] [It is not quite clear which conference Dr Mitchell is here referring to. In the conference held at Stirling in December 1578, the Second Book of Discipline was discussed section by section. The results are preserved not only by Spottiswoode, as mentioned

was not at that time, nor till considerably later, secured to the clauses in the Act affirming the powers of the larger presbytery.

I have said elsewhere that in chapters xxv. and xxvi. of the Westminster Confession of Faith we have a doctrine affirmed as to the church and the communion of saints which seems to me to be more thoroughly catholic than that which is set forth in the Articles of the Irish Episcopal Church, of the teaching of which the compilers of our Confession have so largely availed themselves. In addition to one invisible church to which all the true elect of God are affirmed to belong, and particular visible churches composed of *professing* Christians in particular nations (both of which are expressly owned in both formularies), the Westminster Confession recognises one visible church to which all throughout the world who profess

above (p. 227 n.), but also by Calderwood (iii. 433-442), neither of whom, however, says that these results were then noted as having been expressly approved by the king. The heads agreed upon at the Holyrood conference on 17th February 1585-86 do not include anything which can be regarded as the draft of the clause of the Act of 1592 concerning the power and jurisdiction of " particulare kirkis " (Calderwood's History, iv. 491-494). The articles defining the jurisdiction of provincial assemblies, presbyteries, and particular kirks, agreed on by the king in conference with some of the brethren sent to him by the General Assembly in May 1586, are transferred almost *verbatim* to the Act of Parliament of 1592 (Booke of the Universall Kirk, Bannatyne Club edit., ii. 665, 666 ; Calderwood's History, iv. 567, 568 ; Acts of Parliament, iii. 541, 542).]

faith in Christ are to feel that they belong, and with the members of which they are bound, as God gives them opportunity, to cultivate union and communion. " The catholic or universal church, which is invisible, consists of the whole number of the elect that have been, are, or shall be gathered into one, under Christ the head thereof; and is the spouse, the body, the fulness of Him that filleth all in all. The visible church, which is also catholic or universal under the Gospel (not confined to one nation as before under the law), consists of all those throughout the world that profess the true religion, and of their children, and is the kingdom of the Lord Jesus Christ, the house and family of God, out of which there is no ordinary possibility of salvation. Unto this catholic visible church Christ hath given the ministry, oracles, and ordinances of God for the gathering and perfecting of the saints in this life to the end of the world; and doth by His own presence and Spirit, according to His promise, make them effectual thereunto. This catholic church hath been sometimes more, sometimes less, visible ; and particular churches which are members thereof are more or less pure, according as the doctrine of the Gospel is taught and embraced, ordinances administered, and public worship performed more or less purely in them. . . . All saints that are united to Jesus Christ their head, by His Spirit and by faith, have fellowship with Him in His graces, sufferings, death, resurrection, and glory. And, being united to one another in love, they have communion in each other's gifts and graces, and are obliged to the performance of such duties, public and private, as do conduce to their mutual good." In other words, every true member of the church, be he hearer or office-bearer, holds his place in the body for the good of all, and is bound to use his gifts and opportunities to promote, as far as he can, the spiritual and temporal good of all. A single sentence from the Westminster Directory for Church Government is all I need to give, in supplement of this statement of the Confession, to put you in full possession of their authors' views and aspirations. " When their number [*i.e.*, the membership of a congregation] is so great that they cannot conveniently meet in one place, it is expedient that they be divided according to the respective bounds of their dwellings into distinct and fixed congregations for the better administration of such ordinances as belong unto them, and the discharge of mutual duties; wherein all, according to their several places and callings, are to labour to promote whatever appertains to the power of godliness and credit of religion, that the whole

land, in the full extent of it, may become the
kingdom of our Lord and of His Christ."

The sum of all this may be given in the
words of Henderson, in the conclusion of his
treatise on ' The Government and Order of the
Church of Scotland,' the only other treatise
which has any right to be set alongside of
the Books of Discipline. " In the authoritie of
these assemblies, parochial, presbyteriall, pro-
vinciall, and nationall, and in the subordination
of the lesser unto the greater, or of more particular elderships to the larger and generall
eldership, doth consist the externall order,
strength, and steadfastnesse of the Church of
Scotland. . . . Here there is a superiority without tyrannie, for no minister hath a papall or
monarchicall jurisdiction over his own flock, far
lesse over other pastors and over all the congregations of a large dioces. Here there is
paritie without confusion and disorder, for the
pastors are in order before the elders, and the
elders before the deacons; the church [*i.e.*, each
congregation] is subordinate to the presbyterie,
the presbyterie to the synod, and the synod to
the nationall assembly. One pastor also hath
priority [of esteem] before another, for age, for
zeale, for gifts, for his good deservings of the
church, each one honouring him whom God
hath honoured, and as he beareth the image of

God which was to bee seen among the apostles
themselves.   But none hath power or jurisdiction above others : even as in nature one eye
hath not power over another, only the head
hath power over all, even as Christ over His
church. . . . And lastly, here there is a
subjection without slaverie, for the people are
subject to the pastors and assemblies, yet there
is no assemblie wherein everie particular church
hath not interest and power ; nor is there anything done but they are, if not actually, yet
virtually called to consent unto it."[1]   This is
presbytery in theory, and there is no reason
why we should not approximate to the ideal in
practice more closely than some recent repre-
sentations imply, save that we come short of
what we ought to be as men and as Christians,
and that would suffice to mar any form of
government that could be devised by the wit
of men.

[1] The Government and Order of the Church of Scotland, 1641,
pp. 60, 64, 65.

CHAPTER XI.

ALESIUS.

WE owe it to the Rev. Christopher Anderson, the author of the 'Annals of the English Bible,' that attention has been once more turned to the deeply interesting story of Alexander Alane, or Alesius. Principal Lorimer, in his 'Scottish Reformation,' has thrown further light on him. And Dr Merle D'Aubigné, who appears to have minutely examined most of his tracts and commentaries, has wrought into his graphic but imaginative narrative much of the information which they have been the chief means of handing down to us. It was after his expatriation that he received from Melanchthon the name of Alesius, or the wanderer.

This highly distinguished but long forgotten *alumnus* of St Andrews University was born in Edinburgh on the 23rd of April 1500, of honest parents, and received the first rudiments of his

education in his native city. It was probably
while he was still there that he had vouchsafed
on his behalf those wonderful interpositions of
Providence, which remained through life engraven
on his heart, and which he thus relates in his
preface to his Commentary on the Second Epistle
of Paul to Timothy, published at Leipzig in 1551.
" Certe ab infantia [Diabolus] me saepe incautum
opprimere voluit, et perdere non tam insidiis et
crudelitate hostium, quam praecipitio in ignem
et aquam. Verum ille, qui servavit me inter
omnia pericula et infantem de gradibus patris
mei cadentem in acervum lapidum advectorum
ad extruendum supremum tabulatum in oedibus,
et reptantem manibus in cacumine altissimi
montis, ex cujus declivi vel praerupto, divinitus
in alterum latus in quo facilis erat descensus,
subito perveni." [1] With even more than his usual
licence, Dr D'Aubigné thus recounts this adventure : He " was fond of going with other boys of
his own age to the heights which environ Edinburgh. The great rock on the summit of which
the castle stands, the beautiful Calton Hill, and
the picturesque hill called Arthur's Seat, in turn

---

[1] [Alesius thus proceeds : " Et in mari inter tempestates et 18
diebus subtus terram in teterrimo specu inter bufones et serpentes
custodivit (oportet enim me haec alicubi commemorare pro gratitudine erga Deum). Hic igitur Salvator omnium, maxime fidelium,
perficiet id quod per me facere instituit " (In Alteram ad Timotheum
expositio. Autore Alexandro Alesio. D. Lipsiae, 1551, sign. A 2).]

attracted them. One day, it was in 1512, Alexander and his friends, having betaken themselves to the last - named hill, amused themselves by rolling over and over down a slope which terminated in a precipice. Suddenly the lad found himself on the brink; terror deprived him of his senses; some hand grasped him and placed him in safety, but he never knew by whom or by what means he had been rescued. The priests gave the credit of this escape to the paper with which they had provided him, but Alexander himself attributed it to God and his father's prayers." [1]

[1] D'Aubigné's Reformation in the Time of Calvin, vi. 13, 14. [D'Aubigné is here following, or rather embellishing, the account which Alesius thus gives in another of his works: " Pueri, me adhuc puero, quasdam sententias excerptas ex Joanne, scriptas in membrana, ut illam, in principio erat verbum, Ecce agnus Dei, &c., Sic Deus dilexit mundum, Ego sum resurrectio et vita, &c., ac similes, vel auro et argento inclusas circa collum gestabant, non tam ornamenti causa, quàm quod magnam vim et virtutem in his collo-carent contra incantationes et pericula, in quae diabolus saepe pueros incautos solet conjicere. Memini frequenter, et quoties reminiscor, toto corpore cohorresco, me in praerupto altissimi montis manibus et pedibus reptantem, ac proximum praecipitio, subito translatum nescio à quo aut quomodo, in alium locum : et alia vice ex eminentiori deambulacro aedium patris cadentem inter acervum lapidum poliendorum ad aedificium, servatum esse divinitus.

"Non tribuo hanc salutem sententiis ex Joanne, quas forsan aliorum puerorum more circumferebam : sed fidei parentum, qui harum sententiam mente circumferebant, et pro me orabant. Sed tamen, ut mihi videtur, magis deceret nobilitatem Christianam, has et similes sententias in auro et lapidibus preciosis insculptas à collo dependentes circumferre, quàm ethnicorum Regum ac Caesarum imagines" (Commentarius in Evangelium Joannis. Basileae, 1553. Epistola Dedicatoria, pp. 14-16).]

Alesius, or Alane as he was still called, being
of good abilities, was early sent to the university,
and seems to have been one of the first set of
students who entered St Leonard's College (the
college founded by Prior John Hepburn, with the
consent of Archbishop Alexander Stuart) after its
opening in 1512. His studies appear to have
been prosecuted there in the usual way, and in
1515 he became a determinant, or took the degree of B.A.;[1] and, probably after acting for a
few years as a regent in the college, he was
drafted as a novice into the priory, and ultimately
became one of its canons. When John Major
came to St Andrews in 1523 as principal of the
Pædagogium, he, like Hamilton and some others
who ultimately shared the same opinions, studied
theology under him, and made great progress,
especially in the study of the schoolmen and the
fathers of the Christian church. He was, like
most of the young scholastics of his time, fond
of disputation; and if he listened to those lectures
on the gospels which Major gave to the press
some years after, he probably imbibed from his
teacher that combative attitude towards the new

---

[1] [In a list of names without a heading, he appears as "Alexr.
Allane na. Lau.," which shows that of the nations into which the
members of the university were then classified, he belonged to
Lothian. In the list of determinants he appears as "Allexr. Alan."
Opposite his name and the names of his class-fellows is the word
"pauperes," which shows that they paid no fees.]

opinions which at this period of his life he showed. D'Aubigné says : " His keenest desire was to break a lance with Luther. . . . As he could not measure himself personally with the man whom he named *arch-heretic,* Alesius had refuted his doctrine in a public discussion held at the university. The theologians of St Andrews had covered him with applause.[1] . . . Alesius, alive to these praises and a sincere catholic, thought that it would be an easy task for him to convince young Hamilton of his errors. . . . Armed cap - a - pie, crammed with scholastic learning, and with all the formulæ ' quo modo sit, quo modo nonsit,' " he had various discussions with him. " Hamilton had before him nothing but the Gospel, and he replied to all the reasonings of his antagonist with the clear, living, and profound word of the Scriptures. . . . Alesius, struck and embarrassed, was silenced, and felt as if ' the morning star were rising in his heart. It was not merely his understanding that was convinced, the breath of a new life penetrated his soul." [2] He continued from time to time to visit the reformer while he lived, and to cherish

[1] He himself at a later period ingenuously acknowledges that his arguments in great part were borrowed from the treatise of an English bishop, namely Fisher, Bishop of Rochester, who at the request of Henry VIII. had replied to Luther's attack on that monarch.

[2] D'Aubigné's Reformation in the Time of Calvin, vi. 59, 60.

his memory after he had been so cruelly put to death.

When the opinions and martyrdom of Hamilton were the subject of conversation among the canons, several of the younger of whom were attached to him, Alesius refused to condemn him. He was not yet by any means, as Dr Lorimer would have it, a Lutheran; he was not yet prepared to separate himself from the old church; but he saw and mourned over her corruptions, and longed, and in a quiet way laboured, for the removal of them, and also yearned for the revival of a more earnest Christian spirit, and more correct moral conduct among those over whom his influence extended. From that day no one could induce him to express approval of the proceedings which had been taken against Hamilton, or to pronounce an unfavourable judgment on the articles for which he had been condemned to death.

This silence brought him under the suspicion of his more bigoted associates, and gave special offence to his superior, Prior Patrick Hepburn (the nephew of Prior John, who had founded St Leonard's College), a violent, coarse, immoral young noble, emulous of the debaucheries and vices, as well as of the cultured *hauteur*, of the young French ecclesiastics of rank among whom his youth had been passed. Knox has given a graphic if rather coarse account of the revelries of this young man and his gay associates, more in keeping with what we should have expected from the sons of Tarquin in heathen Rome than from the *élite* of the young ecclesiastics of a primatial Christian city, and under the eye of an aged archbishop.[1] The representation of Alesius is only the more credible because it is the more restrained, and the one representation corroborates the other, and proves to what a low ebb morality had sunk among the ministers of the old church in Scotland before it was swept away. Not only did this bold bad man set at nought the laws of God and the canons of his church, and make a boast of doing so among his boon companions, but even when the archbishop sought to separate him from his unlawful connection, the prior collected his armed retainers, and would have fought with him had not the Earl of Rothes and the Abbot of Arbroath, the primate's hopeful nephew, come between the two bands and patched up a sort of truce between their leaders.

The Christian lives and healthful influence of the younger canons could not but be felt to be a standing rebuke by their superior, and doubtless were one main cause why he bore them so deep a grudge and gave way to such savage outbursts

---

[1] Laing's Knox, i. 40, 41.

of temper in his intercourse with them. He is said to have denounced them, and especially Alesius, to the aged primate, and probably with the view of entrapping him into some unguarded expression of approval of the new opinions, he got him appointed to preach the sermon at the opening of a synod of bishops and priests which was held at St Andrews probably in the Lent of the year 1529. Alesius, while carefully avoiding everything which might give needless offence to his hearers, thought, to use his own words, that in such presence, and speaking in the Latin language, he would not discharge his duty unless he earnestly exhorted those set in authority over the churches to the practice of piety, the observance of good morals, the study of Christian doctrine, and the pious teaching and governing of their churches. He confesses that he earnestly inveighed against immoral priests, but he adds that as he had said nothing in a disloyal spirit, or more harshly than the facts warranted, and had attacked no one by name, the sermon gave no offence to good men. But his irate and domineering prior imagined that the sermon was specially aimed at him, and was intended to hold him up to the ridicule of the assembled prelates and clergy. Having already defied the archbishop, Hepburn could not brook such a liberty on the part of one of his own subordinates. An

opportunity soon occurred to him of paying back
with interest the insult which he imagined had
been done to him.

It so happened that the whole college of
canons resolved, for many and grave reasons, to
lodge a complaint with the king respecting the
harshness and cruelty of their superior. When
this came to Hepburn's ears, he rushed with a
band of armed attendants into the sacred chapter-
house where the canons were assembled, and
when admonished by Alesius, who probably presided in the meeting, not in the heat of passion
to be guilty of any foolish prank, he ordered the
speaker to be seized by his armed attendants,
and drawing his sword would have run it through
him had not two of the canons forcibly dragged
him back and turned aside his weapon. The
affrighted and timid canon cast himself at his
superior's feet and entreated him to spare his
life, but in return only received a kick in the
breast which nearly proved fatal to him. When
he had partially recovered from this, and was
being hurried off to prison, another dastardly
attack was made on him, but that was parried
by the prior's own retainers, who saw that he
was beside himself with rage and fury. After
this all the other canons were seized and imprisoned, but on the remonstrance of certain
noble friends they were ordered to be released

by the king, who was then in St Andrews and was informed of what had taken place.

The king's order was speedily carried out in regard to all save Alesius; but he, notwith-standing all remonstrances of friends, was not only detained in custody, but was even thrust into a more filthy dungeon, called by the suf-ferer, in one of his treatises, *teterrimo specu subtus terram inter bufones et serpentes*,[1] and in another a *latrinâ*,[2] or sink, to which I know nothing at all corresponding in St Andrews save the underground chamber near the college hall,[3] and the roughly-hewn cavern still subsisting in the rock to the north of the house at the end of Castle Street, going down by the southern en-trance by thirty or more somewhat irregular steps through the rock, and terminating in a small chamber of rounded or oval form, having an opening in its roof originally little more than a foot in diameter, but now considerably enlarged, and to which on the other side a covered pas-sage from the castle leads down. They might well abandon hope who entered there, and pos-sibly one at least of its uses was for literally immuring those who were never again to have

---

[1] [See it so described in the passage quoted, *supra*, p. 240 n.]

[2] [He calls it a *latrinâ* in his 'Responsio ad Cochlei Calumnias,' sign. A v.

[3] [Now known as Bishop's Hall.]

further intercourse with their fellow-men. In
this or some other equally horrible place the
poor canon was confined for eighteen or twenty
days; and when, after repeated remonstrances
on the part of the king and the magistrates of
the city, the prior was obliged to produce his
victim, he enjoined him strictly on no account
to utter one word about the shameful maltreatment to which he had been subjected. Alesius,
however, had suffered too horribly in this place
to let slip the opportunity so unexpectedly presented to him of telling the worst to the friendly
magistrates, and entreating them to save him
from all further risk of a repetition of this bar-
barous cruelty. But the magistrates, though
friendly, were easily persuaded that all was now
to go right. As soon, however, as they were
got out of the way under this persuasion, the
prior upbraided the poor canon for having
divulged the whole disgusting truth which he
had enjoined him to conceal, and ordered him
to be again placed in confinement, in which he
was left to languish for nearly a year. But
this confinement was in a less objectionable
place, and apparently within the precincts of
the priory; and when the prior was absent the
canons occasionally had the prisoner brought
out from his ward, and even permitted him, as
in former times, to take a leading part in the

services at the altar. On one occasion the
prior, coming back unexpectedly, and seeing
what occurred in his absence, ordered Alesius
at once into confinement, threatening on the
morrow to have him off to the old filthy place
where his life had been so nearly sacrificed
before, and where he was to be entrusted to
the care of a more remorseless jailer.

As soon as their superior left them for the
night the canons, satisfied that all hope of preserving the life of their comrade in St Andrews
was at an end, and that if he did not seek
safety by instant flight horrible torments and
certain death awaited him, gathered round him
and urged him to escape. On his expressing
a wish to consult with other friends before taking
a step so serious, they pressed him only the more
urgently to flee and leave the country at once,
as he would certainly be pursued, and, if over-
taken, brought back for condign punishment.
The sequel I give in his own unvarnished statement, which is to me more touching from its
very simplicity than the highly embellished
rechauffées of D'Aubigné : " Etsi maximo dolore
afficiebar cum cogitarem mihi è patria, qua
nihil dulcius est bene institutis naturis, disce-
dendum esse, tamen, et necessitati, et tot bon-
orum virorum consiliis parendum duxi."[1]   And

[1] Responsio ad Cochlei Calumnias, sign. A vj.

then follows a parting scene only less affecting
than that of St Paul from the disciples on the
seashore at Tyre, and proving that even yet
all good was not extinguished from the hearts
of those under the rule of this vicious prior,
and encouraging the hope, which was afterwards fully realised, that the best of them
would ultimately find a more congenial home
in a new and purified church. Only the
apostle, though in a heathen land, could kneel
down in open day on the seashore to pray with
his friends, and they without challenge could
accompany him to the ship which waited to receive him; while these men, though living in a
professedly Christian land, had secretly to bring
out their friend from the place of confinement
and comfort him, and then send him away alone
into the thick darkness to pursue his weary
journey under cover of night to that broad firth
which bounds Fifeshire on the north, if haply
he might find on its shores some boat to ferry
him across, or on its bosom some friendly craft
to convey him without loss of time beyond
the reach of his implacable persecutor. "Clam
igitur educunt me domo, instruunt et viatico.
Ita cum lachrymantes inter nos vale dixissemus,
et illi suavissima commemoratione illustrium
virorum et sanctorum qui similiter è patria
tyrannidi cesserunt, maesticiam meam non nihil

levassent, media jam nocte in densissimis tene-
bris solus iter ingredior." [1] Sadly he plodded
on his way through the darkness, oppressed
with forebodings, for he knew of no hospitable
retreat in other lands; he had neither friend
nor acquaintance among foreigners; he could
speak no language but his native tongue and
Latin; and he had some reason to fear that he
might be classed with those vagabonds who had
been driven out from various Continental states
because of their fanatical opinions, and were
justly suspected even by Protestants in Germany. But in the multitude of distracting
thoughts within him he encouraged himself in
the Lord his God and in Christ his Saviour.
Ere morning had well dawned his journey was
completed, and he got safely on shipboard,
where, according to his own account, *quidam
homo germanus* [2]—that is, according to some, a
certain man a German; according to others, a
certain man a kinsman—received him very affec-
tionately, and afterwards nursed him with great
kindness during the sea-sickness from which he
suffered throughout the stormy vogage.

On the day following his escape, when the
vessel which sheltered him had already sailed,
there came horsemen to the shore, sent by the
prior from St Andrews, to make search for the

---

[1] Responsio ad Cochlei Calumnias, sign. A vj.   [2] Ibid.

fugitive. When they returned without success to
their master, he is reported to have summoned
before him a certain citizen of Dundee, whom he
suspected to have aided in providing a ship for
the canon. This merchant citizen [1] took with
him another true-hearted favourer of the Reformation, James Scrymgeour, provost of the town ;
and on the former denying that he had given
the assistance which he was accused of doing to
Alesius, and which probably he could deny with
a good conscience, his sons in St Andrews and
Dundee having been too prudent to involve him
in their little plot, the provost spoke out boldly
to the haughty prior, and said : Why make a
work about this ? I, myself, if I had known that
Alexander was preparing to go away, would with
the greatest pleasure have furnished him both
with a ship and with provisions for his voyage,
that he might be put in safety beyond the reach
of your cruelty. Assuredly, had he been my
brother I would long ago have rescued him from

---

[1] No doubt James Wedderburn, merchant at the West Kirk Style
of Dundee, who carried on a large trade with the Continent, and
was known to be friendly to those holding the reformed opinions.
One of his sons was then studying at St Andrews, and probably had
been the means of communication between the canons and Dundee
to secure beforehand a speedy departure for their fugitive friend.
[For many interesting details concerning the sons of this Dundee
merchant, see Dr Mitchell's Wedderburns and their Work, 1867 ;
and also his edition of The Gude and Godlie Ballatis, 1897, pp.
xvii-xxxii, lxxxiii-civ.]

those perils and miseries in which you have involved him.

Thus Alexander Alesius was driven from his much-loved native land, destined never to return to it more, or again to see the friends and relations to whom he was so warmly attached. " Could any one then have whispered in the ear of the disconsolate exile that he was on the road to far more extensive usefulness " and freedom ; that he would gain many friends in foreign lands, and would not only be spared to labour there for more than thirty years, but would also be honoured to be the first to plead by his writings for the free circulation of the Scriptures in his native Scotland, and one of the first to help on Cranmer in England, and Hermann von Wied, the reforming Archbishop of Cologne, in Germany ; that he would be privileged to attend, as one of the Protestant representatives, many of the most important colloquies of the leaders of the old and the new church on the Continent, to be the intimate friend of Luther and Melanchthon, to labour as a professor of theology in two German universities, and to live and die in the greatest honour and respect among those with whom he laboured,—"how incredible would it all have seemed to him ! " Yet it was thus God meant it, and thus He brought it to pass ; and if there was one among the Scottish exiles of those times who was less embittered towards his persecutors than another, or more ready to yield to them in things indifferent or of minor importance, if only he could gain their hearts for Christ and His cause in matters of highest moment, it was he.

The ship in which Alesius sailed was bound for France, probably for Dieppe or Rouen, with which towns the trade of Scotland was carried on, and where many Scottish merchants resided or had factors ; but she had not gone far on her way from port when a violent westerly gale carried her across the German Ocean, drove her into the Sound, and made it necessary to get her into the harbour at Malmö in Scania, in order to refit her. There, as well as at the French ports named, there was a community of Scottish merchants, probably by this time enjoying the ministrations of John Gaw or Gall, another St Andrews *alumnus*, early won over to the cause of the Reformation. The community of Malmö, a year or two before, had given its adhesion to the same cause, and its leading ministers, as well as the Scottish chaplain, were, therefore, prepared to welcome and treat with all kindness their exiled co-religionist, as he himself, twenty - five years after, feelingly narrates.[1]   After being refitted

---

[1] [In his Introduction (pp. xviii-xx) to Gau's 'Richt Vay to the Kingdom of Heuine,' Dr Mitchell says : " The treatise ' De Apostolicis Traditionibus,' in which he [*i.e.*, Alesius] has given an

at Malmö, the vessel proceeded on her voyage to France, where Alesius left, and plodding his way along the northern coast, visited Belgium, where he would meet with friendly Scots at Bruges, and probably also at Antwerp.

He then passed up the Rhine to Cologne, where, as already suggested, he was favourably received by the Archbishop, Hermann von Wied, who afterwards became a friend of the Reformation, though at this time, like Alesius himself, not yet decided altogether to break with the old church. It is no doubt to this visit he refers in the following passage of the treatise from which I have repeatedly quoted: " When lately at Cologne I conversed familiarly with a

account of his visit, and of the manner in which he was received by his countrymen and the reforming preachers of Malmö, is one of the rarest of his minor treatises, and is not to be found in any of our Scottish libraries, nor in the British Museum, nor even in the library of the University of Leipsic, in which he was so long an honoured professor. . . . Neither the name of Gau nor that of any other of his countrymen then in the city is given by Alesius. . . . Principal Lorimer has ingeniously conjectured that Gau may have come out to act as chaplain to his countrymen at Malmö. And I am inclined to accept the conjecture to a modified extent. . . . At any rate, we find that before the close of 1533 he was in Denmark, and had got such an accurate knowledge of the Danish language that he had translated and published a treatise of considerable length from Danish into his native Scotch." In the Appendix to the same Introduction (p. xlv) Dr Mitchell explains that "modern Danish scholars express doubts whether, in the early part of the 16th century, any nation, save the German as represented by the Hanseatic League, was organised as a distinct community at Malmö."]

certain man of the highest learning and authority, and perceived how deeply he was grieved by the disturbed state of the church in Germany. I began to exhort him to interpose his judgment in certain matters of dispute, because I hoped that milder views might gain the ascendancy if princes and people only had such monitors excelling in learning and authority. When I had argued long in support of my opinion, heaving a sigh, but making no formal reply to my arguments, he bade me listen to an apologue : When the lion, worn out with old age, could no longer obtain his prey by hunting, he fell on the device of inviting the beasts to visit him in his den. There came to him a bear, a wolf, and a fox. The bear entered first, and being affably received by the lion, and conducted round the den, he was asked how he was pleased with the amenity of the place. Being no courtier, the bear answered bluntly that he could never stay in such a filthy hole, among heaps of decaying carcasses. The lion, enraged, chid the bear for finding fault with the amenity of the royal den, and tearing him up, cast away his carcass among the others. The wolf, who had been standing by, seeing in what danger he was, thought by artifice to soothe the haughty mind of the lion. He accordingly approached, was led round the den, and was asked whether the smell of the heap of carcasses was unpleasant to him.

R

The wolf replied, in a carefully considered speech, that he had never seen anything more pleasant. This artifice, however, was of no avail to the wolf. The lion meted out the same treatment to him as to the bear, tearing him up for his impudent flattery. The fox, who had witnessed all this, and how both the simplicity of the bear and the flattery of the wolf had given equal offence to the lion, was in great perplexity what to answer when it came to his turn. He went forward, however, and being interrogated as the others had been whether the smell of the den was disagreeable, he replied modestly that he could not express any opinion on the point, as he was labouring under a cold in the head." Alesius waited to hear from his host the moral or application of the apologue, but this was not given by him. He preferred to leave it to his own good sense, merely counselling him to be cautious of engaging in such discussions for the present. Ultimately, however, both came to see that there is a time to speak as well as a time to keep silence; and it is interesting to note that to the last both observed similar moderation in their statements of doctrine, both evinced the same desire, by conciliation to gain opponents, rather than to provoke them, notwithstanding all the hard usage they both met with from their secular and ecclesiastical superiors.

Soon after this Alesius appears to have passed

on from Cologne to Wittenberg, and there for a time to have resumed the study of theology, as well as of Greek and Hebrew, under Melanchthon and the other gifted teachers in that university. Luther he does not seem to have met for a time, or to have been acquainted with his writings when he published his *first*[1] treatises. Melanchthon cherished a special affection for Alesius and the Scottish exiles who soon after followed him to Wittenberg, believing that they were the descendants of those Scoti who had sent the early Christian missionaries to Germany, and that it became him to repay to them the great kindness the heathen Germans had received from their forefathers in the distant past.[2]

It was while he was thus occupied that Alesius heard of the cruel edict of the Scottish bishops, and it hardly admits of doubt that he submitted to Melanchthon, and got corrected by him, his little treatise against their decree, forbidding the New Testament Scriptures to be used by the laity

---

[1] [This sentence is interlined, and the word which seems to be *first* is rather indistinct.]

[2] In the preceding narrative I have availed myself of the details which Alesius has given us of his labours and sufferings in his commentaries and lesser treatises, and especially in two of the smallest of them, both published in 1533, the one bearing the title—"Alexandri Alesii Epistola contra decretum quoddam Episcoporū in Scotia, quod prohibet legere Noui Testamenti libros lingua vernacula"; the other "Alexandri Alesii Scotti Responsio ad Cochlei Calvmnias."

in the vernacular. It is a very pithy and forcible
bit of pleading for the right of the Christian laity
to possess and study the Scriptures in their own
tongue. This remarkable treatise struck the true
key-note in the contest it ushered in, and helped
it on to victory—a victory which was substantially
to be gained ere Knox had taken his place among
the combatants on the side of the Reformation
at all.[1]

To this epistle Cochlaeus replied without loss
of time,[2] and ere the year was out Alesius rejoined in that Responsio ad Cochlei calumnias,[3]
in which he has given so touching an account of
his own maltreatment, so interesting a statement
of his own opinions in matters of faith and church
polity, and so trenchant a reply to the sophistries
and slanders of his opponent.[4]

---

[1] [The nature of the arguments used by Alesius in this epistle may
be learned from the lengthy extracts quoted in Christopher Anderson's Annals of the English Bible, 1845, ii. 430-437.]

[2] [This reply by Cochlaeus, which is dated 6th June 1533, is
entitled: "An Expediat Laicis, legere Noui Testamenti libros
lingua Vernacula? Ad Serenissimvm Scotiæ Regem Iacobum V.
Disputatio inter Alexandrum Alesium Scotum, & Iohannem Coch-
læum Germanum. Anno dñi M.D. XXXIII." A beautiful copy of
this very rare work was secured at the Laing sale for the library
of the Church of Scotland. There is also a copy in the Signet
Library. A few extracts may be found in Anderson's Annals, ii.
439-441.]

[3] [A beautiful copy of this excessively rare tract was also secured
for the Church library at the Laing sale.]

[4] [For a translation by Dr Mitchell of that part of the Responsio
which relates to the opinions of Alesius, see Appendix E.]

This able and, for the age, singularly temperate reply made a deep impression in England as well as in Scotland, and doubtless prepared the way for that offer of employment there which two years subsequently was made him by Cranmer, whom, in his moderation and earnest desire to avoid a total rupture between the old church and the new life, he then so much resembled. But whatever its merits, the disputatious Cochlaeus —" der gewaffnete mann," as Luther sneeringly terms him—was determined that his opponent should not have the last word in the dispute, and accordingly in August 1534 he published at Leipsic his Apologia pro Scotiae Regno adversus personatum Alexandrum Alesium Scotum.[1] In this treatise he repeats the assertion in his previous one that Melanchthon, not Alesius, was the author of these epistles. He charges Alesius with putting lies into the mouth of a foreigner to the discredit of his native country, and tells him that if he had the power he would gladly send him away to Scotland with his hands tied behind his back to be ignominiously punished as a traitor and a public slanderer. His opponent's minute and temperate narrative of facts appears to have

[1] [Dr Mitchell possessed copies of several of the other tracts of Cochlaeus, as well as of this : " Pro Scotiae Regno Apologia Iohannis Cochlei, adversvs personatum Alexandrum Alesium Scotum. Ad Sereniss. Scotorū regē. M.D.XXXIIII." It ends : " Excusum Lipsiae apud Michaelem Blum."]

made no impression on him. He is content magisterially to pronounce it absurd and incredible, and inconsistent with itself as well as with probability. He appears in his ire to forget that the king of Scots and his subjects were better able to judge of its truthfulness than he, a foreigner, could be ; and that after saying all he could for the bishops and superior clergy in his former reply, he had been obliged to conclude with the damaging admission that possibly there were " bishops and prelates who, neither in sanctity of life nor in acquaintance with sacred learning, responded to or satisfied their dignity and office."

The epistles of Cochlaeus, if abusive and less cogent in reasoning, as well as less relieved by any sparkle of wit or racy anecdote than those of Alesius, are certainly written in a more easy and flowing Latin style, and, in that respect at least, the Scottish prelates had no reason to be ashamed of the champion who had volunteered his services in their cause. Nor were they wanting in those more substantial expressions of their satisfaction which Cochlaeus, like most of the controversialists of his time, evidently coveted. The Archbishops of St Andrews and Glasgow testified their gratitude for his services by sending him liberal presents. The king wrote him a letter, a contemporary transcript of which is still extant, and also, as is stated by Cochlaeus

himself in a letter to a Polish archbishop, sent
him some more material tokens of his regard.[1]
And even the messenger who had brought over
the copies of his first epistle received, as it now
appears, a present of fifty pounds Scots.[2]   Alesius,
though in quite another way, did not lack his
reward, and it came in the way which he valued
most—the treatises he had written, to a certain
extent at least, got into circulation both in Scotland and in England.   They cheered the hearts
of the faithful under all the terrible trials to
which they were subjected in the later years of
James's reign, when he seems to have abandoned
his former kindliness, and surrendered himself in
a great measure to the priests and to vicious
indulgences.   They carried conviction to the
minds of many, and gradually ripened opinion

[1] [Alesius says : " I was at Antwerp whan a contryman of myne,
whose name was John Foster, did send a somme of mony unto
Cochleus by a marchant from the Bisshop of S. Andrews, which
geveth him yerely so long as he liveth a certen stipend.   And it
chanced by the goodnes of God, wherby He discloseth the
wickednes of these hipocytes (*sic*), that a pistle of Cochleus which
he sent unto a certen bisshop of Pole came unto my handes, wherin
he complayneth that he hath gret losse and evel fortune in setting
forth of bokes, for as moch as no man wil wetesaue to rede his
bokes.   And he beggeth a yerely stipend of the bisshops of Pole,
saing that he hath bene nobly rewarded of the King of Scottys and
of the Archbisshop of S. Andrews and of the Bisshop of Glasguo "
(' Of the Auctorite of the Word of God ').]

[2] [From the Treasurer's Accounts, as quoted by M'Crie, it appears that the servant who brought over his book received £10
(M'Crie's Knox, 1855, p. 321 n.).]

to demand the right to do publicly what many had learned to do secretly — to study the Word of God, and especially the New Testament, in their native tongue. This right was authorised by an Act of the Scottish Parliament passed in 1543,[1] when Cardinal Betoun was in disgrace, and the Archbishop of Glasgow was left alone to protest against it. This Act was the first real victory of the reformed party in Scotland, and it was mainly due to the able and temperate pleading of Alesius that this great boon, or indeed I may say this indefeasible right of Christian laymen, was granted. The same subject had been reverted to by him in his more elaborate treatise, De authoritate Verbi Dei, which was published in 1542 in Latin, and some time after was translated into English.[2]

One other episode in this controversy remains still to be adverted to. This is the intervention of the great humanist, Erasmus, — an incident in his history on which his biographers with one consent have observed a judicious silence. Nevertheless, the fact is as undoubted as melan-

[1] [15th March 1542-43 (Acts of Parliament, ii. 415).]

[2] [The title is: "De Avthoritate Verbi Dei Liber Alexandri Alesij, contra Episcopum Lundensem. An. M.D.XLII." The preface is dated: "Francfordiae ad Oderam. Calend. Maijs. an. Domini M.D.XL." The colophon is: "Argentorati apvd Cratonem Mylivm an. M.D.XLII. mense Septembri." The translation, which is in black-letter, bears no date, place, or printer's name. For a copy of its title, see *infra*, p. 268 n.]

choly that he—who had done so much to promote
the freer circulation and profounder study of the
Greek original of the New Testament, and had
even ventured, under the patronage of Pope
Leo X., to bring out a Latin version of the
New Testament more true to the original than
the Vulgate version, that those who knew only
Latin might understand more fully the meaning
of the original—in his old age, when irritated by
the course of events, and by his controversies
with Luther, consented to recommend this scurrilous pamphleteer to his friends in Scotland.
His own letter is not now extant, or, if extant,
is not at present accessible; but the answer sent
to him by the Scottish king has been preserved,
like his letter to Cochlaeus, among the MSS. in
the British Museum.   It is sufficient to prove
the fact that Erasmus did intervene, and commend to his Scottish friends a writer who repre-
sents Luther's translation of the New Testament,
which more than any other book has made Germany what it is, as the "pabulum mortis, fomes
peccati, velamen malitiae, praetextus falsae liber-
tatis, inobedientiae praesidium, disciplinae cor-
ruptio, morum depravatio, concordiae dissipatio
. . . vitiorum scaturigo . . . rebellionis in-
cendium . . . charitatis peremptio . . . veri-
tatis perduellio."

In 1535 Alesius, having received encourage-

ment from the agents of the English king then
negotiating an alliance with the Protestant
princes of Germany, came over to England with
a letter of recommendation from Melanchthon.[1]
He was favourably received by Archbishop
Cranmer, by Crumwell the Vicar-General, and
by the king himself, who appointed him king's
scholar, and instructed Crumwell, as Chancellor
of the University of Cambridge, to give him a
place as a reader in divinity there. He accordingly went into residence in Queen's College,
the same college which shortly before had been
the home of Erasmus while lecturing in the
university on Greek, and towards the end of
the year he began a course of lectures on the
Hebrew Psalter. He is supposed to have been
the first who delivered lectures in Cambridge on
the Hebrew Scriptures, but he was not suffered
to do it long in peace. It could not be concealed
that he was a favourer of the new opinions and a
friend of Melanchthon, and that he had, in fact,
been recommended by him to the king and the
chancellor of the university. By the time he had
entered on the exposition of Psalm viii. he was
challenged by one of the champions of the old
learning to a public disputation, and courage-

[1] [Alesius says that he was the bearer of the Loci Theologici,
which he had persuaded Melanchthon to dedicate to Henry VIII.
(Foreign Calendar, Elizabeth, i. 525).]

ously accepted the challenge; but when the day appointed for the discussion arrived, his opponent did not venture to meet him in open fight. He preferred to plot against him in secret, and to foment tumult among the scholars, till Alesius, finding that his life was in danger, and that he could not count on the protection of the university authorities, deemed it his duty to leave Cambridge and return to London.[1]

For the next three years he remained there, supporting himself chiefly by the practice of medicine, which he studied under a London physician of note. He occasionally, however, gave assistance to his reforming friends in the varying fortunes of these unquiet times. He did so notably in a convocation or a meeting of the superior clergy in 1536 or 1537,[2] being put

---

[1] [He was in London during the time of the trial and execution of Anne Boleyn. He sent Elizabeth an account of a dream or vision which he then had. See Appendix F.]

[2] [There is "great uncertainty" as to whether this meeting took place in 1536 or 1537 (Hardwick's Reformation, 1883, p. 182 n.). The year 1537 is given by Alesius in his ' De Avthoritate Verbi Dei' (p. 18), and is repeated in the translation. In the latter it is said : "Contrary to all my expectacion I chanced to fall agayn into such a disputacyon as I was in before, and in maner with like adversarys. . . . Unto this disputacion I came sodenly unprepared, for as I did mete bi chance in the streate the right excellent Lord Crumwel going unto the Parlament Howse in the yeare 1537, he whan he sawe me called me unto him, and toke me with him to the Parlament House to Westmyster (*sic*), where we fownd all the bisshops gathered together."]

forward by Cranmer and Crumwell as the chief spokesman on the reforming side, the opinions of which he defended with considerable force and ability, so far as the notes of the debates preserved by Foxe in his 'Acts and Monuments' enable us to judge.[1] His appearance on this occasion brought him into sharp collision with Stokesley, Bishop of London. On the other hand, it secured for him the warm friendship of Cranmer and Latimer, towards both of whom he continued to the last to cherish a deep affection, and of whose martyrdom he spoke with so much grief when he published his Commentary on the First Book of Psalms. While in England, as Thomasius tells us, he married an English lady, by name Catherine de Mayn; and when Henry VIII. once more veered round to his

[1] Cattley's Foxe, v. 381-384. [The whole of this account, as Cattley points out, is taken by Foxe almost *verbatim* from a statement made by Alesius himself in his rare tract entitled, *Of the Auctorite of the Word of God agaynst the Bisshop of London, wherein are conteyned certen disputacyons had in the Parlament Howse betwene the Bisshops, abowt the nomber of the Sacraments, and other things very necessary to be known: made by Alexander Alane Scot and sent to the Duke of Saxon.* Christopher Anderson says that this translation of the tract De Authoritate Verbi Dei Liber was made by Edmund *Allen*. So completely had the original name of Alesius dropped out of knowledge that Anderson actually charges the printer with committing "a strange blunder in the title." Believing that *Ales* was the real name of Alesius, he thought that the printer had divided the name of the author between the author and the translator ('Annals of the English Bible,' ii. 479 n.).]

former moorings, and passed the bloody statute of the six articles, insisting *inter alia* on the doctrine of Transubstantiation and the celibacy of the clergy, Alesius, like several other married priests, had to consult his safety and that of his family by a hurried retreat to the Continent.[1]

Among those who had to leave England about the same time were John M'Alpine[2] and John Fyffe —or, as they were henceforth to be surnamed by Melanchthon, Joannes Macchabaeus and Joannes Fidelis—both, like Alesius himself, Scotsmen, the former having been prior of the Dominican monastery at Perth, and the latter an *alumnus* and teacher in St Leonard's College. They had, along with several other known favourers of the Reformation, been obliged to leave Scotland at an earlier period, and after finding a temporary shelter in England, apparently at Salisbury, under the protection of Bishop Shaxton, who was then a favourer of the reformed opinions, were, like Alesius himself, to find their ultimate home and special work on the Continent—the one in the University of Copenhagen, the other in the University of Frankfort on the Oder. They seem to have gone first to Wittenberg, and while the others for a time resumed their studies there, Alesius almost immediately on his return was

[1] [For the circumstances of his departure, see Appendix G.]
[2] [For M'Alpine, see Gau's Richt Vay, Introd., p. xii.]

selected by Melanchthon to accompany him to
the colloquy at Worms, and then to that at
Regensburg, which were attended not only by
the Lutheran and the Catholic theologians, but
also by Bucer, Calvin, and other reforming divines
of Strassburg. So it came about that Alesius,
who had suffered exile in the cause of the Reformation in Scotland, and still had striven to promote it, was probably the first of our countrymen
to be brought into contact with Calvin, who was
ultimately to exercise so marked an influence on
the form and mode of that Reformation, and who
too was then an exile both from his native land
and from the scene of his earlier labours. To
the last Alesius seems to have been the one of
his pupils to whom the gentle and timid Melanchthon most closely clung, and it was by his recommendation that in the very year of his return to
the Continent he was promoted to be Professor
of Divinity in the University of Frankfort on the
Oder. And it is something of which a Scotchman
and a St Andrean may be proud, that the university of that little principality of Brandenburg,
which has since expanded into the great kingdom
of Prussia, was indebted for two of its first Protestant professors of divinity to Scotland and to
St Andrews.

His stay at Frankfort, however, was but short,
a controversy having arisen between him and one

of his colleagues about the propriety of attaching civil punishments to adultery and other offences against the seventh commandment. In 1542, or early in 1543, he resigned his professorship, and transferred his family to Leipsic. Melanchthon, who, though concurring in his opinions, blamed his hasty resignation, yet exerted himself to procure an appointment for him in the great Saxon university; so also did Ludovicus Fachsius, at once the Burgomaster and the head of the Faculty of Law, of whose kindness he makes special mention in the dedication to his sons of his edition of Melanchthon's Catechism, which he had used when superintending their religious instruction.[1]

The remaining twenty-one years of his life were spent busily and usefully in this famous university,

[1] "I owe much," he says, "to your father, who received me most hospitably at my first coming hither, and, in name of Duke Maurice (now Elector of Saxony), invited me to give my services to this famous university, and retained me here some years after, when I was called elsewhere" (*i.e.*, probably Königsberg), "promising me the favour and grace of the most illustrious prince elector. Finally, after the war, he encouraged me, then hesitating, to write to the elector to beg the restitution of my books and other effects, which I had lost at the time of the siege of this city, kindly offering his best services in rendering my supplicatory letter to the prince, by which, however, he only succeeded in securing that the elector, when departing from his own dominions to attend the imperial diet, should give instructions on the matter to his counsellors whom he had left at home, and should deliver to be sent on to me a letter full of kindness through Damianus Sybothendorff, secretary to his highness."

though he suffered somewhat severely during the
Schmalkaldic war and the seige of Leipsic. It
was there that most of his theological treatises
were elaborated and published. He was twice
at least chosen Rector of the university—viz., in
1555 and in 1561.[1] In 1542, as already stated,
he published in Latin the arguments he had
used in his disputation with Stokesley, Bishop
of London, on the authority of the Word of God,
and against the doctrine of the seven sacraments,
both confirming his former arguments as to the
rights of the Christian laity, and maintaining the
supremacy of Scripture over tradition. He had
previously published his inaugural dissertation in
the University of Frankfort, ' De restituendis
scholis,' in which he advocated at length the
great need for university training for the ministers
of the protestant churches, and gave a detailed
account of his own opinions, which he affirmed
were then in full accord with those of the
Lutheran churches. In 1543, probably before he
was fully settled at Leipsic, it is said that on

---

[1] On the former of which occasions he inscribed the following
paragraph in the matriculation book of the university : " Anno
MDLV, die 23 Aprilis, qui Divo Georgio sacer est, et quo existimo
me natum esse, supputatis retro LV annis, ego Alexander Alcsius,
gente Scotus, Patriâ Edinburgensis, atavis consulibus, qui duobus
regibus, Jacobo Quinto, et Henrico Octavo, et quatuor electoribus,
Johanni Friderico, Mauricio et Augusto, Ducibus Saxoniae, et
Joachimo Electori Brandeburgensi inservivi, invitus suscepi officium rectoris universitatis scholae in inclytâ urbe Lipsiâ."

hearing the news of the favourable change which had taken place in Scotland on the death of James V. and the accession of Arran to the regency, he, like many other Scottish exiles, had serious thoughts of returning home, and availing himself to the uttermost of this unexpected opportunity which seemed to be opening for carrying forward the work of the Reformation in the land which was still dear to him. But before he had fully made up his mind to follow this course, he fortunately heard that the fickle regent had already begun to change his policy, and that though the privilege of freely reading the Scriptures in the vernacular, for which he had so earnestly contended, was legally secured, the triumph of the Reformation was by no means so near at hand as at first he had been led to suppose. Shortly after this, roused by the tidings of fresh persecutions which had reached him from Scotland, and especially by the account of the cruel executions of the humble martyrs of Perth by the cardinal and his party on St Paul's day, 1543-44, Alesius on 23rd April wrote to Melanchthon in the following terms :—

"Three days ago there were here several countrymen of mine, who declare that the cardinal rules all things at his pleasure in Scotland, and governs the governor himself. In the town of St Johnston he hung up four respectable citizens, for no other cause than because they had requested a monk, in the middle of his sermon, not to depart in his doctrine from the sacred text, and not to mix up notions of his own with the words of Christ. Along with these a most respectable matron, carrying a sucking child in her arms, was haled before the tribunal and condemned to death by drowning. They report that the constancy of the woman was such that, when her husband was led to the scaffold and mounted the ladder, she followed and mounted along with him, and entreated to be allowed to hang from the same beam. She encouraged him to be of good cheer, for in a few hours, said she, I shall be with Christ along with you. They declare also that the governor was inclined to liberate them, but that the cardinal suborned the nobles to threaten that they would leave him if the condemned were not put to death. When the cardinal arrived with his army at Dundee, from which the monks had been expelled, all the citizens took to flight; and when he saw the town quite deserted he laughed, and re-marked that he had expected to find it full of Lutherans." [1]

---

[1] Lorimer's Scottish Reformation, 1860, pp. 112, 113. [The Perth martyrs are noticed above, pp. 53, 54. See also Laing's Knox, i. 117, 118, 523-526.]

Before the expiry of that year Alesius addressed to the chief nobles, prelates, barons, and to the whole people of Scotland, his Cohortatio ad concordiam pietatis ac doctrinæ Christianæ defensionem. This piece, Dr Lorimer tells us, "is instinct throughout with the spirit of true Christian patriotism, as well as with genuine evangelical earnestness and fervour. Lamenting the distractions of the kingdom by opposing political factions — the French faction and the English — he [like the author of the Complaynt of Scotland a few years later] implores his countrymen to lay aside these divisions, and demonstrates by many examples from classical history the dangers of national disunion, and the duty of patriotic concord in defence of the safety and honour of their common country. His expostulations against the oppression and cruelty of the bishops, and his allusions to the martyrs who had suffered in the cause of truth, are full of interest; and his digression, in particular, upon the character and martyrdom of Patrick Hamilton, is a noble burst of eloquence and pathos. When he exhorts to national union he means union in the truth — union in the one great work of purifying religion and reforming the corruptions of the church of God. What urgent need there was of such a work he demonstrates at much length, and with great freedom and faithfulness. Unless the church of Christ be reformed it must perish from the earth, and those are its worst enemies, not its real friends, who oppose such indispensable reform."[1] "Everywhere," he says, "we see the church driven forward to such reform. Ask even those who are most solicitous for its welfare, and they will tell you that the church can no longer be safe or free from troubles unless it be strengthened by the removal of abuses. If this, then, is a measure of absolute necessity unless we would see the whole church go to ruin; if all men confess that this should be done, if facts themselves call with a loud voice that some care should be taken to relieve the labouring [bark of the] church, to purify her depraved doctrine, and to reform her whole administration, — why, I demand, are those maligned and vilified who discover and point out the church's faults and failings? The proper remedies could not possibly have been applied till the disease was known; and yet the men who point it out, warn of its virulence and danger, and wish to alleviate or entirely remove it, are hated and

[1] Lorimer's Scottish Reformation, 1860, pp. 115, 116. [The quotations from the Cohortatio which follow agree substantially with those given by Dr Lorimer, but many of the variations in the phraseology show that Dr Mitchell had the original as well as Lorimer's translation before him when he wrote.]

persecuted as much as if they had been themselves the cause of all." With equal vigour he repels the cry of innovation raised against the reformers and their teaching. Their work was rather an honest attempt at restoration. What they sought, he said, "was just such a change as would take place in the manners of an age if the gravity, modesty, and frugality of ancient times were to take the place of levity, lewdness, luxury, and other vices. Such a change might be termed the introduction of what was novel, but in fact it was only the reintroduction of what was old and primitive. Let us," he exclaims, "have innovation everywhere if only we can get the true for the false, seriousness for levity, and solid realities for empty dreams." " It is no new doctrine we bring, but the most ancient, nay rather the eternal truth, for it proclaims that Jesus Christ, the Son of God, came into the world to save sinners, and that we are saved by faith in Him. Of Him even Moses wrote, and to Him give all the prophets witness, that whosoever believeth in Him shall receive remission of sins. This is the old doctrine which runs through all the ages. Those which are really new are the doctrines which have obscured or contaminated it, brought in by those entrusted with the care of the vineyard of the Lord, and who, like the keepers of the vineyard in the Gospel parable, have maltreated and slain many of the Lord's messengers."

This was the last service, so far as we know, which Alesius was able to render to the cause of the Reformation in his native land, and it did not fail in due time to produce abundant and lasting fruit. As Major before him, so Knox after him, strenuously contended for union of Scotsmen among themselves; and after that, but only after that, for a league with England rather than with France. They laboured, and others entered into their labours, and, proceeding on the same lines on which they had worked, at last brought the conflict to a triumphant issue. Tidings of their success filled Alesius with joy in the land of his exile. Even these, however, failed in his old age to tempt him back to the home of his youth, or the scene of those early struggles which were so deeply engraven on his memory and heart. And, so far as we know, he received no call to return from those who were then at the head of affairs in Scotland, though unquestionably he was more deeply read in theology than any one of them, and though, as unquestionably, the faculty of divinity was for several years but poorly supplied in the universities of Scotland, and preachers of ability, culture, and learning were very rare in the land.

His life, especially after the close of the Schmalkaldic war, seems to have passed tranquilly and
happily at the great Lutheran University of Leipsic. He was loved and honoured by his colleagues and by his prince, and, as I have already
hinted, he was the bosom friend and unremitting
correspondent of Melanchthon. As his services
had been called into requisition by the Preceptor
Germaniæ at the colloquies of Worms and Regensburg, so were they sought and got at the
colloquy of Saxon theologians for the preparation
of the Leipsic Interim in 1548, at that of Naumburg in 1554, at that of Nuremberg in 1555, and
that of Dresden in 1561. "In all these"—the
Leipsic professor, who on the occasion of the first
centenary of his second rectorship pronounced
an oration on him, affirms that—"he so conducted
himself that no one could charge him with want
of perseverance in building up the truth, or of
judiciousness in examining the errors of others,
or of faithfulness and dexterity in the counsels he
gave." M'Kenzie, who has inserted a sketch of
his career in his 'Lives of Eminent Scotsmen,'
assures us that in the conference of Naumburg
he acquitted himself to the admiration of the
whole assembly, for which he is highly commended by Camerarius in his 'Life of Melanchthon'; and further, that in the year 1555 the
disciples of Andrew Osiander having raised great

dissensions in the city of Nuremberg respecting the doctrine of justification, Melanchthon made choice of Alesius as the fittest person to appease them by his wisdom and learning, and that his management answered Melanchthon's expectations, though Alesius himself had previously taken a side in the controversy. In the Majoristic controversy, Alesius, like Melanchthon, so far sided with Major as to maintain against the extreme Lutherans the necessity of good works, not to justification, but to final salvation; and in 1560 he seems to have discussed this question in one of his so-called *disputationes*.

With respect to his private life, we are told by Thomasius that he had by his English wife one son, whose name was Caspar, and who died while still a youth, and had a monument erected by his father to his memory, bearing the simple inscription, "Caspari. Filiolo. Alexander. Alesius. Doctor. Lugens. Posuit." He had at least two daughters. One named Christina, Thomasius tells us, was married to a German bearing the classical name Marcus Scipio: she outlived her husband, and died in 1604, in the fifty-ninth year of her age. The name of the other daughter does not seem to have been known to Thomasius, but as he states that she was given in marriage in 1557, we can have no doubt that she is the same Anna whose wedding is referred to in a

letter of Alesius to Melanchthon, recently unearthed, and inviting him and other friends in
Wittenberg to the wedding.[1]

Alesius himself died on the 17th March 1565,
and was buried at Leipsic; but no stone was
raised, or, if raised, now remains, to tell where
his ashes repose. In all probability it was in
his son's grave, in the church of St Paul,
in the city of Leipsic, that his ashes were laid
to rest. The only monuments to his memory
reared at the time and still existing are those
furnished by our own John Johnston — second
master of St Mary's College, and colleague of
Andrew Melville — in his Latin poems on the
Scottish martyrs and confessors, and entitled
Περι Στεφανων, and by Beza in his 'Icones.'
Johnston, joining together Macchabaeus and Alesius, says:—

> " Sors eadem exilii nobis, vitaeque laborumque,
>   Ex quo nos Christi conciliavit amor.
> Una salus amborum, unum et commune periclum ;
>   Pertulimus pariter praestite cuncta Deo.
> Dania te coluit   Me Lipsia culta docentem.
>   Audiit, et sacros hausit ab ore sonus." [2]

Beza says, " He was a man dear to all the learned,
who would have been a distinguished ornament
of Scotland if that country had recovered the
light of the Gospel at an earlier period ; and who,

---

[1] See Appendix H.
[2] M'Crie's Knox, 1855, p. 462.

when rejected by both Scotland and England, was most eagerly embraced by the evangelical church of Saxony, and continued to be warmly cherished and esteemed by her to the day of his death." The man who was held in such high esteem by the reforming Archbishops of Cologne and Canterbury; who was the bosom friend of Melanchthon; who was highly thought of by Luther, and warmly eulogised by Beza and Johnston, was certainly not one whose memory his countrymen should willingly let die. He was unquestionably the most cultured, probably also the most liberal and conciliatory, of the Scottish theologians of the sixteenth century. He was the first to plead publicly before the authorities of the nation for the right of every household and every individual to have access to the Word of God in the vernacular tongue, and to impress on parents the sacred duty of sedulously inculcating its teaching on their children, and therefore, as Christopher Anderson has said, "the man who struck the first note in giving a tone to that character," for which his native country has since been known, and often since commended, as Bible-loving Scotland. Had his countrymen not so long lost sight of him, perhaps some stone of remembrance might have been found to his memory in Germany; but surely, though he was so long an exile, the chief memorial of his birth and death ought to be in Edinburgh or St Andrews. " There, in reference to the cause he advocated, no inappropriate emblem " would be " a father and his child reading the same sacred volume; and, for a motto, in remembrance of his position at the moment, perhaps his own memorable quotation of the Athenian, ' Strike, but hear me.' " [1]

[1] Anderson's Annals of the English Bible, 1845, ii. 485. For a list of the published writings of Alesius see Appendix I.

APPENDIX A (p. 19).

THE PÆDAGOGIUM, OR ST MARY'S COLLEGE, ST ANDREWS.[1]

St Mary's College, if in one sense the youngest, is in another sense the oldest, college within the University. It occupies the earliest site of the University, and gathers up into itself not only the old *Pædagogium*, but also a still older college. In January 1418 . . . a certain *Robertus de Monte Rosarum* mortified a site on the south side of South Street, with the buildings thereon, as a college for the study of theology and arts. This was the strip of ground on which the eastern portion of the Library, as well as the new south wing, now stands, but on which, in the oldest bird's-eye view of the city, a sort of collegiate building is represented as standing. That was undoubtedly the College, or Hall, or " Inns " of St John, to which repeated reference is made in the oldest manuscript records of the University. It had probably a lecture-room, rooms for the students to lodge in, and a chapel also, dedicated to St John the Evangelist, in which daily service was maintained, but, so far as we now know, it was very poorly endowed.

In 1430 Bishop Wardlaw, the illustrious founder of the University, mortified as a site for a *Pædagogium* or common

---

[1] [This is taken from a paper on " St Mary's College," contributed by Dr Mitchell to the " Student's Handbook to the University of St Andrews," 1895, pp. 12-15.]

school for the faculty of arts the strip of land and buildings thereon immediately to the west of St John's College—the frontage now covered by the western portion of the Library, the porch of St Mary's College, and the Principal's house. After the erection and endowment of St Salvator's College by Bishop Kennedy, and of St Leonard's College by Prior Hepburn, the attendance on the *Pædagogium*, which was but slenderly endowed, seems to have fallen off, and the number of its regents to have been curtailed. Archbishop Alexander Stewart, the favourite pupil of Erasmus, and one of the most accomplished of our long line of chancellors, was the first who formed the purpose of enlarging and endowing Bishop Wardlaw's foundation, but his life was prematurely brought to a close on the fatal field of Flodden. His successor, Andrew Forman, appears to have taken no interest in the work on which Stewart had set his heart. But James Betoun, who came next in succession, acted a nobler part. He brought with him from Glasgow John Major—the one great schoolman of whom Scotland in the sixteenth century could boast, who had upheld the reputation of his country in the University of Paris as an able and successful teacher of the philosophy and theology of the day. Major and Patrick Hamilton—the one the representative of the old, the other of the new learning—were incorporated into the University of St Andrews on the same day (9th June 1523); and, for at least two years, the former presided over the *Pædagogium*, and probably lectured both on philosophy and theology. In 1525-26 he returned to Paris, partly that he might publish there his commentaries on the Gospels, and partly that he might act again as a teacher in that wider sphere; but a few years later, on a vacancy occurring in the principality of St Salvator's College, he returned to St Andrews, and continued in that more lucrative charge till his death.

It was mainly in his last years, however, that James Betoun set himself in right earnest to complete the work which Archbishop Stewart had begun. At his solicitation Pope Paul III., on 12th February 1537, issued a bull annexing the teinds of the church of Tannadice, in Forfarshire, and of the wealthier church of Tyninghame, in East Lothian, to the old foundation, and erecting it into a privileged college under the title of the Blessed Mary of the Assumption. In this college, medicine, law, and theology, as well as arts, were henceforth to be taught, and the privilege was granted to it of conferring degrees in all lawful faculties, and of conferring them on those who had gained their knowledge elsewhere as well as on those who had studied within the college—in fact, making it almost a university within the University, and conceding to it more extensive powers than were conceded to many universities. His first work was to replace the decaying buildings of the *Pædagogium* by others more massive and commodious. That work was far from finished at the time of his death, and having been intermitted by his successor [the cardinal], was only completed by Archbishop Hamilton, who, with papal sanction, reconstituted the college and added to its endowments.

Early, however, in 1538, the first staff of teachers entered on their work as a college organised and equipped "*ut militans Dei ecclesia indies abundet viris litterarum scientiâ præditis,*" and few institutions through a long and eventful history have more illustriously fulfilled this object, though in another sense than its founders meant, and handed on the torch of sacred learning from generation to generation. Bannerman, who succeeded Major, had the honour of reorganising the old institution and starting it on its new career. Archibald Hay, who came next, was the child of the Renaissance, and more in earnest about religion than many of that school; and, had his life been spared, and the cardinal given heed to his counsels, the old Church might have been able to make a better fight for privilege or for life in the struggle which ensued. John Douglas, his successor, bridged the passage from the old to the new without any violent break, probably taking part with Wynram in the composition of Archbishop Hamilton's Catechism, as he did afterwards in the preparation of the Reformed Confession of

Faith and the First Book of Discipline. He was a man of the ancient academic type, content to live in single blessedness, to treat his pupils, who also lived in college, with the familiarity and affection of a father. He had the honour of training the youthful Andrew Melville, and perhaps it was with some presentiment of his future eminence that, as he held the precocious youth between his knees at the college fire, he fondly said, "My sillie fatherless and motherless chyld, it is ill to wit what God may mak of thee yit."

God watched over that weakly youth, and prospered his studies at Paris, Poictiers, and Geneva, so that with a mind stored with all the learning of his time, he returned to his native land to complete the reformation of its universities, and to delight successive generations of students by his stores of learning and wit, and by his accessibility and generosity. It was to meet his ideas of what a theological school should be that the college was set apart "allenarly" for the study of theology, and furnished with professors of the Old and the New Testament, who were to "expone" the various books of Scripture as well as to read them in the original, comparing the Hebrew of the Old Testament with the Septuagint and the Chaldee paraphrases, and the Greek of the New Testament with the old Syriac translation, while the principal was to teach the *loci communes* or the systematic theology of the age. The first assistants in the "wark of theology" were Mr John Robertson, who acted as *professor Novi Testamenti*, and his own nephew, James Melville, who taught Hebrew and the Old Testament, and to whom we owe that graphic diary which gives us several interesting glimpses of college life in those early days. To John Robertson succeeded Mr John Johnston, author of Latin poems in praise of our reformers and martyrs, and of Latin verses descriptive of the line of our Scottish kings.

Melville was by no means an illiberal theologian, and he and Johnston wrote to the Protestant churches of France urging moderation on them in controversies which were then being discussed with great bitterness. Both lived with and

for their pupils, and secured in an unusual degree their
reverence and affection. Both ultimately lost the favour of
the king ; and Melville, after being cruelly used in London,
had to spend his declining years in the French Protestant
University of Sedan.

APPENDIX B (p. 30).

CITATIO PATRICII HAMILTON

e Formulari vetere Andreano.

*Citatio super suspecto de heresi ad faciendum purgationem
alias ad videndum [ipsum] hereticum declarari.*

JACOBUS etc., Decano Christianitatis nostre de L[audonia]
Universisque et singulis aliis Dominis rectoribus, vicariis
perpetuis, capellanis curatis et non curatis per provinciam
nostram S[ti Andree] ubilibet constitutis, Illique vel illis ad
quem vel ad quos presentes litere pervenerint, Salutem cum
benedictione divina : Quia per fidelem inquisitionem aliter
de mandato nostro legitime receptam compertum extitit
quendam Magistrum P[atricium] H[amilton] de heresi mul-
tiplici suspectum, quem citandum et desuper accusandum
antea decrevimus, sed medio tempore relictâ patriâ ad alia
et extera se transtulit loca, nuper autem vagante fama ad
aures nostras clamorosa insinuatione pervenit Ipsum nuper-
rime in patriam reversum et quod primo statim adventu
non debite missus nec prerogativis aut privilegiis debitis
munitus, sed propriâ auctoritate et temerariâ presumptione,
predicationis officium de heresi ei designata acceptare ausus
est, et suas hereticas pravitates et perversas Martini Lutheri
heretici alias ab ecclesia damnati et suorum fautorum ac
sequacium opiniones promulgare, docens seminansve et
pertinaciter affirmans, ac populum Christianum de eisdem

T

instruere non erubescit, indeque simplices et illiteratos hujus regni Christi fideles qui in se et progenitoribus per tanta temporis curricula, spatio viz. mille et trecentorum annorum et ultra in ecclesiâ Dei constantissime militaverunt, a verâ nostrâ orthodoxâ fide et catholica ecclesia seducere, et quantum in eo est pervertere nititur et proponit, dicendo predicando et temerario ausu inter alia palam et publice affirmando :—

Legibus, canonibus, patrum sanctionibus et decretis, humanis quoque constitutionibus non esse obtemperandum ; Claves et censuras ecclesie contempnendas, nec sacramentis ejusdem fidendum, Templa non esse frequentanda, nec ymagines adorandas, pro defunctorum animabus non esse exorandum ; nec decimas Deo et ecclesie solvendas ; pro bonis operibus nullum fore salutis premium nec pro malis cruciatum ; Nostros progenitores in ecclesia Dei et ejusdem sacramentis fidentes in malâ et iniquâ fide esse mortuos et in inferno sepultos :—

Aliaque dictu et recitatu saltem inter Christianos et fideles horrenda et nephanda predicat docet et affirmat in Dei viventis claviumque ecclesie ac nostre fidei orthodoxe contemptum, regni et reipublice ejusdem damnum scandalum et, digna Dei ultione, si premissis favere incipiat, sperandam ruinam, animabusque perpetrantium gravissimum periculum nisi remedio succurratur oportuno : In quibus omnibus et singulis idem Magister P. communi voce et famâ ex publicâ et notoria ejusdem predicatione orta de heresi suspectus reputatur, habetur et divulgatur. Consilio igitur desuper recepto ipsum citandum et de premissis experiendum decrevimus : Quare vobis et vestrum cuilibet nos precipimus et mandamus, quatenus citetis legitime dictum Magistrum P. H. primo, secundo, tertio et peremptorie etc. quod compareat personaliter coram [nobis] nostrisque consulibus Dñis Episcopis, Abbatibus, Prioribus, sacrarum literarum Professoribus, et Religiosis, aliisque nobis pro tempore assistentibus, in ecclesiâ nostrâ Metropolitanâ S[ti Andree] regni Scotie primatiali, die *N* mensis

N proxime futuris, horâ decimâ antemeridiana vel eo circa,
ad respondendum nobis ex officio de et super suis pertinaciter dictis, affirmatis, predicatis, divulgatis, tentis et
disputatis contra nostram orthodoxam fidem et sanctam
ecclesiam catholicam ; et propterea ad videndum et
audiendum ipsum hereticum declarari, et penâ condignâ
a canonibus propterea latâ et imperatâ puniendum fore et
puniri debere ; superque adherentiâ et favoribus prestitis
peregrinis opinionibus et pravitatibus dicti Martini Lutheri,
heretici ab ecclesiâ damnati, et suorum sequacium ; ac aliis
interrogandis similiter reddendis, et tanquam heretice pra-
vitatis fautorem et male de fide sentientem accusandum fore
et accusari ac condempnari debere. Testimonia quoque et
probationes, si necesse fuerit, desuper recipi, jurari, et
admitti ; ac in premissis omnibus et singulis summarie et
de plano sine strepitu et figurâ judicii prout juris fuerit
procedendum fore et procedi debere; Vel ad allegandum
causam rationabilem quare premissa fieri non deberent ;
Cum intimatione debita, ut moris est, intimamus eidem
quod sive dictis die et loco comparere curaverit sive non
comparuerit Nos nihilominus in premissis omnibus et
singulis procedere volumus et intendimus justitiâ mediante ;
Imprimis absentiâ seu contumaciâ in aliquo non obstante ;
et ne periculum sit in mora, et ut interim hujus hereses in
hoc regno hucusque ab omni tali labe et hereticâ peste per
tanta temporis spatia sano, et post Christi Salvatoris sus-
ceptam fidem inviolabiliter preservato, non oriantur nec per
Christi fideles audiantur, vobis omnibus et singulis supra-
dictis, modo et forma premissis precipimus et mandamus,
quatenus auctoritate nostra inhibentes omnibus et singulis
Christi fidelibus cujuscunque dignitatis, status, gradus,
ordinis aut conditionis existant, ne dicto Magistro P. sic
ut premittitur, de heresi suspecto, favorem, assistentiam,
societatem, colloquium seu gratam audientiam praebeant ;
nec in suis temerariis et insolentibus predicationibus dis-
putationibus seu conventiclis publice vel occulte quovis
quesito colore vel ingenio conveniant seu presentiam exhi-

beant ; sed sibi et suis saltem de premissis fautoribus resis-
tere studeant, resistentiamque faciant et procurent ; ab illo
quoque edendo, bibendo aut communicando in premissis
abstineant, donec de heresi et infamia desuper ortâ
purgetur, et eundem vitent sub penâ excommunicationis
majoris ; Quam contrarium facientes incurrere volumus et
decernimus ipso facto. Et quos vos, etc. Datum, etc.

APPENDIX C (p. 46).

CARDINAL BETOUN'S INCONTINENCE.

"WHILE . . . he was possessed," Mr M'Bain tells us, "of
eminent qualities, he led, in many respects, anything but a
moral life. His favourite mistress was Marion Ogilvie,
daughter of Sir James, afterwards Lord, Ogilvie of Airlie,
to whom [as Abbot of Arbroath] he granted a liferent lease
of the lands of Burnton of Ethie, and other lands near the
place, for a small sum of money *and other causes*. This was
on the 22nd of May 1528. On the 20th of July 1530, he
granted her a liferent lease of the Kirkton of St Vigeans,
with the muir-fauld and the toft of St Vigeans, and a piece
of common land lying to the south of the church. On 17th
February 1533-34, she obtained a nineteen years' lease of
the eighth part of the lands of Auchmithie [lying to the
north-east of Ethie], with the brew-house there, and the
lands belonging to it, and on 10th March 1534[-35] there
is the record of a feu to her of a piece of land in the
'Sandpots,' for the construction of a toral or ustrina lying
'beyond and near the red wall of the monastery commonly
so called'" (Eminent Arbroathians, 1897, pp. 37, 38). For
these facts Mr M'Bain has the authority of the 'Registrum
de Aberbrothoc,' Bannatyne Club, ii. 482, 500, 519, 521.

On p. 482 are the words : " Pro certa summa pecunie et aliis causis assedat pro toto tempore vite Mariote Ogylwy subtenentibus coadjutoribus et assignatis," &c. Mr M'Bain adds : " It is not known by whom Ethie House was built, but it was [one of the mansions belonging to the abbey and] a favourite residence of David Beaton and Marion Ogilvie, his mistress. . . . After Beaton's death a natural daughter of his by Marion Ogilvie laid claim to the furniture in Ethie House, if not to the house itself. . . . But Ethie was not the only place in the neighbourhood occupied by David Beaton and Marion Ogilvie. In 1542 he acquired the barony of Melgund, and erected the castle in which he and his mistress and their children resided. The Beaton and the Ogilvie arms are still to be seen in one of the rooms. The initials ' D.B.' are over one window, and ' M.O.' over the other ; while on the corbal of the stair leading to this room are the Ogilvie arms, and the initials ' M.O.' . . . David Beaton settled the property of Melgund on his mistress in liferent, and on his eldest son David in fee " (Eminent Arbroathians, pp. 38, 39).

[According to Dr Joseph Robertson, " Cardinal Beaton had five bastards" ('Concilia Scotiæ,' ii. 302). There is record evidence, however, to show that he had at least seven. On the 4th of November 1539, three of his sons were legitimated in the following terms : " Rex dedit literas legitimationis Jacobo Betoun, Alexandro Betoun et Johanni Betoun, bastardis, filiis naturalibus Davidis archiepiscopis S. Andree, &c." (Register of Great Seal, iii. No. 2037). He had also a son David (Ibid., No. 1931), and three daughters, Elizabeth (Ibid., Nos. 1274, 2330), Margaret, and Agnes (Ibid., iv. Nos. 1353, 2740 ; ' Liber Officialis Sancti Andree,' Abbotsford Club, p. 158).]

APPENDIX D (p. 124).

CONDITIONS ON WHICH THE USE OF THE CHURCH OF THE
WHITE LADIES AT FRANKFORT WAS GRANTED TO THE
ENGLISH EXILES.

"Nun war bey Ankunft der Engelländer eine Kirche in
Frankfurt, die einigen französischen Protestanten zum
Gebrauch eingeräumt war, welche nun auch zum Behuf
der Engelländer in Vorschlag gebracht, und am 14 Julii
ihnen wirklich angewiesen wurde. Doch machte der Rath
gewisse Ordnungen, und suchte die Sache also einzurichten,
das allerlei Disputen, die etwa entstehen mögten, der Weg
verlaget wurde. Die vornehmsten waren diese : (*a*) dass
die Engelländer und Franzosen einerley Lehre und Ceremonien führen sollten ; Daher sollten jene (*b*) der Franzosen
Glaubensbekäntniss, das diese N.B. dem Rath überreichet
hatten, unterschreiben. (*c*) Liessen sich die Engelländer
gefallen, dass das Volk bey dem gemeinen Gebet das
Amen nicht mehr laut sagen sollte, wie sonst in der Kirche
von Engelland üblich ist. (*d*) Dass die Prediger das weisse
Chorhemde, nebst vielen andern in Engelland eingeführten
Ceremonien abschaffen sollten, als welche den Einwohnern,
die solcher Dinge ungewohnt wären, einstossig seyn könnten.
Und was der gleichen Umstände mehr waren, welche die
Engelländer, um desto eher zum Stande zu kommen, frei-
willig eingiengen."—J. Hildebrand Withof, 'Vertheidigung
der. . . . Nachricht wie es mit V. Pollane erstem Reform-
irten Prediger zu Frankfurt-am-Mayn . . . zugegangen,'
1753, folio.

APPENDIX E (p. 260).

THE THEOLOGICAL AND ECCLESIASTICAL OPINIONS OF ALESIUS.

(From the 'Responsio ad Cochlei Calvmnias.')

"WITH all his scribbling, he [*i.e.*, Cochlaeus] has never yet, so far as I know, disclosed what are his own opinions about Christian doctrine ; and therefore his empty and scurrilous treatises miss their mark, and are justly held in derision by learned men. . . . But I, renowned monarch, that you may know that my alliance is with the Church of Christ and not with any other factions, do not refuse before you and other good men to give a simple and clear account of my faith as I formerly wrote to you, for I believe the prophetical and apostolical Scriptures, and embrace the consensus of the holy fathers whom the Church approves. I also reverence the ecclesiastical authority, being one who, especially in doubtful matters, will obey and follow its decisions. Does Cochlaeus ask anything further? I myself will add, I approve of nothing seditious. With my whole heart and soul I abhor the ravings of the Anabaptists. No new doctrine, unsupported by the testimony of the ancient Church, is acceptable to me. Further still, as I do not undertake the defence of Luther, so, on the other hand, I do not approve of all the dreams of the monks which have been received, not only contrary to the decision of the Scripture, but also to the authority of the ancient church. Moreover, I cannot approve of the cruelty which is everywhere being practised against those who, following the judgment of Scripture and of the fathers, reject or censure any manifest abuse or error that in the course of time may have crept into the Church. Such is my faith, O Cochlaeus, use it if you are pleased with it ; if not, show me a better.

If the unjust punishments inflicted on the truly pious afford
you pleasure, you are not only a miserable, but a con-
temptible wretch.   I neither can nor will ever knowingly
burden or pollute my conscience by approving of these
parricides.   I saw in my own country the punishment of
one, born in a most honourable station, and innocent of
any serious crime, Patrick [Hamilton].   I saw burned at
Cologne two men of pious and orthodox sentiments, and
most averse to the fanatical opinions of the Anabaptists.
Nor can I express in words how deeply I was grieved by
these mournful spectacles.   And I did not grieve only over
the fate of those who were punished, in whom because, as
the poet says, 'grace shone through their very anguish,'
their singular bravery and constancy brought some alleviation to my grief ; but much more did I grieve over the fate
of the Church, which is disordered in many ways, and
likely yet to be more so, by the practice of such cruelty.
Finally, there is no doubt that the State will, in God's
appointed time, have to suffer heaviest punishment for
its guilt in permitting such parricides ; yet I do not im-
pugn the laws as to the punishment of heretics, if only
there is due cognition of each case, and care is taken
that those who are really innocent of perverting the true
Christian faith may not be punished."

Then follows a paragraph of great importance in itself,
and of almost as much from the light it casts on its author's
state of mind, and, perhaps, also on Melanchthon's, at that
particular time :—

" I myself also desire moderation in certain things on the
part of the Lutherans, and reasonableness.   To this they
may be recalled if the matters in dispute are duly examined
into.   It is the duty of the bishops to do their utmost that
learned men of either side should lovingly confer together
on Christian doctrine, that some one certain form of doctrine,
founded only upon the Word of God and the teaching of
the primitive fathers, should be framed ; and if this were
done, the Church might easily be brought to coalesce again

into one body. Nor do I doubt that good men on both sides are so disposed that they would not only willingly proffer their opinions, but also yield their individual convictions if they should hear more weighty reasons from the other side. For it is tyrannical, and specially unbecoming in a theologian, to do that which the son reproves in the tyrant, his father, in the tragedy. He wishes, the son says, to speak but to hear nothing in reply. At present the good men who are most desirous to provide some remedy for public evils keep silence, and secretly bewail the fate of the Church, not only alarmed by fear of those in power, but crushed by a sort of despair in this so great madness of slanderers, who have become so domineering that they would suffer no one but themselves to gain a hearing."

[APPENDIX F (p. 267).

THE DREAM OR VISION OF ALESIUS CONCERNING THE DECAPITATION OF ANNE BOLEYN.

I TAKE to witness Christ, who shall judge the quick and the dead, that I am about to speak the truth. On the day upon which the Queen was beheaded, at sunrise between two and three o'clock, there was revealed to me (whether I was asleep or awake I know not) the Queen's neck after her head had been cut off, and this so plainly that I could count the nerves, the veins, and the arteries.

Terrified by this dream, or vision, I immediately arose, and, crossing the river Thames, I came to Lambeth (this is the name of the Archbishop of Canterbury's palace), and I entered the garden in which he was walking.

When the archbishop saw me, he inquired why I had come so early, for the clock had not yet struck four. I answered that I had been horrified in my sleep, and I told him the whole occurrence. He continued in silent wonder for a while, and at length broke out into these words, " Do not you know what is to happen to-day?" and when I answered that I had remained at home since the date of the Queen's imprisonment, and knew nothing of what was going on, the archbishop then raised his eyes to heaven and said, " She who has been the Queen of England upon earth will to-day become a queen in heaven." So great was his grief that he could say nothing more, and then he burst into tears.

Terrified at this announcement, I return[ed] to London sorrowing. Although my lodging was not far distant from the place of execution, yet I could not become an eye-witness to the butchery of such an illustrious lady, and of the exalted personages who were beheaded along with her. —(Foreign Calendar, Elizabeth, i. 528).]

[APPENDIX G (p. 269).

THE DEPARTURE OF ALESIUS FROM ENGLAND.

As soon as the king [*i.e.*, Henry VIII.] began to hate her [*i.e.*, Anne Boleyn], laws hostile to the purer doctrine of the Gospel appeared. When I could not bear these with a good conscience, nor could my profession allow me to dissemble them (for I was filling the office of the ordinary reader in the celebrated University of Cambridge by the king's orders), I came to the Court, and asked for my dismissal by means of Crumwell. But he retained me for about three years with empty hopes, until it was decreed and confirmed by law that married priests should be separated from their wives and punished at the king's pleasure. But before this law was published, the Bishop of Canterbury

sent Lord Pachet [*i.e.* Paget] from Lambeth to me at London.
. . . He directed me to call upon the archbishop early in
the morning. When I called upon him, "Happy man that
you are," said he, "you can escape! I wish that I might
do the same; truly my see would be no hindrance to me.
You must make haste to escape before the island is blocked
up, unless you are willing to sign the decree, as I have,
compelled by fear. I repent of what I have done. And if
I had known that my only punishment would have been
deposition from the archbishopric (as I hear that my Lord
Latimer is deposed), of a truth I would not have subscribed.
I am grieved, however, that you have been deprived of your
salary for three years by Crumwell;[1] that you have no funds
for your travelling expenses, and that I have no ready
money. Nor dare I mention this to my friends, lest the
king should become aware that warning had been given
by me for you to escape, and that I have provided you with
the means of travelling. I give you, however, this ring as
a token of my friendship. It once belonged to Thomas
Wolsey, and it was presented to me by the king when he
gave me the archbishopric."

When I heard what the bishop had to say, I immediately
caused my property to be sold, and I concealed myself in
the house of a German sailor until the ship was ready, in
which I embarked, dressed as a soldier, along with other
German troops, that I might not be detected. When I
had escaped a company of searchers, I wrote to Crumwell
(although he had not behaved well towards me) and warned
him of the danger in which he stood at that time, and about
certain other matters. For this I can vouch the testimony
of John Ales, Gregory, and the Secretary, and Pachet him-

---

[1] [In Crumwell's accounts there are payments of £5 to Alesius on
each of the following dates: 4th January 1536-37, 28th March, 28th
May, and 24th October 1537; of 10 merks, on 19th February 1537-38;
and of £5, on 13th October 1538, to Ric. Morison, which he gave "by
my lord's command" to Alesius (Letters and State Papers, Henry
VIII., vol. xiv. part ii. 328-338).]

self. But Christopher Mount said that Crumwell did not dare to speak to me when I was going away and soliciting my dismissal, nor could he venture to give me anything, lest he should be accused to the king, but that he would send the sum that he owed me into Germany.[1]

The next intelligence, however, which I heard of him was that he had undergone capital punishment by order of the king ; to whom he had written, when in prison, saying that he was punished by the just judgment of God, because he had loved the king more than God ; and that out of deference to his sovereign he had caused many innocent persons to be put to death, not sparing your [*i.e.*, Elizabeth's] most holy mother, nor had he obeyed her directions in promoting the doctrine of the Gospel.—(Foreign Calendar, Elizabeth, i. 532-534).]

APPENDIX H (p. 281).

ALESIUS' INVITATION OF MELANCHTHON TO HIS DAUGHTER'S WEDDING.

NOCKAU, 11 *August* 1557.

ALEXANDER ALESIUS AU MELANCHTHON.

S.D. Quod fœlix faustumque sit. Dilectissima filia mea Anna, cui nomen in baptismo indidit bonæ memoriæ primo-genita vestra, desponsata est honesto iuveni Martino Luxso-lario (nam solem etiam pro insigni habet), doctoris Martini filio, petente id sua matre per cognatos et affines, et suaden-tibus communibus amicis nostris. Dictus est autem dies

---

[1] [Alesius arrived at Wittenberg on the 9th of July 1539, and from thence informed Crumwell that he was encouraged to hope that he would receive a post in the University there (Letters and State Papers, Henry VIII., vol. xiv. part i. 583, 584). Melanchthon wrote to the Elector's chancellor, on the 1st of December 1539, recommending him for the University of Frankfort (Corpus Reformatorum, iii. 842-844).]

nuptiarum ultimus Augusti, circa quod tempus vos ad colloquium profecturum (*sic*) spero. Peto igitur reverenter et
amanter, ut una cum honestissima coniuge vestra, genero,
filia ac nepte nuptias vestra praesentia ornare velitis. Existimo autem magistrum Paulum, amanuensem vestrum, una
venturum, sed tamen ut eum cum uxore invitetis meis verbis
ad nuptias oro. Scitis autem summum sacerdotem et ponti-
ficem nostrum filium Dei, qui primos parentes in paradyso
copulavit, et non minore magnificentia quam sapientia et
potencia suam ordinationem contra sophistica et tyrannidem
diaboli et multiplicem ingratitudinem nostram defendit, ut
totam actionem, ita etiam invitacionem hospitum et com-
munia officia sua presentia et primo miraculo compro-
basse[t] ac monstrasse[t], quantum dilectetur (*sic*) istis con-
gressibus. Nos autem parentes et amici, sponsi et sponsae,
una cum eis, pro hoc officio et molestia profectionis grati-
tudinem pollicemur per omnem occasionem.

Ex pago Nockau postridie Laurentii 1557.

ALEXANDER ALESIUS.

Adresse: Clarissimo et ornatissimo viro d. Philippo Mel-
anchthoni, suo præceptori carissimo.

APPENDIX I (p. 283).

THE WORKS OF ALESIUS.

THE following is a list of the published writings of Alesius,
so far as I have been able to trace them :—

1. Epistola contra decretum quoddam Episcoporum in
Scotia, 1533. [For a full copy of the title see p. 259 n.
No place, date, or printer's name is given on the title-page.
This small 8vo consists of only 14 leaves. It begins:
'Inclyto Regis Scotorum D. Iacobo Quinto Duci Albaniæ,

Principi Hiberniæ & Orchadum Domino suo clementissimo
Allexander Alesius S. D." At the end there is the date,
"Anno. M.D.XXXIII." In Cooper's 'Athenae Cantabrigienses' (i. 239), 1542 and 1543 are given as the dates of other
two editions.]

2. Responsio ad Cochlei Calumnias, 1533. [The full title
is : "Alexandri Alesii Scotti Responsio ad Cochlei Calvmnias." No place, date, or printer's name is given.]

3. Oratio de Gratitudine et Restituendis Scholis. Lipsiæ (?),
1541. [In the 'Athenae Cantabrigienses,' the 'Oratio de
Gratitudine' and the 'De Restituendis Scholis' are entered
as separate works published in Leipsic in 1541. They may,
however, have been also issued as one. In the 'Corpus
Reformatorum,' xi. 251-257, is printed the "Oratio de Gratitudine M. Alexandri Alesii Scoti, Decani, in promotione
Magistrorum anno M.D.XXXIV." The full title of the other
is : "De Restitvendis Scholis Oratio habita ab Alexdro
(*sic*) Alesio, in celebri Academia Frācofordiana ad Oderam.
An. M.D.XL. Mense Iunio. Francofordiæ apud Ioannem
Hanaw." The dedication ends : "Francofordiæ ad Oderam
calēdis Iunij. An. M.D.XL." There are only 19 leaves in
this small tract.]

4. De Auctore et Utilitate Psalmorum. 1542.

5. De Auctoritate Verbi Dei contra Episcopum Lundensem. 1542. [See p. 264 n.]

6. Of the Auctorite of the Word of God agaynst the
Bisshop of London. [For a full copy of the title, see p. 268
n. This small 8vo black-letter tract of 46 leaves bears no
place, date, or printer's name. In the British Museum
Catal., *Leipsic* is given as the probable place of printing,
and 1537 as the supposed date. Perhaps the date has been
inferred from the opening sentence of the tract : "Abowt
V yere agone I wrote to the noble king of Scottys the father
of my contry complanning of a certen proclamacyon wherin
the bisshops had forbidden the Holy Scripture to be redd in
the mother tong." It is rather curious that in the Latin
version this sentence runs thus : "Ante *biennium* scripsi

inclyto regi Scotorum patri meæ patriæ, et questus sum de edicto quodam, quo episcopi prohibebant lectionem sacrorum librorum lingua patria."]

7. Cohortatio ad concordiam pietatis ac doctrinæ Christianæ defensionem. Lipsiæ, 1544.

8. [De Argvmento Epistolae ad Romanos Dispvtatio prima, pvblice proposita in celebri Academia Lipsensi, et in ordinaria dispvtatione defensa, praesidente Alexandro Alesio, sacrae theologiae doctore. Lipsiae in officina Valenttini Papae. anno M.D.XLVII. This small 8vo tract of 8 leaves is printed in italics.]

9. Ordo Distributionis Sacramenti Altaris in Regno Angliæ. 1548. [This is a translation of 'The Order of the Communion,' which has been re-printed for the Parker Society in 'The Two Liturgies of Edward VI.' In the British Museum Catal., it is mentioned that the translator's address to the reader is signed: 'A. A. S. D. Th.'—*i.e.*, "Alexander Alesius, Scotus, Doctor Theologiæ." See also Coverdale's Remains, Parker Society, p. 525 n.]

10. Epitome Catechismi D. P. Melanchthonis cui addita est expositio symboli et Orationis Dominicæ. 1550.

11. Commentarius in Epistolam Primam Si Pauli ad Timotheum. Lipsiæ, 1550.

12. Commentarius in Epistolam Secundam Si Pauli ad Timotheum. Lipsiæ, 1551. [The exact title of this is : "In Alteram ad Timotheum Expositio. Avtore Alexandro Alesio. D. Lipsiæ, excvdebat Georgivs Hantzsch anno M.D.LI."]

13. Ordinatio Ecclesiæ in Regno Angliæ. 1551. [This is a translation of the 'First Liturgy of Edward VI.' As a translation it is somewhat adversely criticised in the 'Liturgical Services of Queen Elizabeth,' Parker Society, pp. xxiv-xxvii. The full title is : "Ordinatio Ecclesiae, sev Ministerii Ecclesiastici, in Florentissimo Regno Angliæ, conscripta sermone patrio, & in Latinam linguam bona fide conuersa, & ad consolationem ecclesiarum Christi, ubicunque locorum ac gentium, his tristissimis temporibus, edita, ab Alexandro

Alesio Scoto sacrae theologiae doctore. Lipsiae in officina
VVolfgangi Gvnteri. Anno M.D.LI." The copy of this 4to
in the Edinburgh University Library belonged to Drum-
mond of Hawthornden. In the 'Athenae Cantabrigienses,'
1619 and 1690 are given as the dates of two 8vo editions.]

14. Commentarius in Epistolam S. Pauli ad Titum.
Lipsiæ, 1552. [The full title of this is : "Epistolae ad
Titvm Expositio, in qva pleraque tractantur per quæstiones,
ut à pueris facilius percipi, & retineri possint. Nulla est
autem sententia in tota Epistola praetermissa, quae non sit
explicata : Et de Syntaxi, & Figura sermonis, ac genuina
significatione dictionū passim disputatur. Praelecta Lipsiae,
ab Alexandro Alesio. D. Lipsiae, in officina typographica
Georgii Hantzsch. M.D.LII."]

15. Refutatio errorum Andreæ Osiandri de Justificatione.
Wittembergæ, 1552. [The full title is : "Alexandri Alesii
Doctoris Theologiae diligens refutatio errorum, quos sparsit
nuper Andreas Osiander in libro, cui titulum fecit : De
Vnico Mediatore Christo. Edita VVitebergæ ex officina
Ioannis Lufftij anno 1552." In the 'Athenae Cantabrigi-
enses' it is stated that an edition was also printed at
Leipsic in 1553.]

16. Commentarius in Evangelium Joannis. Lipsiæ, 1552.
Basilii, 1553. [The full title is : "Commentarivs in Euan-
gelium Ioannis, praelectvs in celebri Academia Lipsensi, ab
Alexandro Alesio D. Theologo, anno Domini 1552. Cum
locuplete rerum & uerborum memorabilium indice.
Basileae, per Ioannem Oporinum." The colophon is :
"Basileae, ex officina Ioannis Oporini, anno salutis humanae
M.D.LIII. Mense Martio." This volume contains over 600
pages.]

17. Disputatio in XIIII. cap. Rom. Disputt. et Orr. aliquot
Francoforti habitæ 1540 et 1541. [The full title is : "In
Capvt XIIII. Epistolae Pavli ad Romanos, Dispvtatio
Alexandri Alesii Theologiae D. Lipsiae, M.D.XLVI." This
tract of 6 leaves, with the exception of the title-page and
the heading, is printed in italics.]

18. Omnes Disputationes Alexandri Alesii in Epistolam Si Pauli ad Romanos. Lipsiæ, 1553. [The full title is: "Omnes Dispvtationes D. Alexandri Alesii de tota Epistola ad Romanos diversis temporibvs propositae ab ipso in celebri Academia Lipsensi, et a mvltis doctis viris expetitae, iam tandem collectae per Georgivm Hantsch, et editae in gratiam stvdiosorvm. Cvm praefatione Philippi Melanchthonis. M.D.LIII." In the British Museum Catal. Wittenberg is entered as the supposed place of publication. In the sale catal. of the Makellar Library there is the item: "Alesius (Alex. Scotus) De Paulina Argumentatione, capiti secundo ad Romanos, Ideo inexcusabilis es, o Homo quis-quis es qui Judicus (*sic*), Disputatio Sexta, . . . s. l. anno 1549." See also *supra*, Nos. 8 and 17.]

19. Primus Liber Psalmorum Davidis. Lipsiæ, 1550, 1554.

20. Disputationes Tres De Mediatore et Justificatione hominis. Lipsiæ, 1554.

21. Responsio ad Tapperum de Missâ et Cœna Domini. Lipsiæ. [In the 'Athenae Cantabrigienses,' 1565 is given as the date of publication.]

22. Contra horrendas Serveti Blasphemias Disputationes Tres. Lipsiæ, 1554. [These disputations were probably issued separately and were supplemented by a fourth. In the 'Athenae Cantabrigienses' there is the entry: "Contra Michaelem Servetum ejusque blasphemias disp. iii. Leipsic, 8vo. 1554"; and also this other: "Contra horrendas Serveti blasphemias disputatio quarta. Leipsic, 8vo. 1555."]

23. Disputatio de Perpetuo Consensu Ecclesiæ. Lipsiæ, 1553(?), 1556.

24. Ad libellum Ludovici Nogarolæ comitis De Traditionibus Apostolicis et earum necessitate Responsio Alexandri Alesii D. Lip. 1556. [For the rarity of this tract see *supra*, p. 255 n. In his Introduction to Gau, Dr Mitchell gives as the alternate title: "Apostolicæ institutiones a Ludovico Nogarola Com. in parvum libellum collectæ et ab Alexandro Alesio in Disputationem propositæ in celebri Academia Lipsiensi. Lipsiæ, Excudebat Georgius Hantzsch, 1556." 8vo.]

25. Responsio ad Duos et triginta Articulos Theologorum Lovaniensium. Lipsiæ, 1559. [In the sale catalogue of the Makellar Library 1545 is given as the year of publication. In the 'Athenae Cantabrigienses' 1549 is given.]

26. Assertio Doctrinæ Ecclesiæ Catholicæ de Sancta Trinitate, cum confutatione erroris Valentini Gentilis. 1564 (?). [British Museum Catalogue gives Geneva, 1567.]

27. Edinburgi Regiæ Scotorum Urbis Descriptio. Banna-tyne Club Miscellany, vol. i. [This description of Edinburgh was sent by Alesius to Sebastian Munster for his " Cosmog-raphy," printed at Basle in 1550, and republished in 1572. There are translations of it in Mackenzie's Lives and Char-acters of Scots Writers, ii. 400, 401 ; and in Chambers' Minor Antiquities of Edinburgh ; and in Hume Brown's Scotland before 1700.]

28. [Congratulatory letter to Queen Elizabeth, dated at Leipsic, 1st September 1559. The original holograph of twenty pages and a slip is still preserved. A translation of most of it is given in the Calendar of Foreign State Papers, Reign of Elizabeth, i. 524-534.]

[There are copies of Nos. 5, 12, 14, 15, 16 (1553), and 18 in St Andrews University Library ; of No. 2 in the Church of Scotland Library, Edinburgh ; of No. 16 (1553) in the Signet Library ; of No. 8 in the Advocates' ; of Nos. 2, 3 (De Restituendis Scholis), 5, 13, 16 (1553), and 17 in the Edinburgh University Library ; and of Nos. 1, 6, 7, 9, 10, 12, 13, 15, 16 (1553), 18, 19 (1554), 23 (1556), and 26 in the British Museum. Nos. 27 and 28 are in all important public libraries. At Laing's sale, No. 1 brought £6, 5s. ; No. 2, £17, 17s. ; No. 5, £6 ; No. 6, £4 ; No. 13, £10 ; No. 15, £5, 17s. 6d. ; No. 16, £5, 10s. ; and No. 18 (with which was bound up " Sarcerius de Scholasticae Theologiae Vanitate "), £6. In the 'Athenae Cantabrigienses,' the following six items, which are not in the above list, are mentioned : " Disputatio de Justitia Dei et Justitia hominis coram Deo. Leipsic, 1553." " De utriusque naturae officiis in Christo." " De distincta Christi hypostasi." " Preface to Gardiner upon obedience. Translated from English to Latin." "De Balaei Vocatione. Translated from English." "Ordinationes Anglorum Ecclesiae per Bucerum. Translated from English to Latin." In connection with the last, see 'Liturgical Services of Queen Elizabeth,' Parker Society, p. xxv, n. 3.]

[ADDENDA.

PAGE 20. *Patrick Hamilton's admission to the Faculty of Arts in St Andrews University.*—The entry in the 'Acta Facultatis Artium' runs thus: "Congregatione artium facultatis, in Nouis Scolis eiusdem tenta tercio die mensis Octobris, anno Domini millesimo quingentesimo vigesimo quarto, Magister Johannes Ba[l]four regentium senior Collegij Sancti Saluatoris in quodlibetarium est electus; et Magister Patricius Hamiltone, abbas de Ferne, Rossensis diocesis, in facultatem est receptus."

Page 117. *Two sacraments only.*—In the Preface to the Book of Common Order it is said that "for the ministration of the two sacraments, our Booke giveth sufficient proofe" (Dunlop's Confessions, ii. 395; Laing's Knox, iv. 164). In the Confession used in the English congregation at Geneva only two are referred to (Dunlop's Confessions, ii. 9; Laing's Knox, iv. 172); in "the Maner to Examine Children" their number is said to be two (Laing's Knox, vi. 344); and in Calvin's Catechism, printed with the Book of Common Order, it is emphatically declared that there are two only (Dunlop's Confessions, ii. 233).

Page 121. *The language of Rev.* xiv. 11.—In the text of the Confession the passage runs thus: "For sik as now delyte in vanity, cruelty, filthynes, superstition or idolatry, sal be adjudged to the fire unquencheable: in quhilk they sall be tormented for ever, asweill in their awin bodyes, as in their

saules, quhilk now they give to serve the devill in all abhom-
ination" (Dunlop's Confessions, ii. 96, 97). As printed in
Laing's Knox (ii. 120) the word "inextinguishable," and in
the Acts of Parliament (ii. 534 ; iii. 22) the word "unstanche-
abill," is used instead of "unquencheable." In Dunlop,
however, there is in addition, at the bottom of the page, in
smaller type : "Rev. 14. 10. The same shall drynke the
wyne of the wrath of God, which is poured in the cuppe of
hys wrath. And he shall be punyshed in fyre and brymstone
before the holy angells, and before the Lambe. And the
smooke of theyr torment ascendeth up evermore, and they
have no rest daye nor nyght, whyche worshyppe the beast
and hys ymage."

Page 153. *Readers or exhorters.*—The name *exhorter* does
not occur in the First Book of Discipline ; but that "sort of
readers" therein mentioned as having "some gift of exhortation" (Dunlop's Confessions, ii. 537 ; Laing's Knox, ii. 200)
soon came to be known as exhorters, and are so named in
various Acts of Assembly ; see, for example, the Act of 1564
quoted on p. 128. They are distinguished from readers in
the 'Register of Ministers, Exhorters, and Readers,' printed
for the Maitland Club ; but, as David Laing has pointed out,
the title of exhorter as indicating an advanced class seems
to have been soon and silently dropped. "On comparing
the list of the persons so styled in 1567 with that of 1574,
we find some of them had become ministers, but the greater
number are entered simply as readers" (Wodrow Miscellany, p. 323).

Page 233. *Conference between the two parties.*—Besides
the three conferences mentioned in the footnote, there was
another held in the early summer of 1578. The results, as
recorded in the Booke of the Universall Kirk (ii. 414, 415)
and in Calderwood's History (iii. 412, 413), embrace nothing
about the kirk-session, beyond the perpetuity of the persons
of the elders.

Page 259. *Alesius at Wittenberg.*—Through the influence
of Luther and Melanchthon, the Elector of Saxony had con-

ferred on Alesius the prebend of Aldenburgh. Being in greats straits for money, and having been disappointed of help otherwise, he was constrained to write from Wittenberg, on the 12th of December 1533, to Spalatinus, requesting him to obtain payment of the moiety of the prebend (Corpus Reformatorum, ii. 690, 691).

Page 261. *The disputatious Cochlaeus.*—On the suggestion of Melanchthon, an attack in verse was made on Cochlaeus for his injustice to Alesius ; but the timorous author so dreaded Cochlaeus that, instead of writing in his own name, he personated Alesius (Corpus Reformatorum, iv. 1025, 1026).

Page 265. *Erasmus and Cochlaeus.*—Summaries of the letters which James V. wrote, on the 1st of July 1534, to Erasmus, to Cochlaeus, and to the King of the Romans, are in the Letters and State Papers of Henry VIII., vol. vii. p. 358.

Page 267. *Alesius as a physician.*—" I determined with my self to serve the tyme and to change the preaching of the crosse with the scyence of physic wherin I had a litle sight before, and thus I went unto a very well-lerned phisycian called Doctor Nicolas, which hath practised phisyk in London thes many yeares with high prayse, whose company I dyd use certen yeares, wherby I did both see and lern many things, even the principal poyntes concerning that science. In so moch that at length certen of my frindes did move me to take in hand to practise, which thing I did I trust not unluckyly " (Of the Auctorite of the Word of God agaynst the Bisshop of London).

Page 268. *Latimer and Cranmer.*—For the opinion of Alesius on Latimer and Cranmer, see Dr Mitchell's Westminster Assembly, 1883, p. 14 n., and p. 23 n.

Page 268 n. *Ales or Alesius.*—Christopher Anderson may be excused for supposing that Ales was the real name of Alesius ; but less can be said for those editors of State Papers and compilers of important Library Catalogues who have helped to perpetuate the error long after it was pointed out by Principal Lorimer in his Patrick Hamilton.

Page 269. *John M'Alpine and John Fyffe.*—From a correction which Dr Mitchell has made in his own copy of the 'Gude and Godlie Ballatis,' 1897, p. cv, it seems that he had come to the conclusion that it was M'Alpine and *Macdowal*, not *Fyffe*, who were protected by Bishop Shaxton. Cf. Lorimer's Patrick Hamilton, pp. 186, 187.]

CORRIGENDA.

P. 119, line 4 from bottom. *After* contained *insert* in.
P. 240, line 14. *For* oedibus *read* aedibus.

INDEX.

THE END.

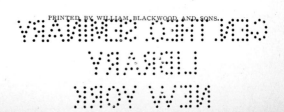

Baird Lectures.

THEISM. Being the Baird Lecture for 1876. By ROBERT FLINT, D.D., LL.D., Professor of Divinity in the University of Edinburgh. Ninth Edition, Revised. Crown 8vo, 7s. 6d.

ANTI-THEISTIC THEORIES. Being the Baird Lecture for 1877. By the SAME AUTHOR. Fifth Edition. Crown 8vo, 10s. 6d.

THE EARLY RELIGION OF ISRAEL. As set forth by Biblical Writers and Modern Critical Historians. Being the Baird Lecture for 1888-89. By JAMES ROBERTSON, D.D., Professor of Oriental Languages in the University of Glasgow. Demy 8vo, 12s.

THE APOSTOLIC MINISTRY IN THE SCOTTISH CHURCH. The Baird Lecture for 1897. By ROBERT HERBERT STORY, D.D. (Edin.), F.S.A. Scot., Principal of the University of Glasgow, Principal Clerk of the General Assembly, and Chaplain to the Queen. Crown 8vo, 7s. 6d.

Croall Lectures.

AGNOSTICISM. Being the Croall Lecture for 1887-88. By ROBERT FLINT, D.D., LL.D. In 1 vol. demy 8vo.
[*In the press.*

RECENT ARCHÆOLOGY AND THE BIBLE. Being the Croall Lecture for 1898. By THOMAS NICOL, D.D., Professor of Divinity and Biblical Criticism in the University of Aberdeen; Author of 'Recent Explorations in Bible Lands.' Demy 8vo, 9s. net.

THE POETRY AND THE RELIGION OF THE PSALMS. The Croall Lecture, 1893-94. By JAMES ROBERTSON, D.D. Demy 8vo, 12s.

WILLIAM BLACKWOOD & SONS, EDINBURGH AND LONDON.

EDINBURGH GIFFORD LECTURES.

PHILOSOPHY AND DEVELOPMENT OF RELIGION.
Being the Edinburgh Gifford Lectures for 1894. By OTTO
PFLEIDERER, D.D., Professor of Theology at Berlin University.
In 2 vols. post 8vo, 15s. net.

Summary of Contents:—Religion and Morality—And Science—The
Belief in God—God in the Natural Order of the World—In the Moral
and Religious Order of the World—The Religious View of Man—The
Religious View of the World—The Preparation of Christianity in
Judaism—The Gospel of Jesus Christ—The Primitive Christian Com-
munity—The Apostle Paul—Jewish and Christian Hellenism—The
Christianity of the Alexandrian Fathers—Of Augustine and of the
Roman Church—Of Luther and of Protestantism.

PHILOSOPHY OF THEISM. Being the Gifford Lectures
delivered before the University of Edinburgh in 1894-95. By
ALEXANDER CAMPBELL FRASER, Hon. D.C.L. Oxford; Emeritus
Professor of Logic and Metaphysics in the University of Edinburgh. Second Edition, Amended. Post 8vo, 6s. 6d. net.

Summary of Contents:—The Universal Problem—Three Primary
Data: Ego, Matter, and God—Universal Materialism—Panegoism—
Pantheism—Pantheistic Unity and Necessity: Spinoza—Final Scep-
ticism: David Hume—God latent in Nature—Ideal Man an Image of
God — What is God? — Perfect Goodness Personified — Omnipotent
Goodness—Omnipresent Divine Adaptation—Philosophical or Theo-
logical Omniscience — Final Faith — Evil on this Planet — Theistic
Optimism — Human Progress — Miraculous Interference — The Final
Venture of Theistic Faith—A RETROSPECT.

ELEMENTS OF THE SCIENCE OF RELIGION. PART
I.—MORPHOLOGICAL. PART II.—ONTOLOGICAL. Being the Gifford Lectures delivered before the University of Edinburgh in
1896-98. By C. P. TIELE, Theol. D., Litt. D. (Bonon.). Hon.
M.R.A.S., &c., Professor of the Science of Religion in the University of Leyden. In 2 vols., post 8vo, 7s. 6d. net each.

Summary of Contents:—MORPHOLOGICAL—Conception, Aim, and
Method of the Science of Religion—Conception of the Development of
Religion—Stages, Directions, and Laws of Development—Influence of
the Individual in the Development of Religion — Essentials of the
Development of Religion. ONTOLOGICAL — Manifestations and Con-
stituents of Religion—Conceptions of Faith—Philosophy and Religious
Doctrine—The Constant Element in all Conceptions of God—Rela-
tionship between God and Man—Worship, Prayers, and Offerings—
Religion as a Social Phenomenon—The Being or Essence of Religion—
The Origin of Religion—The Place of Religion in Spiritual Life.

WILLIAM BLACKWOOD & SONS, EDINBURGH AND LONDON.

Catalogue

of

Messrs Blackwood & Sons'

Publications

PERIODS OF EUROPEAN LITERATURE. Edited by
PROFESSOR SAINTSBURY.

THE FLOURISHING OF ROMANCE AND THE RISE OF ALLE-
GORY. (12TH AND 13TH CENTURIES.) By GEORGE SAINTSBURY, M.A.,
Professor of Rhetoric and English Literature in Edinburgh University.
Crown 8vo, 5s. net.
THE LATER RENAISSANCE. By DAVID HANNAY. Crown 8vo,
5s. net.
THE FOURTEENTH CENTURY. By F. J. SNELL. Crown 8vo,
5s. net.
THE AUGUSTAN AGES. By OLIVER ELTON. Crown 8vo, 5s. net.
THE ROMANTIC TRIUMPH. By T. S. OMOND. Crown 8vo.
[*Shortly.*
THE TRANSITION PERIOD. By G. GREGORY SMITH. Crown 8vo.
[*In the press.*

The other Volumes are:—

THE DARK AGES . . . Prof. W. P. Ker.
THE EARLIER RENAISSANCE. The Editor.
THE FIRST HALF OF THE SEVENTEENTH
CENTURY . . Prof. H. J. C. Grierson.

THE MID-EIGHTEENTH
CENTURY . . . . J. Hepburn Millar.
THE ROMANTIC REVOLT Prof.C.E.Vaughan.
THE LATER NINETEENTH
CENTURY . . . . The Editor.

PHILOSOPHICAL CLASSICS FOR ENGLISH READERS.
Edited by WILLIAM KNIGHT, LL.D., Professor of Moral Philosophy
in the University of St Andrews. In crown 8vo Volumes, with Portraits,
price 3s. 6d.

Contents of the Series. — DESCARTES, by
Professor Mahaffy, Dublin. — BUTLER, by
Rev. W. Lucas Collins, M.A.—BERKELEY,
by Professor Campbell Fraser. — FICHTE,
by Professor Adamson, Glasgow. — KANT,
by Professor Wallace, Oxford.—HAMILTON,
by Professor Veitch, Glasgow.—HEGEL, by
the Master of Balliol.—LEIBNIZ, by J. Theodore Merz.—VICO, by Professor Flint, Edinburgh. — HOBBES, by Professor Croom
Robertson. — HUME, by the Editor. —
SPINOZA, by the Very Rev. Principal Caird,
Glasgow.—BACON: Part I. The Life, by
Professor Nichol.—BACON: Part II. Philosophy, by the same Author.—LOCKE, by
Professor Campbell Fraser.

FOREIGN CLASSICS FOR ENGLISH READERS. Edited by
Mrs OLIPHANT. CHEAP RE-ISSUE. In limp cloth, fcap. 8vo, price 1s.
each.

DANTE, by the Editor. — VOLTAIRE,
by General Sir E. B. Hamley, K.C.B.
— PASCAL, by Principal Tulloch. — PE-
TRARCH, by Henry Reeve, C.B.—GOETHE,
by A. Hayward, Q.C.—MOLIÈRE, by the
Editor and F. Tarver, M.A.—MONTAIGNE,
by Rev. W. L. Collins.—RABELAIS, by Sir
Walter Besant. — CALDERON, by E. J.
Hasell.—SAINT SIMON, by C. W. Collins.
CERVANTES, by the Editor. — CORNEILLE
AND RACINE, by Henry M. Trollope. —
MADAME DE SÉVIGNÉ, by Miss Thackeray.
— LA FONTAINE, AND OTHER FRENCH
FABULISTS, by Rev. W. Lucas Collins,
M.A.— SCHILLER, by James Sime, M.A.
—TASSO, by E. J. Hasell.—ROUSSEAU,
by Henry Grey Graham. — ALFRED DE
MUSSET, by C. F. Oliphant.

ANCIENT CLASSICS FOR ENGLISH READERS. Edited by
the REV. W. LUCAS COLLINS, M.A. CHEAP RE-ISSUE. In limp cloth,
fcap. 8vo, price 1s. each.

Contents of the Series.—HOMER: ILIAD,
by the Editor.—HOMER: ODYSSEY, by the
Editor.—HERODOTUS, by G. C. Swayne.—
CÆSAR, by Anthony Trollope.—VIRGIL, by
the Editor. — HORACE, by Sir Theodore
Martin.—ÆSCHYLUS, by Bishop Copleston.
—XENOPHON, by Sir Alex. Grant.—CICERO,
by the Editor.—SOPHOCLES, by C. W. Col-
lins.—PLINY, by Rev. A. Church and W. J.
Brodribb.—EURIPIDES, by W. B. Donne.—
JUVENAL, by E. Walford. — ARISTOPHANES,
by the Editor.—HESIOD AND THEOGNIS, by
J. Davies.—PLAUTUS AND TERENCE, by the
Editor. — TACITUS, by W. B. Donne.—
LUCIAN, by the Editor.—PLATO, by C. W.
Collins. — GREEK ANTHOLOGY, by Lord
Neaves.—LIVY, by the Editor.—OVID, by
Rev. A. Church. — CATULLUS, TIBULLUS,
AND PROPERTIUS, by J. Davies.—DEMOS-
THENES, by W. J. Brodribb.—ARISTOTLE,
by Sir Alex. Grant.—THUCYDIDES, by the
Editor.—LUCRETIUS, by W. H. Mallock.—
PINDAR, by Rev. F. D. Morice.

CATALOGUE

OF

MESSRS BLACKWOOD & SONS'

PUBLICATIONS.

ALISON.
    History of Europe. By Sir ARCHIBALD ALISON, Bart., D.C.L.
        1. From the Commencement of the French Revolution to
            the Battle of Waterloo.
                LIBRARY EDITION, 14 vols., with Portraits. Demy 8vo, £10, 10s.
                ANOTHER EDITION, in 20 vols. crown 8vo, £6.
                PEOPLE'S EDITION, 13 vols. crown 8vo, £2, 11s.
        2. Continuation to the Accession of Louis Napoleon.
                LIBRARY EDITION, 8 vols. 8vo, £6, 7s. 6d.
                PEOPLE'S EDITION, 8 vols. crown 8vo, 34s.
    Epitome of Alison's History of Europe. Thirtieth Thou-
        sand, 7s. 6d.
    Atlas to Alison's History of Europe. By A. Keith Johnston.
                LIBRARY EDITION, demy 4to, £3, 3s.
                PEOPLE'S EDITION, 31s. 6d.
    Life of John Duke of Marlborough. With some Account of
        his Contemporaries, and of the War of the Succession. Third Edition. 2 vols.
        8vo. Portraits and Maps, 30s.
    Essays : Historical, Political, and Miscellaneous. 3 vols.
        demy 8vo, 45s.

ACROSS FRANCE IN A CARAVAN : BEING SOME ACCOUNT
    OF A JOURNEY FROM BORDEAUX TO GENOA IN THE "ESCARGOT," taken in the Winter
    1889-90. By the Author of 'A Day of my Life at Eton.' With fifty Illustrations
    by John Wallace, after Sketches by the Author, and a Map. Cheap Edition,
    demy 8vo, 7s. 6d.

ACTA SANCTORUM HIBERNIÆ ; Ex Codice Salmanticensi.
    Nunc primum integre edita opera CAROLI DE SMEDT et JOSEPHI DE BACKER, e
    Soc. Jesu, Hagiographorum Bollandianorum ; Auctore et Sumptus Largiente
    JOANNE PATRICIO MARCHIONE BOTHAE. In One handsome 4to Volume, bound in
    half roxburghe, £2, 2s.; in paper cover, 31s. 6d.

ADOLPHUS. Some Memories of Paris. By F. ADOLPHUS.
    Crown 8vo, 6s.

AFLALO. A Sketch of the Natural History (Vertebrates) of
    the British Islands. By F. G. AFLALO, F.R.G.S., F.Z.S., Author of 'A Sketch
    of the Natural History of Australia,' &c. With numerous Illustrations by Lodge
    and Bennett. Crown 8vo, 6s. net.

AIKMAN.
 Manures and the Principles of Manuring. By C. M. AIKMAN,
 D.Sc., F.R.S.E., &c., Professor of Chemistry, Glasgow Veterinary College;
 Examiner in Chemistry, University of Glasgow, &c. Crown 8vo, 6s. 6d.
 Farmyard Manure : Its Nature, Composition, and Treatment.
 Crown 8vo, 1s. 6d.

ALLARDYCE.
 The City of Sunshine. By ALEXANDER ALLARDYCE, Author of
 'Earlscourt,' &c. New Edition. Crown 8vo, 6s.
 Balmoral : A Romance of the Queen's Country. New Edition.
 Crown 8vo, 6s.

ALMOND. Christ the Protestant ; and other Sermons. By
 HELY HUTCHINSON ALMOND, M.A. Oxon., Hon. LL.D. Glasgow ; Head-master of
 Loretto School. Crown 8vo, 5s.

ANCIENT CLASSICS FOR ENGLISH READERS. Edited
 by Rev. W. LUCAS COLLINS, M.A. Price 1s. each. *For List of Vols. see p. 2.*

ANDERSON. Daniel in the Critics' Den. A Reply to Dean
 Farrar's 'Book of Daniel.' By ROBERT ANDERSON, LL.D., Barrister-at-Law,
 Assistant Commissioner of Police of the Metropolis ; Author of 'The Coming
 Prince,' 'Human Destiny,' &c. Post 8vo, 4s. 6d.

AUTOBIOGRAPHY OF A CHILD. Crown 8vo, 6s.

AYTOUN.
 Lays of the Scottish Cavaliers, and other Poems. By W.
 EDMONDSTOUNE AYTOUN, D.C.L., Professor of Rhetoric and Belles-Lettres in the
 University of Edinburgh. New Edition. Fcap. 8vo, 3s. 6d.
 CHEAP EDITION. 1s. Cloth, 1s. 3d.

 An Illustrated Edition of the Lays of the Scottish Cavaliers.
 From designs by Sir NOEL PATON. Cheaper Edition. Small 4to, 10s. 6d.

 Bothwell : a Poem. Third Edition. Fcap., 7s. 6d.

 Poems and Ballads of Goethe. Translated by Professor
 AYTOUN and Sir THEODORE MARTIN, K.C.B. Third Edition. Fcap., 6s.

 Memoir of William E. Aytoun, D.C.L. By Sir THEODORE
 MARTIN, K.C.B. With Portrait. Post 8vo, 12s.

BEDFORD & COLLINS. Annals of the Free Foresters, from
 1856 to the Present Day. By W. K. R. BEDFORD, W. E. W. COLLINS, and other
 Contributors. With 55 Portraits and 59 other Illustrations. Demy 8vo, 21s. *net*.

BELLAIRS. Gossips with Girls and Maidens, Betrothed and
 Free. By LADY BELLAIRS. New Edition. Crown 8vo, 3s. 6d. Cloth, extra
 gilt edges, 5s.

BELLESHEIM. History of the Catholic Church of Scotland.
 From the Introduction of Christianity to the Present Day. By ALPHONS BEL-
 LESHEIM, D.D., Canon of Aix-la-Chapelle. Translated, with Notes and Additions,
 by D. OSWALD HUNTER BLAIR, O.S.B., Monk of Fort Augustus. Cheap Edition.
 Complete in 4 vols. demy 8vo, with Maps. Price 21s. net.

BENTINCK. Racing Life of Lord George Cavendish Bentinck,
 M.P., and other Reminiscences. By JOHN KENT, Private Trainer to the Good-
 wood Stable. Edited by the Hon. FRANCIS LAWLEY. With Twenty-three full-
 page Plates, and Facsimile Letter. Third Edition. Demy 8vo, 25s.

BICKERDYKE. A Banished Beauty. By JOHN BICKERDYKE,
 Author of 'Days in Thule, with Rod, Gun, and Camera,' 'The Book of the All-
 Round Angler,' 'Curiosities of Ale and Beer,' &c. With Illustrations. Cheap
 Edition. Crown 8vo, 2s.

BINDLOSS. In the Niger Country. By HAROLD BINDLOSS.
With 2 Maps. Demy 8vo, 12s. 6d.

BIRCH.

Examples of Stables, Hunting-Boxes, Kennels, Racing Establishments, &c. By JOHN BIRCH, Architect, Author of 'Country Architecture,' &c. With 30 Plates. Royal 8vo, 7s.

Examples of Labourers' Cottages, &c. With Plans for Improving the Dwellings of the Poor in Large Towns. With 34 Plates. Royal 8vo, 7s.

Picturesque Lodges. A Series of Designs for Gate Lodges, Park Entrances, Keepers', Gardeners', Bailiffs', Grooms', Upper and Under Servants' Lodges, and other Rural Residences. With 16 Plates. 4to, 12s. 6d.

BLACKIE.

The Wisdom of Goethe. By JOHN STUART BLACKIE, Emeritus Professor of Greek in the University of Edinburgh. Fcap. 8vo. Cloth, extra gilt, 6s.

John Stuart Blackie: A Biography. By ANNA M. STODDART. With 3 Plates. Third Edition. 2 vols. demy 8vo, 21s.
POPULAR EDITION. With Portrait. Crown 8vo 6s.

BLACKMORE.

The Maid of Sker. By R. D. BLACKMORE, Author of 'Lorna Doone,' &c. New Edition. Crown 8vo, 6s. Cheaper Edition. Crown 8vo, 3s. 6d.

Dariel: A Romance of Surrey. With 14 Illustrations by Chris. Hammond. Crown 8vo. 6s.

BLACKWOOD.

Annals of a Publishing House. William Blackwood and his Sons; Their Magazine and Friends. By Mrs OLIPHANT. With Four Portraits. Third Edition. Demy 8vo. Vols. I. and II. £2, 2s.

—— Vol. III. John Blackwood. By his Daughter, Mrs GERALD PORTER. With 2 Portraits and View of Strathtyrum. Demy 8vo, 21s.

Blackwood's Magazine, from Commencement in 1817 to November 1899. Nos. 1 to 1009, forming 166 Volumes.

Index to Blackwood's Magazine. Vols. 1 to 50. 8vo, 15s.

Tales from Blackwood. First Series. Price One Shilling each, in Paper Cover. Sold separately at all Railway Bookstalls.
They may also be had bound in 12 vols., cloth, 18s. Half calf, richly gilt, 30s. Or the 12 vols. in 6, roxburghe, 21s. Half red morocco, 28s.

Tales from Blackwood. Second Series. Complete in Twenty-four Shilling Parts. Handsomely bound in 12 vols., cloth, 30s. In leather back, roxburghe style, 37s. 6d. Half calf, gilt, 52s. 6d. Half morocco, 55s.

Tales from Blackwood. Third Series. Complete in Twelve Shilling Parts. Handsomely bound in 6 vols., cloth, 15s.; and in 12 vols. cloth, 18s. The 6 vols. in roxburghe, 21s. Half calf, 25s. Half morocco, 28s.

Travel, Adventure, and Sport. From 'Blackwood's Magazine.' Uniform with 'Tales from Blackwood.' In Twelve Parts, each price 1s. Handsomely bound in 6 vols., cloth, 15s. And in half calf, 25s.

New Educational Series. *See separate Educational Catalogue.*

BLACKWOOD.

New Uniform Series of Novels (Copyright).

Crown 8vo, cloth. Price 3s. 6d. each. Now ready:—

THE MAID OF SKER. By R. D. Blackmore.
WENDERHOLME. By P. G. Hamerton.
THE STORY OF MARGRÉDEL. By D. Storrar Meldrum.
MISS MARJORIBANKS. By Mrs Oliphant.
THE PERPETUAL CURATE, and THE RECTOR. By the Same.
SALEM CHAPEL, and THE DOCTOR'S FAMILY. By the Same.
A SENSITIVE PLANT. By E. D. Gerard.
LADY LEE'S WIDOWHOOD. By General Sir E. B. Hamley.
KATIE STEWART, and other Stories. By Mrs Oliphant.
VALENTINE AND HIS BROTHER. By the Same.
SONS AND DAUGHTERS. By the Same.

MARMORNE. By P. G. Hamerton.
REATA. By E. D. Gerard.
BEGGAR MY NEIGHBOUR. By the Same.
THE WATERS OF HERCULES. By the Same.
FAIR TO SEE. By L. W. M. Lockhart.
MINE IS THINE. By the Same.
DOUBLES AND QUITS. By the Same.
ALTIORA PETO. By Laurence Oliphant.
PICCADILLY. By the Same. With Illustrations.
LADY BABY. By D. Gerard.
THE BLACKSMITH OF VOE. By Paul Cushing.
MY TRIVIAL LIFE AND MISFORTUNE. By A Plain Woman.
POOR NELLIE. By the Same.

Standard Novels. Uniform in size and binding. Each complete in one Volume.

FLORIN SERIES, Illustrated Boards. Bound in Cloth, 2s. 6d.

TOM CRINGLE'S LOG. By Michael Scott.
THE CRUISE OF THE MIDGE. By the Same.
CYRIL THORNTON. By Captain Hamilton.
ANNALS OF THE PARISH. By John Galt.
THE PROVOST, &c. By the Same.
SIR ANDREW WYLIE. By the Same.
THE ENTAIL. By the Same.
MISS MOLLY. By Beatrice May Butt.
REGINALD DALTON. By J. G. Lockhart.

PEN OWEN. By Dean Hook.
ADAM BLAIR. By J. G. Lockhart.
LADY LEE'S WIDOWHOOD. By General Sir E. B. Hamley.
SALEM CHAPEL. By Mrs Oliphant.
THE PERPETUAL CURATE. By the Same.
MISS MARJORIBANKS. By the Same.
JOHN: A Love Story. By the Same.

SHILLING SERIES, Illustrated Cover. Bound in Cloth, 1s. 6d.

THE RECTOR, and THE DOCTOR'S FAMILY. By Mrs Oliphant.
THE LIFE OF MANSIE WAUCH. By D. M. Moir.
PENINSULAR SCENES AND SKETCHES. By F. Hardman.

SIR FRIZZLE PUMPKIN, NIGHTS AT MESS, &c.
THE SUBALTERN.
LIFE IN THE FAR WEST. By G. F. Ruxton.
VALERIUS: A Roman Story. By J. G. Lockhart.

BON GAULTIER'S BOOK OF BALLADS. Fifteenth Edition. With Illustrations by Doyle, Leech, and Crowquill. Fcap. 8vo, 5s.

BOWHILL. Questions and Answers in the Theory and Practice of Military Topography. By Major J. H. BOWHILL. Crown 8vo, 4s. 6d. net. Portfolio containing 34 working plans and diagrams, 3s. 6d. net.

BRADDON. Thirty Years of Shikar. By Sir EDWARD BRADDON, K.C.M.G. With Illustrations by G. D. Giles, and Map of Oudh Forest Tracts and Nepal Terai. Demy 8vo, 18s.

BROWN. The Forester: A Practical Treatise on the Planting and Tending of Forest-trees and the General Management of Woodlands. By JAMES BROWN, LL.D. Sixth Edition, Enlarged. Edited by JOHN NISBET, D.Œc., Author of 'British Forest Trees,' &c. In 2 vols. royal 8vo, with 350 Illustrations, 42s. net.

BROWN. A Manual of Botany, Anatomical and Physiological. For the Use of Students. By ROBERT BROWN, M.A., Ph.D. Crown 8vo, with numerous Illustrations, 12s. 6d.

BRUCE.

In Clover and Heather. Poems by WALLACE BRUCE. New and Enlarged Edition. Crown 8vo, 3s. 6d.
A limited number of Copies of the First Edition, on large hand-made paper, 12s. 6d.

Here's a Hand. Addresses and Poems. Crown 8vo, 5s. Large Paper Edition, limited to 100 copies, price 21s.

BUCHAN. Introductory Text-Book of Meteorology. By ALEX-
ANDER BUCHAN, LL.D., F.R.S.E., Secretary of the Scottish Meteorological
Society, &c. New Edition. Crown 8vo, with Coloured Charts and Engravings.
[*In preparation.*

BURBIDGE.
Domestic Floriculture, Window Gardening, and Floral Decora-
tions. Being Practical Directions for the Propagation, Culture, and Arrangement
of Plants and Flowers as Domestic Ornaments. By F. W. BURBIDGE. Second
Edition. Crown 8vo, with numerous Illustrations, 7s. 6d.
Cultivated Plants : Their Propagation and Improvement.
Including Natural and Artificial Hybridisation, Raising from Seed Cuttings,
and Layers, Grafting and Budding, as applied to the Families and Genera in
Cultivation. Crown 8vo, with numerous Illustrations, 12s. 6d.

BURKE. The Flowering of the Almond Tree, and other Poems.
By CHRISTIAN BURKE. Pott 4to, 5s.

BURROWS.
Commentaries on the History of England, from the Earliest
Times to 1865. By MONTAGU BURROWS, Chichele Professor of Modern History
in the University of Oxford ; Captain R.N. ; F.S.A., &c. ; "Officier de l'In-
struction Publique," France. Crown 8vo. 7s. 6d.
The History of the Foreign Policy of Great Britain. New
Edition, revised. Crown 8vo, 6s.

BURTON.
The History of Scotland : From Agricola's Invasion to the
Extinction of the last Jacobite Insurrection. By JOHN HILL BURTON, D.C.L.,
Historiographer-Royal for Scotland. Cheaper Edition. In 8 vols. Crown 8vo,
3s. 6d. each.
History of the British Empire during the Reign of Queen
Anne. In 3 vols. 8vo. 36s.
The Scot Abroad. Cheap Edition. Crown 8vo, 3s. 6d.
The Book-Hunter. Cheap Edition. Crown 8vo, 3s. 6d.

BUTE. The Altus of St Columba. With a Prose Paraphrase
and Notes. By JOHN, MARQUESS OF BUTE, K.T. In paper cover, 2s. 6d.

BUTE, MACPHAIL, AND LONSDALE. The Arms of the
Royal and Parliamentary Burghs of Scotland. By JOHN, MARQUESS OF BUTE,
K.T., J. R. N. MACPHAIL, and H. W. LONSDALE. With 131 Engravings on
wood, and 11 other Illustrations. Crown 4to. £2, 2s. net.

BUTLER.
The Ancient Church and Parish of Abernethy, Perthshire.
An Historical Study. By Rev. D. BUTLER, M.A., Minister of the Parish. With
13 Collotype Plates and a Map. Crown 4to, 25s. net.
John Wesley and George Whitefield in Scotland ; or, The
Influence of the Oxford Methodists on Scottish Religion. Crown 8vo, 5s.
Henry Scougal and the Oxford Methodists ; or, The Influence
of a Religious Teacher of the Scottish Church. Fcap. 8vo, 3s. 6d.

BUTT.
Theatricals : An Interlude. By BEATRICE MAY BUTT. Crown
8vo, 6s.
Miss Molly. Cheap Edition, 2s.
Eugenie. Crown 8vo, 6s. 6d.
Elizabeth, and other Sketches. Crown 8vo, 6s.
Delicia. New Edition. Crown 8vo, 2s. 6d.

CADELL. Sir John Cope and the Rebellion of 1745. By the
late General Sir ROBERT CADELL, K.C.B., Royal (Madras) Artillery. With 2
Maps. Crown 4to, 12s. 6d. net.

CAFFYN. Seventy-One not Out, the Reminiscences of William
Caffyn, Member of the All England and United Elevens, of the Surrey County
Eleven, of the Anglo-American Team of 1859, and of the Anglo-Australian Teams
of 1861 and 1863. Edited by "Mid-On." With numerous Illustrations.
Crown 8vo, 6s.

CAIRD. Sermons. By JOHN CAIRD, D.D., Principal of the
University of Glasgow. Seventeenth Thousand. Fcap. 8vo, 5s.

CALDWELL. Schopenhauer's System in its Philosophical Significance (the Shaw Fellowship Lectures, 1893). By WILLIAM CALDWELL, M.A.,
D.Sc., Professor of Moral and Social Philosophy, Northwestern University,
U.S.A.; formerly Assistant to the Professor of Logic and Metaphysics, Edin.,
and Examiner in Philosophy in the University of St Andrews. Demy 8vo,
10s. 6d. net.

CALLWELL. The Effect of Maritime Command on Land
Campaigns since Waterloo. By Major C. E. CALLWELL, R.A. With Plans.
Post 8vo, 6s. net.

CAMPBELL. Balmerino and its Abbey. A Parish History.
With Notices of the Adjacent District. By JAMES CAMPBELL, D.D., F.S.A. Scot.,
Minister of Balmerino; Author of 'A History of the Celtic Church in Scotland.'
A New Edition. With an Appendix of Illustrative Documents, a Map of the
Parish, and upwards of 40 Illustrations. In 1 vol. demy 8vo.   [*In the press.*

CAPES.
Our Lady of Darkness. By BERNARD CAPES. Crown 8vo, 6s.
The Adventures of the Comte de la Muette during the Reign
of Terror. Crown 8vo, 6s.

CHARTERIS. Canonicity; or, Early Testimonies to the Exist-
ence and Use of the Books of the New Testament. Based on Kirchhoffer's
'Quellensammlung.' Edited by A. H. CHARTERIS, D.D., Professor of Biblical
Criticism in the University of Edinburgh. 8vo, 18s.

CHENNELLS. Recollections of an Egyptian Princess. By
her English Governess (Miss E. CHENNELLS). Being a Record of Five Years'
Residence at the Court of Ismael Pasha, Khédive. Second Edition. With Three
Portraits. Post 8vo, 7s. 6d.

CHRISTISON. Early Fortifications in Scotland: Motes, Camps,
and Forts. Being the Rhind Lectures in Archæology for 1894. By DAVID
CHRISTISON, M.D., F.R.C.P.E., Secretary of the Society of Antiquaries of Scotland. With 379 Plans and Illustrations and 3 Maps. Fcap 4to, 21s. net.

CHURCH AND FAITH. Being Essays on the Teaching of the
Church of England. By Dr WACE, Dean FARRAR, Dr WRIGHT, Rev. R. E.
BARTLETT, Principal DRURY, Canon MEYRICK, Professor MOULE, Chancellor
SMITH, MONTAGUE BARLOW, Sir RICHARD TEMPLE, Bart., E. H. BLAKENEY, and
J. T. TOMLINSON. With Introduction by the LORD BISHOP OF HEREFORD. Post
8vo, 7s. 6d. net.

CHURCH SERVICE SOCIETY.
A Book of Common Order: being Forms of Worship issued
by the Church Service Society. Seventh Edition, carefully revised. In 1 vol.
crown 8vo, cloth, 3s. 6d.; French morocco, 5s. Also in 2 vols. crown 8vo,
cloth, 4s.; French morocco, 6s. 6d.
Daily Offices for Morning and Evening Prayer throughout
the Week. Crown 8vo, 3s. 6d.
Order of Divine Service for Children. Issued by the Church
Service Society. With Scottish Hymnal. Cloth, 3d.

CLOUSTON. The Lunatic at Large. By J. STORER CLOUSTON.
Crown 8vo, 6s.

COCHRAN. A Handy Text-Book of Military Law. Compiled
chiefly to assist Officers preparing for Examination; also for all Officers of the
Regular and Auxiliary Forces. Comprising also a Synopsis of part of the Army
Act. By Major F. COCHRAN, Hampshire Regiment Garrison Instructor, North
British District. Crown 8vo, 7s. 6d.

COLLINS. The Don and the Undergraduate. A Tale of St
Hilary's College, Oxford. By W. E. W. COLLINS. Crown 8vo, 6s.

COLQUHOUN. The Moor and the Loch. Containing Minute
Instructions in all Highland Sports, with Wanderings over Crag and Corrie,
Flood and Fell. By JOHN COLQUHOUN. Cheap Edition. With Illustrations.
Demy 8vo, 10s. 6d.

CONDER.

The Bible and the East. By Lieut.-Col. C. R. CONDER,
R.E., LL.D., D.C.L., M.R.A.S., Author of 'Tent Work in Palestine,' &c. With
Illustrations and a Map. Crown 8vo, 5s.

The Hittites and their Language. With Illustrations and
Map. Post 8vo, 7s. 6d.

The Hebrew Tragedy. In 1 vol. fcap. 8vo.   [*In the press.*]

CORNFORD. R. L. Stevenson. "Modern English Writers."
By L. COPE CORNFORD. Crown 8vo, 2s. 6d.

COUNTY HISTORIES OF SCOTLAND. In demy 8vo volumes of about 350 pp. each. With Maps. Price 7s. 6d. net.

Fife and Kinross. By ÆNEAS J. G. MACKAY, LL.D., Sheriff
of these Counties.

Dumfries and Galloway. By Sir HERBERT MAXWELL, Bart.
M.P.

Moray and Nairn. By CHARLES RAMPINI, LL.D., Sheriff-
Substitute of these Counties.

Inverness. By J. CAMERON LEES, D.D.

Roxburgh, Selkirk, and Peebles. By Sir GEORGE DOUGLAS,
Bart.

Prehistoric Scotland and its Place in European Civilisation.
Being a General Introduction to the "County Histories of Scotland." By
ROBERT MUNRO, M.A., M.D., Author of 'Prehistoric Problems,' 'The Lake-
Dwellings of Europe,' &c. With numerous Illustrations.

Aberdeen and Banff. By WILLIAM WATT, Editor of Aberdeen
'Daily Free Press.'   [*In the press.*]

CRAWFORD. Saracinesca. By F. MARION CRAWFORD, Author
of 'Mr Isaacs,' &c., &c. Cheap Edition. Crown 8vo, 3s. 6d.

CRAWFORD.

The Doctrine of Holy Scripture respecting the Atonement.
By the late THOMAS J. CRAWFORD, D.D., Professor of Divinity in the University
of Edinburgh. Fifth Edition. 8vo, 12s.

The Fatherhood of God, Considered in its General and Special
Aspects. Third Edition, Revised and Enlarged. 8vo, 9s.

The Preaching of the Cross, and other Sermons. 8vo, 7s. 6d.

The Mysteries of Christianity. Crown 8vo, 7s. 6d.

CROSS. Impressions of Dante, and of the New World; with a
Few Words on Bimetallism. By J. W. CROSS, Editor of 'George Eliot's Life, as
related in her Letters and Journals.' Post 8vo, 6s.

CUMBERLAND. Sport on the Pamirs and Turkistan Steppes.
By Major C. S. CUMBERLAND. With Map and Frontispiece. Demy 8vo, 10s. 6d.

CURSE OF INTELLECT. Third Edition. Fcap. 8vo, 2s. 6d. net.

CUSHING. The Blacksmith of Voe. By PAUL CUSHING, Author
of 'The Bull i' th' Thorn,' 'Cut with his own Diamond.' Cheap Edition. Crown
8vo, 3s. 6d.

DARBISHIRE. Physical Maps for the use of History Students.
By BERNHARD V. DARBISHIRE, M.A., Trinity College, Oxford. Two Series:—
Ancient History (9 maps); Modern History (12 maps).   [*In the press.*]

DAVIES. Norfolk Broads and Rivers; or, The Waterways, Lagoons, and Decoys of East Anglia. By G. CHRISTOPHER DAVIES. Illustrated with Seven full-page Plates. New and Cheaper Edition. Crown 8vo, 6s.

DESCARTES. The Method, Meditations, and Principles of Philo-sophy of Descartes. Translated from the Original French and Latin. With a New Introductory Essay, Historical and Critical, on the Cartesian Philosophy. By Professor VEITCH, LL.D., Glasgow University. Eleventh Edition. 6s. 6d.

DOUGLAS.

The Ethics of John Stuart Mill. By CHARLES DOUGLAS, M.A., D.Sc., M.P., late Lecturer in Moral Philosophy, and Assistant to the Professor of Moral Philosophy in the University of Edinburgh. Post 8vo, 6s. net.

John Stuart Mill: A Study of his Philosophy. Crown 8vo, 4s. 6d. net.

DOUGLAS. Chinese Stories. By ROBERT K. DOUGLAS. With numerous Illustrations by Parkinson, Forestier, and others. New and Cheaper Edition. Small demy 8vo, 5s.

DOUGLAS. Iras: A Mystery. By THEO. DOUGLAS, Author of 'A Bride Elect.' Cheaper Edition, in Paper Cover specially designed by Womrath. Crown 8vo, 1s. 6d.

DZIEWICKI. Entombed in Flesh. By M. H. DZIEWICKI. Crown 8vo, 3s. 6d.

ELIOT.

George Eliot's Life, Related in Her Letters and Journals. Arranged and Edited by her husband, J. W. CROSS. With Portrait and other Illustrations. Third Edition. 3 vols. post 8vo, 42s.

George Eliot's Life. With Portrait and other Illustrations. New Edition, in one volume. Crown 8vo, 7s. 6d.

Works of George Eliot (Standard Edition). 21 volumes, crown 8vo. In buckram cloth, gilt top, 2s. 6d. per vol.; or in roxburghe binding, 3s. 6d. per vol.
ADAM BEDE. 2 vols.—THE MILL ON THE FLOSS. 2 vols.—FELIX HOLT, THE RADICAL. 2 vols.—ROMOLA. 2 vols.—SCENES OF CLERICAL LIFE. 2 vols.—MIDDLEMARCH. 3 vols.—DANIEL DERONDA. 3 vols.—SILAS MARNER. 1 vol.—JUBAL. 1 vol.—THE SPANISH GIPSY. 1 vol.—ESSAYS. 1 vol.—THEOPHRASTUS SUCH. 1 vol.

Life and Works of George Eliot (Cabinet Edition). 24 volumes, crown 8vo, price £6. Also to be had handsomely bound in half and full calf. The Volumes are sold separately, bound in cloth, price 5s. each.

Novels by George Eliot. New Cheap Edition. Printed on fine laid paper, and uniformly bound.
Adam Bede. 3s. 6d.—The Mill on the Floss. 3s. 6d.—Scenes of Clerical Life. 3s.—Silas Marner: the Weaver of Raveloe. 2s. 6d.—Felix Holt, the Radical. 3s. 6d.—Romola. 3s. 6d.—Middlemarch. 7s. 6d.—Daniel Deronda. 7s. 6d.

Essays. New Edition. Crown 8vo, 5s.

Impressions of Theophrastus Such. New Edition. Crown 8vo, 5s.

The Spanish Gypsy. New Edition. Crown 8vo, 5s.

The Legend of Jubal, and other Poems, Old and New. New Edition. Crown 8vo, 5s.

Silas Marner. New Edition, with Illustrations by Reginald Birch. Crown 8vo, 6s.

Scenes of Clerical Life. Pocket Edition, 3 vols. pott 8vo, 1s. net each; bound in leather, 1s. 6d. net each. Illustrated Edition, with 20 Illustrations by H. R. Millar, crown 8vo, 2s. 6d. Popular Edition, royal 8vo, n paper cover, price 6d.

ELIOT.
   Adam Bede. Pocket Edition. In 3 vols. pott 8vo, 3s. net;
bound in leather, 4s. 6d. net. Popular Edition, royal 8vo, in paper cover, price 6d.

   Wise, Witty, and Tender Sayings, in Prose and Verse. Selected
from the Works of GEORGE ELIOT. New Edition. Fcap. 8vo, 3s. 6d.

ELTON. The Augustan Ages. "Periods of European Litera-
ture." By OLIVER ELTON, B.A., Lecturer in English Literature, Owen's College,
Manchester. Crown 8vo, 5s. net.

ESSAYS ON SOCIAL SUBJECTS. Originally published in
the 'Saturday Review.' New Edition. First and Second Series. 2 vols. crown
8vo, 6s. each.

FAHIE. A History of Wireless Telegraphy. 1838-1899. By
J. J. FAHIE, Member of the Institution of Electrical Engineers, London, and of
the Société Internationale des Electriciens, Paris; Author of 'A History of
Electric Telegraphy to the Year 1837,' &c. With Illustrations. Crown 8vo, 6s.

FAITHS OF THE WORLD, The. A Concise History of the
Great Religious Systems of the World. By various Authors. Crown 8vo, 5s.

FALKNER. The Lost Stradivarius. By J. MEADE FALKNER,
Author of 'Moonfleet,' &c. Second Edition. Crown 8vo, 6s.

FERGUSON. Sir Samuel Ferguson in the Ireland of his Day.
By LADY FERGUSON, Author of 'The Irish before the Conquest,' 'Life of William
Reeves, D.D., Lord Bishop of Down, Connor, and Drumore,' &c., &c. With
Two Portraits. 2 vols. post 8vo, 21s.

FERGUSSON. Scots Poems. By ROBERT FERGUSSON. With
Photogravure Portrait. Pott 8vo, gilt top, bound in cloth, 1s. net.

FERRIER.
   Philosophical Works of the late James F. Ferrier, B.A.
Oxon., Professor of Moral Philosophy and Political Economy, St Andrews.
New Edition. Edited by Sir ALEXANDER GRANT, Bart., D.C.L., and Professor
LUSHINGTON. 3 vols. crown 8vo, 34s. 6d.

   Institutes of Metaphysic. Third Edition. 10s. 6d.

   Lectures on the Early Greek Philosophy. 4th Edition. 10s. 6d.

   Philosophical Remains, including the Lectures on Early
Greek Philosophy. New Edition. 2 vols. 24s.

FLINT.
   Historical Philosophy in France and French Belgium and
Switzerland. By ROBERT FLINT, Corresponding Member of the Institute of
France, Hon. Member of the Royal Society of Palermo, Professor in the Univer-
sity of Edinburgh, &c. 8vo, 21s.

   Agnosticism. Being the Croall Lecture for 1887-88.
[In the press.

   Theism. Being the Baird Lecture for 1876. Ninth Edition,
Revised. Crown 8vo, 7s. 6d.

   Anti-Theistic Theories. Being the Baird Lecture for 1877.
Fifth Edition. Crown 8vo, 10s. 6d.

   Sermons and Addresses. Demy 8vo, 7s. 6d.

FORD.
   'Postle Farm. By GEORGE FORD. Crown 8vo, 6s.

   The Larramys. Second Edition. Crown 8vo, 6s.

FOREIGN CLASSICS FOR ENGLISH READERS. Edited
by Mrs OLIPHANT. Price 1s. each. *For List of Volumes, see page 2.*

FOSTER. The Fallen City, and other Poems. By WILL FOSTER.
Crown 8vo, 6s.

FRANCILLON. Gods and Heroes; or, The Kingdom of Jupiter.
By R. E. FRANCILLON. With 8 Illustrations. Crown 8vo, 5s.

FRANCIS. Among the Untrodden Ways. By M. E. FRANCIS
(Mrs Francis Blundell), Author of 'In a North Country Village,' 'A Daughter of
the Soil.' 'Frieze and Fustian,' &c. Crown 8vo, 3s. 6d.

FRASER. Philosophy of Theism. Being the Gifford Lectures
delivered before the University of Edinburgh in 1894-96. By ALEXANDER
CAMPBELL FRASER, D.C.L. Oxford ; Emeritus Professor of Logic and Metaphysics in the University of Edinburgh. Second Edition, Revised. Post 8vo,
6s. 6d. net.

GALT. Novels by JOHN GALT. With General Introduction and
Prefatory Notes by S. R. CROCKETT. The Text Revised and Edited by D.
STORRAR MELDRUM, Author of 'The Story of Margrédel.' With Photogravure
Illustrations from Drawings by John Wallace. Fcap. 8vo, 3s. net each vol.
ANNALS OF THE PARISH, and THE AYRSHIRE LEGATEES. 2 vols.—SIR ANDREW
WYLIE. 2 vols.—THE ENTAIL ; or, The Lairds of Grippy. 2 vols.—THE PRO-
VOST, and THE LAST OF THE LAIRDS. 2 vols.
See also STANDARD NOVELS, *p.* 6.

GENERAL ASSEMBLY OF THE CHURCH OF SCOTLAND.
Scottish Hymnal, With Appendix Incorporated. Published
for use in Churches by Authority of the General Assembly. 1. Large type,
cloth, red edges, 2s. 6d.; French morocco, 4s. 2. Bourgeois type, limp cloth, 1s.;
French morocco, 2s. 3. Nonpareil type, cloth, red edges, 6d.; French morocco,
1s. 4d. 4. Paper covers, 3d. 5. Sunday-School Edition, paper covers, 1d.;
cloth, 2d. No. 1, bound with the Psalms and Paraphrases, French morocco, 8s.
No. 2, bound with the Psalms and Paraphrases, cloth, 2s.; French morocco, 3s.

Prayers for Social and Family Worship. Prepared by a
Special Committee of the General Assembly of the Church of Scotland. Entirely
New Edition, Revised and Enlarged. Fcap. 8vo, red edges, 2s.

'Prayers for Family Worship. A Selection of Four Weeks'
Prayers. New Edition. Authorised by the General Assembly of the Church of
Scotland. Fcap. 8vo, red edges, 1s. 6d.

One Hundred Prayers. Prepared by the Committee on Aids
to Devotion. 16mo, cloth limp, 6d.

Morning and Evening Prayers for Affixing to Bibles. Prepared
by the Committee on Aids to Devotion. 1d. for 6, or 1s. per 100.

Prayers for Soldiers and Sailors. Prepared by the Committee
on Aids to Devotion. Thirtieth Thousand. 16mo, cloth limp. 2d. net.

GERARD.
Reata : What's in a Name. By E. D. GERARD. Cheap
Edition. Crown 8vo, 3s. 6d.

Beggar my Neighbour. Cheap Edition. Crown 8vo, 3s. 6d.

The Waters of Hercules. Cheap Edition. Crown 8vo, 3s. 6d.

A Sensitive Plant. Crown 8vo, 3s. 6d.

GERARD.
A Foreigner. An Anglo-German Study. By E. GERARD.
Crown 8vo, 6s.

The Land beyond the Forest. Facts, Figures, and Fancies
from Transylvania. With Maps and Illustrations 2 vols. post 8vo, 25s.

Bis : Some Tales Retold. Crown 8vo, 6s.

A Secret Mission. 2 vols. crown 8vo, 17s.

An Electric Shock, and other Stories. Crown 8vo, 6s.

GERARD.
One Year. By DOROTHEA GERARD. Crown 8vo, 6s.

The Impediment. Crown 8vo, 6s.

A Forgotten Sin. Crown 8vo, 6s.

A Spotless Reputation. Third Edition. Crown 8vo, 6s.

GERARD.
 The Wrong Man. Second Edition. Crown 8vo, 6s.
 Lady Baby. Cheap Edition. Crown 8vo, 3s. 6d.
 Recha. Second Edition. Crown 8vo, 6s.
 The Rich Miss Riddell. Second Edition. Crown 8vo, 6s.

GERARD. Stonyhurst Latin Grammar. By Rev. JOHN GERARD.
 Second Edition. Fcap. 8vo, 3s.

GOODALL. Association Football. By JOHN GOODALL. Edited
 by S. ARCHIBALD DE BEAR. With Diagrams. Fcap. 8vo, 1s.

GORDON CUMMING.
 At Home in Fiji. By C. F. GORDON CUMMING. Fourth
 Edition, post 8vo. With Illustrations and Map. 7s. 6d.
 A Lady's Cruise in a French Man-of-War. New and Cheaper
 Edition. 8vo. With Illustrations and Map. 12s. 6d.
 Fire-Fountains. The Kingdom of Hawaii: Its Volcanoes,
 and the History of its Missions. With Map and Illustrations. 2 vols. 8vo, 25s.
 Wanderings in China. New and Cheaper Edition. 8vo, with
 Illustrations, 10s.
 Granite Crags: The Yō-semité Region of California. Illus-
 trated with 8 Engravings. New and Cheaper Edition. 8vo, 8s. 6d.

GRAHAM. Manual of the Elections (Scot.) (Corrupt and Illegal
 Practices) Act, 1890. With Analysis, Relative Act of Sederunt, Appendix con-
 taining the Corrupt Practices Acts of 1883 and 1885, and Copious Index. By J.
 EDWARD GRAHAM, Advocate. 8vo, 4s. 6d.

GRAND.
 A Domestic Experiment. By SARAH GRAND, Author of
 'The Heavenly Twins,' 'Ideals: A Study from Life.' Crown 8vo, 6s.
 Singularly Deluded. Crown 8vo, 6s.

GRANT. Bush-Life in Queensland. By A. C. GRANT. New
 Edition. Crown 8vo, 6s.

GRAY. Old Creeds and New Beliefs. By W. H. GRAY, D.D.,
 Edinburgh. Crown 8vo, 5s.

GREGG. The Decian Persecution. Being the Hulsean Prize
 Essay for 1896. By JOHN A. F. GREGG, B.A., late Scholar of Christ's College,
 Cambridge. Crown 8vo, 6s.

GRIER.
 In Furthest Ind. The Narrative of Mr EDWARD CARLYON of
 Ellswether, in the County of Northampton, and late of the Honourable East India
 Company's Service, Gentleman. Wrote by his own hand in the year of grace 1697.
 Edited, with a few Explanatory Notes, by SYDNEY C. GRIER. Post 8vo, 6s.
 His Excellency's English Governess. Second Edition. Crown
 8vo, 6s.
 An Uncrowned King: A Romance of High Politics. Second
 Edition. Crown 8vo, 6s.
 Peace with Honour. Second Edition. Crown 8vo, 6s.
 A Crowned Queen: The Romance of a Minister of State.
 Crown 8vo, 6s.
 Like Another Helen. The History of the Cruel Misfortunes
 and Undeserved Distresses of a Young Lady of Virtue and Sensibility, Resident
 in Bengall during the Years 1755-57. Edited by SYDNEY C. GRIER. Second
 Edition. Crown 8vo, 6s.

GROOT.
 A Lotus Flower. By J. MORGAN-DE-GROOT. Crown 8vo, 6s.
 Even If. Crown 8vo, 6s.

HAGGARD. **Under Crescent and Star.** By Lieut.-Col. ANDREW
HAGGARD, D.S.O., Author of 'Dodo and I,' 'Tempest Torn,' &c. With a
Portrait. Second Edition. Crown 8vo, 6s.

HALIBURTON. **Horace in Homespun.** By HUGH HALIBURTON.
A New Edition, containing additional Poems. With Illustrations by A. S. Boyd.
In 1 vol. post 8vo. [*In the press.*

HAMERTON.

Wenderholme: A Story of Lancashire and Yorkshire Life.
By P. G. HAMERTON, Author of 'A Painter's Camp.' New Edition. Crown
8vo, 3s. 6d.

Marmorne. **New Edition.** **Crown 8vo, 3s. 6d.**

HAMILTON.

Lectures on Metaphysics. By Sir WILLIAM HAMILTON,
Bart., Professor of Logic and Metaphysics in the University of Edinburgh.
Edited by the Rev. H. L. MANSEL, B.D., LL.D., Dean of St Paul's; and JOHN
VEITCH, M.A., LL.D., Professor of Logic and Rhetoric, Glasgow. Seventh
Edition. 2 vols. 8vo, 24s.

Lectures on Logic. **Edited by the SAME.** **Third Edition,**
Revised. 2 vols., 24s.

Discussions on Philosophy and Literature, Education and
University Reform. Third Edition. 8vo, 21s.

Memoir of Sir William Hamilton, Bart., Professor of Logic
and Metaphysics in the University of Edinburgh. By Professor VEITCH, of the
University of Glasgow. 8vo, with Portrait, 18s.

Sir William Hamilton: The Man and his Philosophy. Two
Lectures delivered before the Edinburgh Philosophical Institution, January and
February 1883. By Professor VEITCH. Crown 8vo, 2s.

HAMLEY.

The Operations of War Explained and Illustrated. By
General Sir EDWARD BRUCE HAMLEY, K.C.B., K.C.M.G. Fifth Edition, Revised
throughout. 4to, with numerous Illustrations, 30s.

National Defence; Articles and Speeches. Post 8vo, 6s.

Shakespeare's Funeral, and other Papers. Post 8vo, 7s. 6d.

Thomas Carlyle: An Essay. **Second Edition.** **Crown 8vo,**
2s. 6d.

On Outposts. **Second Edition.** **8vo, 2s.**

Wellington's Career; A Military and Political Summary.
Crown 8vo, 2s.

Lady Lee's Widowhood. **New Edition.** **Crown 8vo, 3s. 6d.**
Cheaper Edition, 2s. 6d.

Our Poor Relations. **A Philozoic Essay.** With Illustrations,
chiefly by Ernest Griset. Crown 8vo, cloth gilt, 3s. 6d.

The Life of General Sir Edward Bruce Hamley, K.C.B.,
K.C.M.G. By ALEXANDER INNES SHAND. With two Photogravure Portraits and
other Illustrations. Cheaper Edition. With a Statement by Mr EDWARD
HAMLEY. 2 vols. demy 8vo, 10s. 6d.

HANNAY. **The Later Renaissance.** 'Periods of European
Literature.' By DAVID HANNAY. Crown 8vo, 5s. net.

HARE. **Down the Village Street: Scenes in a West Country**
Hamlet. By CHRISTOPHER HARE. Second Edition. Crown 8vo, 6s.

HARRADEN.

The Fowler. By BEATRICE HARRADEN, Author of 'Ships
that Pass in the Night.' Third Edition. Crown 8vo, 6s.

In Varying Moods: Short Stories. Thirteenth Edition.
Crown 8vo, 3s. 6d.

HARRADEN.
> **Hilda Strafford, and The Remittance Man.** Two Californian Stories. Eleventh Edition. Crown 8vo, 3s. 6d.
>
> **Untold Tales of the Past.** With 40 Illustrations by H. R. Millar. Square crown 8vo, gilt top, 6s.

HARRIS.
> **From Batum to Baghdad,** *viâ* **Tiflis, Tabriz, and Persian** Kurdistan. By WALTER B. HARRIS, F.R.G.S., Author of 'The Land of an African Sultan; Travels in Morocco,' &c. With numerous Illustrations and 2 Maps. Demy 8vo, 12s.
>
> **Tafilet.** The Narrative of a Journey of Exploration to the Atlas Mountains and the Oases of the North-West Sahara. With Illustrations by Maurice Romberg from Sketches and Photographs by the Author, and Two Maps. Demy 8vo, 12s.
>
> **A Journey through the Yemen, and some General Remarks** upon that Country. With 3 Maps and numerous Illustrations by Forestier and Wallace from Sketches and Photographs taken by the Author. Demy 8vo, 16s.
>
> **Danovitch, and other Stories.** Crown 8vo, 6s.

HAY. **The Works of the Right Rev. Dr George Hay, Bishop of** Edinburgh. Edited under the Supervision of the Right Rev. Bishop STRAIN. With Memoir and Portrait of the Author. 5 vols. crown 8vo, bound in extra cloth, £1, 1s. The following Volumes may be had separately—viz. :
> The Devout Christian Instructed in the Law of Christ from the Written Word. 2 vols., 8s.—The Pious Christian Instructed in the Nature and Practice of the Principal Exercises of Piety. 1 vol., 3s.

HEMANS.
> **The Poetical Works of Mrs Hemans.** Copyright Edition. Royal 8vo, with Engravings, cloth, gilt edges, 7s. 6d.
>
> **Select Poems of Mrs Hemans.** Fcap., cloth, gilt edges, 3s.

HENDERSON. **The Young Estate Manager's Guide.** By RICHARD HENDERSON, Member (by Examination) of the Royal Agricultural Society of England, the Highland and Agricultural Society of Scotland, and the Surveyors' Institution. With an Introduction by R. Patrick Wright, F.R.S.E., Professor of Agriculture, Glasgow and West of Scotland Technical College. With Plans and Diagrams. Crown 8vo, 5s.

HERKLESS. **Cardinal Beaton : Priest and Politician.** By JOHN HERKLESS, Professor of Church History, St Andrews. With a Portrait. Post 8vo, 7s. 6d.

HEWISON. **The Isle of Bute in the Olden Time.** With Illustrations, Maps, and Plans. By JAMES KING HEWISON, M.A., F.S.A. (Scot.), Minister of Rothesay. Vol. I., Celtic Saints and Heroes. Crown 4to, 15s. net. Vol. II., The Royal Stewards and the Brandanes. Crown 4to, 15s. net.

HOME PRAYERS. **By Ministers of the Church of Scotland** and Members of the Church Service Society. Second Edition. Fcap. 8vo, 3s.

HORNBY. **Admiral of the Fleet Sir Geoffrey Phipps Hornby,** G.C.B. A Biography. By Mrs FRED. EGERTON. With Three Portraits. Demy 8vo, 16s.

HUEFFER. **The Cinque Ports : A History.** By F. MADOX HUEFFER. With Photogravure and other Illustrations by William Hyde. In 1 vol. royal 4to. *[In the press.*

HUTCHINSON. **Hints on the Game of Golf.** By HORACE G. HUTCHINSON. Ninth Edition, Enlarged. Fcap. 8vo, cloth, 1s.

HYSLOP. **The Elements of Ethics.** By JAMES H. HYSLOP, Ph.D., Instructor in Ethics, Columbia College, New York, Author of 'The Elements of Logic.' Post 8vo, 7s. 6d. net.

IDDESLEIGH. **Life, Letters, and Diaries of Sir Stafford North-** cote, First Earl of Iddesleigh. By ANDREW LANG. With Three Portraits and a View of Pynes. Third Edition. 2 vols. post 8vo, 31s. 6d.
> POPULAR EDITION.—With Portrait and View of Pynes. Post 8vo, 7s. 6d.

JEAN JAMBON. **Our Trip to Blunderland; or, Grand Ex-**
cursion to Blundertown and Back. By JEAN JAMBON. With Sixty Illustrations
designed by CHARLES DOYLE, engraved by DALZIEL. Fourth Thousand. Cloth,
gilt edges, 6s. 6d. Cheap Edition, cloth, 3s. 6d. Boards, 2s. 6d.

JEBB.

A Strange Career. The Life and Adventures of JOHN
GLADWYN JEBB. By his Widow. With an Introduction by H. RIDER HAGGARD,
and an Electrogravure Portrait of Mr Jebb. Third Edition. Demy 8vo, 10s. 6d.
CHEAP EDITION. With Illustrations by John Wallace. Crown 8vo, 3s. 6d.

Some Unconventional People. By Mrs GLADWYN JEBB,
Author of 'Life and Adventures of J. G. Jebb.' With Illustrations. Cheap
Edition. Paper covers, 1s.

JERNINGHAM.

Reminiscences of an Attaché. By HUBERT E. H. JERNINGHAM.
Second Edition. Crown 8vo, 5s

Diane de Breteuille. A Love Story. Crown 8vo, 2s. 6d.

JOHNSTON.

The Chemistry of Common Life. By Professor J. F. W.
JOHNSTON. New Edition, Revised. By ARTHUR HERBERT CHURCH, M.A. Oxon.;
Author of 'Food: its Sources, Constituents, and Uses,' &c. With Maps and 102
Engravings. Crown 8vo, 7s. 6d.

Elements of Agricultural Chemistry. An entirely New
Edition from the Edition by Sir CHARLES A. CAMERON, M.D., F.R.C.S.I., &c.
Revised and brought down to date by C. M. AIKMAN, M.A., B.Sc., F.R.S.E.,
Professor of Chemistry, Glasgow Veterinary College. 17th Edition. Crown 8vo,
6s. 6d.

Catechism of Agricultural Chemistry. An entirely New
Edition from the Edition by Sir CHARLES A. CAMERON. Revised and Enlarged
by C. M. AIKMAN, M.A., &c. 95th Thousand. With numerous Illustrations.
Crown 8vo, 1s.

JOHNSTON. **Agricultural Holdings (Scotland) Acts, 1883 and**
1889; and the Ground Game Act, 1880. With Notes, and Summary of Procedure,
&c. By CHRISTOPHER N. JOHNSTON, M.A., Advocate. Demy 8vo, 5s.

JOKAI. **Timar's Two Worlds.** By MAURUS JOKAI. **Authorised**
Translation by Mrs HEGAN KENNARD. Cheap Edition. Crown 8vo, 6s.

KEBBEL. **The Old and the New: English Country Life.** By
T. E. KEBBEL, M.A., Author of 'The Agricultural Labourers,' 'Essays in History
and Politics,' 'Life of Lord Beaconsfield.' Crown 8vo, 5s.

KENNEDY. **A Life on the Ocean Wave.** By Vice-Admiral Sir
WILLIAM KENNEDY, K.C.B., Author of 'Sport, Travel, and Adventure in New-
foundland and the West Indies.' With Illustrations from Sketches by the
Author. In 1 vol. demy 8vo. [*In the press.*

KERR. **St Andrews in 1645-46.** By D. R. KERR. **Crown**
8vo, 2s. 6d.

KINGLAKE.

History of the Invasion of the Crimea. By A. W. KINGLAKE.
Cabinet Edition, Revised. With an Index to the Complete Work. Illustrated
with Maps and Plans. Complete in 9 vols., crown 8vo, at 6s. each.

—— **Abridged Edition for Military Students.** **Revised by**
Lieut.-Col. Sir GEORGE SYDENHAM CLARKE, K.C.M.G., R.E. Demy 8vo, 15s. net.

———— Atlas to accompany above. Folio, 9s. net.

History of the Invasion of the Crimea. Demy 8vo. Vol. VI.
Winter Troubles. With a Map, 16s. Vols. VII. and VIII. From the Morrow of
Inkerman to the Death of Lord Raglan With an Index to the Whole Work.
With Maps and Plans. 28s

Eothen. **A New Edition, uniform with the Cabinet Edition**
of the 'History of the Invasion of the Crimea.' 6s.
CHEAPER EDITION. With Portrait and Biographical Sketch of the Author.
Crown 8vo, 3s. 6d. Popular Edition, in paper cover, 1s. net.

KIRBY. In Haunts of Wild Game: A Hunter-Naturalist's Wanderings from Kahlamba to Libombo. By FREDERICK VAUGHAN KIRBY, F.Z.S. (Maqaqamba). With numerous Illustrations by Charles Whymper, and a Map. Large demy 8vo, 25s.

KNEIPP. My Water-Cure. As Tested through more than Thirty Years, and Described for the Healing of Diseases and the Preservation of Health. By SEBASTIAN KNEIPP, Parish Priest of Wörishofen (Bavaria). With a Portrait and other Illustrations. Authorised English Translation from the Thirtieth German Edition, by A. de F. Cheap Edition. With an Appendix, containing the Latest Developments of Pfarrer Kneipp's System, and a Preface by E. Gerard. Crown 8vo, 3s. 6d.

LANG.

A History of Scotland from the Roman Occupation. By ANDREW LANG. Demy 8vo. [*Vol. I. in the press.*

Life, Letters, and Diaries of Sir Stafford Northcote, First Earl of Iddesleigh. With Three Portraits and a View of Pynes. Third Edition. 2 vols. post 8vo, 31s. 6d.

POPULAR EDITION. With Portrait and View of Pynes. Post 8vo, 7s. 6d.

The Highlands of Scotland in 1750. From Manuscript 104 in the King's Library, British Museum. With an Introduction by ANDREW LANG. Crown 8vo, 5s. net.

LANG. The Expansion of the Christian Life. The Duff Lecture for 1897. By the Rev. J. MARSHALL LANG, D.D. Crown 8vo, 5s.

LEES. A Handbook of the Sheriff and Justice of Peace Small Debt Courts. With Notes, References, and Forms. By J. M. LEES, Advocate, Sheriff of Stirling, Dumbarton, and Clackmannan. 8vo, 7s. 6d.

LENNOX AND STURROCK. The Elements of Physical Education: A Teacher's Manual. By DAVID LENNOX, M.D., late R.N., Medical Director of Dundee Public Gymnasium, and ALEXANDER STURROCK, Superintendent of Dundee Public Gymnasium, Instructor to the University of St Andrews and Dundee High School. With Original Musical Accompaniments to the Drill by HARRY EVERITT LOSEBY. With 130 Illustrations. Crown 8vo, 4s.

LEWES. Dr Southwood Smith: A Retrospect. By his Granddaughter, Mrs C. L. LEWES. With Portraits and other Illustrations. Post 8vo, 6s.

LINDSAY.

Recent Advances in Theistic Philosophy of Religion. By Rev. JAMES LINDSAY, M.A., B.D., B.Sc., F.R.S.E., F.G.S., Minister of the Parish of St Andrew's, Kilmarnock. Demy 8vo, 12s. 6d. net.

The Progressiveness of Modern Christian Thought. Crown 8vo, 6s.

Essays, Literary and Philosophical. Crown 8vo, 3s. 6d.

The Significance of the Old Testament for Modern Theology. Crown 8vo, 1s. net.

The Teaching Function of the Modern Pulpit. Crown 8vo, 1s. net.

LOCKHART.

Doubles and Quits. By LAURENCE W. M. LOCKHART. New Edition. Crown 8vo, 3s. 6d.

Fair to See. New Edition. Crown 8vo, 3s. 6d.

Mine is Thine. New Edition. Crown 8vo, 3s. 6d.

LOCKHART.

The Church of Scotland in the Thirteenth Century. The Life and Times of David de Bernham of St Andrews (Bishop), A.D. 1239 to 1253. With List of Churches dedicated by him, and Dates. By WILLIAM LOCKHART, A.M., D.D., F.S.A. Scot., Minister of Colinton Parish. 2d Edition. 8vo, 6s.

Dies Tristes: Sermons for Seasons of Sorrow. Crown 8vo, 6s.

LORIMER.
>   The Institutes of Law : A Treatise of the Principles of Juris-
>   prudence as determined by Nature.   By the late JAMES LORIMER, Professor of
>   Public Law and of the Law of Nature and Nations in the University of Edin-
>   burgh.   New Edition, Revised and much Enlarged.   8vo, 18s.
>   The Institutes of the Law of Nations.   A Treatise of the
>   Jural Relation of Separate Political Communities.   In 2 vols. 8vo.   Volume I.,
>   price 16s.   Volume II., price 20s.

LUGARD.   The Rise of our East African Empire : Early Efforts
>   in Uganda and Nyasaland.   By F. D. LUGARD, Captain Norfolk Regiment.
>   With 130 Illustrations from Drawings and Photographs under the personal
>   superintendence of the Author, and 14 specially prepared Maps.   In 2 vols. large
>   demy 8vo, 42s.

LYNDEN - BELL.   A Primer of Tactics, Fortification, Topo-
>   graphy, and Military Law.   By Capt. C. P. LYNDEN - BELL.   With Diagrams.
>   Crown 8vo, 3s. net.

MABIE.
>   Essays on Nature and Culture.   By HAMILTON WRIGHT MABIE.
>   With Portrait.   Fcap. 8vo, 3s. 6d.
>   Books and Culture.   Fcap. 8vo, 3s. 6d.

McCHESNEY.
>   Miriam Cromwell, Royalist : A Romance of the Great Rebel-
>   lion.   By DORA GREENWELL McCHESNEY.   Crown 8vo, 6s.
>   Kathleen Clare : Her Book, 1637-41.   With Frontispiece, and
>   five full-page Illustrations by James A. Shearman.   Crown 8vo, 6s.

M'COMBIE.   Cattle and Cattle-Breeders.   By WILLIAM M'COMBIE,
>   Tillyfour.   New Edition, Enlarged, with Memoir of the Author by JAMES
>   MACDONALD, F.R.S.E., Secretary Highland and Agricultural Society of Scotland.
>   Crown 8vo, 3s. 6d.

M'CRIE.
>   Works of the Rev. Thomas M'Crie, D.D.   Uniform Edition.
>   4 vols. crown 8vo, 24s.
>   Life of John Knox.   Crown 8vo, 6s.   Another Edition, 3s. 6d.
>   Life of Andrew Melville.   Crown 8vo, 6s.
>   History of the Progress and Suppression of the Reformation
>   in Italy in the Sixteenth Century.   Crown 8vo, 4s.
>   History of the Progress and Suppression of the Reformation
>   in Spain in the Sixteenth Century.   Crown 8vo, 3s. 6d.

MACDONALD.   A Manual of the Criminal Law (Scotland) Pro-
>   cedure Act, 1887.   By NORMAN DORAN MACDONALD.   Revised by the LORD
>   JUSTICE-CLERK.   8vo, 10s. 6d.

MACDOUGALL AND DODDS.   A Manual of the Local Govern-
>   ment (Scotland) Act, 1894.   With Introduction, Explanatory Notes, and Copious
>   Index.   By J. PATTEN MACDOUGALL, Legal Secretary to the Lord Advocate, and
>   J. M. DODDS.   Tenth Thousand, Revised.   Crown 8vo, 2s. 6d. net.

MACINTYRE.   Hindu-Koh : Wanderings and Wild Sports on
>   and beyond the Himalayas.   By Major-General DONALD MACINTYRE, V.C., late
>   Prince of Wales' Own Goorkhas, F.R.G.S.   *Dedicated to H.R.H. the Prince of
>   Wales.*   New and Cheaper Edition, Revised, with numerous Illustrations.   Post
>   8vo, 3s. 6d.

MACKENZIE.   Studies in Roman Law.   With Comparative
>   Views of the Laws of France, England, and Scotland.   By LORD MACKENZIE,
>   one of the Judges of the Court of Session in Scotland.   Seventh Edition, Edited
>   by JOHN KIRKPATRICK, M.A., LL.B., Advocate, Professor of History in the
>   University of Edinburgh.   8vo, 21s.

M'PHERSON.   Golf and Golfers.   Past and Present.   By J.
>   GORDON M'PHERSON, Ph.D., F.R.S.E.   With an Introduction by the Right Hon.
>   A. J. BALFOUR, and a Portrait of the Author.   Fcap. 8vo, 1s. 6d.

MAGNUS AND HEADLAM. Prayers from the Poets. A Calendar of Devotion. By LAURIE MAGNUS and CECIL HEADLAM. In 1 vol. fcap. 8vo. [*In the press.*

MAIN. Three Hundred English Sonnets. Chosen and Edited by DAVID M. MAIN. New Edition. Fcap. 8vo, 3s. 6d.

MAIR.

A Digest of Laws and Decisions, Ecclesiastical and Civil, relating to the Constitution, Practice, and Affairs of the Church of Scotland. With Notes and Forms of Procedure. By the Rev. WILLIAM MAIR, D.D., Minister of the Parish of Earlston. New Edition, Revised. Crown 8vo, 9s. net.

Speaking; or, From Voice Production to the Platform and Pulpit. In 1 vol. crown 8vo. [*In the press.*

MARSHMAN. History of India. From the Earliest Period to the present time. By JOHN CLARK MARSHMAN, C.S.I. Third and Cheaper Edition. Post 8vo, with Map, 6s.

MARTIN.

The Æneid of Virgil. Books I.-VI. Translated by Sir THEODORE MARTIN, K.C.B. Post 8vo, 7s. 6d.

Goethe's Faust. Part I. Translated into English Verse. Second Edition, crown 8vo, 6s. Ninth Edition, fcap. 8vo, 3s. 6d.

Goethe's Faust. Part II. Translated into English Verse. Second Edition, Revised. Fcap. 8vo, 6s.

The Works of Horace. Translated into English Verse, with Life and Notes. 2 vols. New Edition. Crown 8vo, 21s.

Poems and Ballads of Heinrich Heine. Done into English Verse. Third Edition. Small crown 8vo, 5s.

The Song of the Bell, and other Translations from Schiller, Goethe, Uhland, and Others. Crown 8vo, 7s. 6d.

Madonna Pia: A Tragedy; and Three Other Dramas. Crown 8vo, 7s. 6d.

Catullus. With Life and Notes. Second Edition, Revised and Corrected. Post 8vo, 7s. 6d.

The 'Vita Nuova' of Dante. Translated, with an Introduction and Notes. Third Edition. Small crown 8vo, 5s.

Aladdin: A Dramatic Poem. By ADAM OEHLENSCHLAEGER. Fcap. 8vo, 5s.

Correggio: A Tragedy. By OEHLENSCHLAEGER. With Notes. Fcap. 8vo, 3s.

MARTIN. On some of Shakespeare's Female Characters. By HELENA FAUCIT, Lady MARTIN. *Dedicated by permission to Her Most Gracious Majesty the Queen.* With a Portrait by Lehmann. Sixth Edition, with a new Preface. Demy 8vo, 7s. 6d.

MARWICK. Observations on the Law and Practice in regard to Municipal Elections and the Conduct of the Business of Town Councils and Commissioners of Police in Scotland. By Sir JAMES D. MARWICK, LL.D., Town-Clerk of Glasgow. Royal 8vo, 30s.

MATHESON.

Can the Old Faith Live with the New? or, The Problem of Evolution and Revelation. By the Rev. GEORGE MATHESON, D.D. Third Edition. Crown 8vo, 7s. 6d.

The Psalmist and the Scientist; or, Modern Value of the Religious Sentiment. Third Edition. Crown 8vo, 5s.

Spiritual Development of St Paul. Fourth Edition. Cr. 8vo, 5s.

The Distinctive Messages of the Old Religions. Second Edition. Crown 8vo, 5s.

Sacred Songs. New and Cheaper Edition. Crown 8vo, 2s. 6d.

MAXWELL.

The Honourable Sir Charles Murray, K.C.B.   A Memoir.
By Sir HERBERT MAXWELL, Bart., M.P., F.S.A., &c., Author of 'Passages in
the Life of Sir Lucian Elphin.' With Five Portraits. Demy 8vo, 18s.

Life and Times of the Rt. Hon. William Henry Smith, M.P.
With Portraits and numerous Illustrations by Herbert Railton, G. L. Seymour,
and Others. 2 vols. demy 8vo, 25s.
POPULAR EDITION. With a Portrait and other Illustrations. Crown 8vo, 3s. 6d.

Scottish Land-Names : Their Origin and Meaning.   Being
the Rhind Lectures in Archæology for 1893. Post 8vo, 6s.

Meridiana : Noontide Essays.   Post 8vo, 7s. 6d.

Post Meridiana : Afternoon Essays.   Post 8vo, 6s.

A Duke of Britain.   A Romance of the Fourth Century.
Fourth Edition. Crown 8vo, 6s.

Dumfries and Galloway.   Being one of the Volumes of the
County Histories of Scotland. With Four Maps. Demy 8vo, 7s. 6d. net.

MELDRUM.

Holland and the Hollanders.   By D. STORRAR MELDRUM.
With numerous Illustrations and a Map. Second Edition. Square 8vo, 6s.

The Story of Margrédel   Being a Fireside History of a Fifeshire Family. Cheap Edition. Crown 8vo, 3s. 6d.

Grey Mantle and Gold Fringe.   Crown 8vo, 6s.

MELLONE. Studies in Philosophical Criticism and Construction.
By SYDNEY HERBERT MELLONE, M.A. Lond., D.Sc. Edin. Post 8vo. 10s. 6d. net.

MERZ. A History of European Thought in the Nineteenth Century. By JOHN THEODORE MERZ. Vol. I., post 8vo, 10s. 6d. net.

MICHIE.

The Larch : Being a Practical Treatise on its Culture and
General Management. By CHRISTOPHER Y. MICHIE, Forester, Cullen House.
Crown 8vo, with Illustrations. New and Cheaper Edition, Enlarged, 5s.

The Practice of Forestry.   Crown 8vo, with Illustrations.   6s.

MIDDLETON.   The Story of Alastair Bhan Comyn ; or, The
Tragedy of Dunphail. A Tale of Tradition and Romance. By the Lady MIDDLE-
TON. Square 8vo, 10s. Cheaper Edition, 5s.

MINTO.

A Manual of English Prose Literature, Biographical and
Critical : designed mainly to show Characteristics of Style. By W. MINTO,
M.A., Hon. LL.D. of St Andrews ; Professor of Logic in the University of Aber-
deen. Third Edition, Revised. Crown 8vo, 7s. 6d.

Characteristics of English Poets, from Chaucer to Shirley.
New Edition, Revised. Crown 8vo, 7s. 6d.

MINTO.

Plain Principles of Prose Composition.   Crown 8vo, 1s. 6d.

The Literature of the Georgian Era.   Edited, with a Biographical Introduction, by Professor KNIGHT, St Andrews. Post 8vo, 6s.

MITCHELL.

The Scottish Reformation.   Its Epochs, Episodes, Leaders,
and Distinctive Characteristics. Being the Baird Lecture for 1899. By the
late ALEXANDER F. MITCHELL, D.D., Emeritus Professor of Church History in St
Andrews University. Edited by D. HAY FLEMING. In 1 vol. crown 8vo.
[In the press.

MODERN ENGLISH WRITERS. In handy crown 8vo
volumes, tastefully bound, price 2s. 6d. each.

Matthew Arnold. By Professor SAINTSBURY. [*Ready*.
Stevenson. By L. COPE CORNFORD. . [*Ready*.

In Preparation.

TENNYSON. By Andrew Lang.	FROUDE. By John Oliver Hobbes.
RUSKIN. By Mrs Meynell.	HUXLEY. By Edward Clodd.
GEORGE ELIOT. By Sidney Lee.	THACKERAY. By Charles Whibley.
BROWNING. By Augustine Birrell.	DICKENS. By W. E. Henley.

MOIR.

Life of Mansie Wauch, Tailor in Dalkeith. By D. M. MOIR.
With CRUIKSHANK's Illustrations. Cheaper Edition. Crown 8vo, 2s. 6d.
Another Edition, without Illustrations, fcap. 8vo, 1s. 6d.

Domestic Verses. Centenary Edition. With a Portrait. Crown
8vo, 2s. 6d. net.

MOMERIE.

Defects of Modern Christianity, and other Sermons. By Rev.
ALFRED WILLIAMS MOMERIE, M.A., D.Sc., LL.D. Fifth Edition. Crown 8vo, 5s.

The Basis of Religion. Being an Examination of Natural
Religion. Third Edition. Crown 8vo, 2s. 6d.

The Origin of Evil, and other Sermons. Eighth Edition,
Enlarged. Crown 8vo, 5s.

Personality. The Beginning and End of Metaphysics, and a Necessary Assumption in all Positive Philosophy. Fifth Ed., Revised. Cr. 8vo, 3s.

Agnosticism. Fourth Edition, Revised. Crown 8vo, 5s.

Preaching and Hearing ; and other Sermons. Fourth Edition,
Enlarged. Crown 8vo, 5s.

Belief in God. Fourth Edition. Crown 8vo, 3s.

Inspiration ; and other Sermons. Second Edition, Enlarged.
Crown 8vo, 5s.

Church and Creed. Third Edition. Crown 8vo, 4s. 6d.

The Future of Religion, and other Essays. Second Edition.
Crown 8vo, 3s. 6d.

The English Church and the Romish Schism. Second Edition.
Crown 8vo, 2s. 6d.

MONCREIFF.

The Provost-Marshal. A Romance of the Middle Shires. By
the Hon. FREDERICK MONCREIFF. Crown 8vo, 6s.

The X Jewel. A Romance of the Days of James VI. Cr. 8vo, 6s.

MONTAGUE. Military Topography. Illustrated by Practical
Examples of a Practical Subject. By Major-General W. E. MONTAGUE, C.B.,
P.S.C., late Garrison Instructor Intelligence Department, Author of 'Campaign-
ing in South Africa.' With Forty-one Diagrams. Crown 8vo, 5s.

MORISON.

Rifts in the Reek. By JEANIE MORISON. With a Photogravure
Frontispiece. Crown 8vo, 5s. Bound in buckram for presentation, 6s.

Doorside Ditties. With a Frontispiece. Crown 8vo, 3s. 6d.

Æolus. A Romance in Lyrics. Crown 8vo, 3s.

There as Here. Crown 8vo, 3s.
* A limited impression on hand-made paper, bound in vellum, 7s. 6d.

Selections from Poems. Crown 8vo, 4s. 6d.

Sordello. An Outline Analysis of Mr Browning's Poem.
Crown 8vo, 3s.

Of "Fifine at the Fair," "Christmas Eve and Easter Day,"
and other of Mr Browning's Poems. Crown 8vo, 3s.

MORISON.
  The Purpose of the Ages. Crown 8vo, 9s.
  Gordon: An Our-day Idyll. Crown 8vo, 3s.
  Saint Isadora, and other Poems. Crown 8vo, 1s. 6d.
  Snatches of Song. Paper, 1s. 6d. ; cloth, 3s.
  Pontius Pilate. Paper, 1s. 6d. ; cloth, 3s.
  Mill o' Forres. Crown 8vo, 1s.
  Ane Booke of Ballades. Fcap. 4to, 1s.

MUNRO.
  John Splendid. The Tale of a Poor Gentleman and the Little
    Wars of Lorn. By NEIL MUNRO. Sixth Edition. Crown 8vo, 6s.
  The Lost Pibroch, and other Sheiling Stories. Fourth
    Edition. Crown 8vo, 3s. 6d.

MUNRO.
  Rambles and Studies in Bosnia-Herzegovina and Dalmatia.
    With an Account of the proceedings of the Congress of Archæologists and
    Anthropologists held at Sarajevo in 1894. By ROBERT MUNRO, M.A., M.D.,
    F.R.S.E., Author of the 'Lake Dwellings of Europe,' &c. With numerous illus-
    trations. Demy 8vo, 12s. 6d. net.
  Prehistoric Problems. With numerous Illustrations. Demy
    8vo, 10s. net.
  Prehistoric Scotland and its Place in European Civilisation.
    Being a General Introduction to the "County Histories of Scotland." With
    numerous Illustrations. Crown 8vo, 7s. 6d. net.

MUNRO. On Valuation of Property. By WILLIAM MUNRO,
    M.A., Her Majesty's Assessor of Railways and Canals for Scotland. Second
    Edition, Revised and Enlarged. 8vo, 3s. 6d.

MURDOCH. Manual of the Law of Insolvency and Bankruptcy:
    Comprehending a Summary of the Law of Insolvency, Notour Bankruptcy,
    Composition - Contracts, Trust - Deeds, Cessios, and Sequestrations; and the
    Winding-up of Joint-Stock Companies in Scotland : with Annotations on the
    various Insolvency and Bankruptcy Statutes ; and with Forms of Procedure
    applicable to these Subjects. By JAMES MURDOCH, Member of the Faculty of
    Procurators in Glasgow. Fifth Edition, Revised and Enlarged. 8vo, 12s. net.

MY TRIVIAL LIFE AND MISFORTUNE: A Gossip with
    no Plot in Particular. By A PLAIN WOMAN. Cheap Edition. Crown 8vo, 3s. 6d.
      By the SAME AUTHOR.
    POOR NELLIE. Cheap Edition. Crown 8vo, 3s. 6d.

NEAVES. Songs and Verses, Social and Scientific. By An Old
    Contributor to 'Maga.' By the Hon. Lord NEAVES. Fifth Edition. Fcap.
    8vo, 4s.

NICHOLSON.
  A Manual of Zoology, for the Use of Students. With a
    General Introduction on the Principles of Zoology. By HENRY ALLEYNE
    NICHOLSON, M.D., D.Sc., F.L.S., F.G.S., Regius Professor of Natural History in
    the University of Aberdeen. Seventh Edition, Rewritten and Enlarged. Post
    8vo, pp. 956, with 555 Engravings on Wood, 18s.
  Text-Book of Zoology, for Junior Students. Fifth Edition.
    Rewritten and Enlarged. Crown 8vo, with 358 Engravings on Wood, 10s. 6d.
  A Manual of Palæontology, for the Use of Students. With a
    General Introduction on the Principles of Palæontology. By Professor H.
    ALLEYNE NICHOLSON and RICHARD LYDEKKER, B.A. Third Edition, entirely
    Rewritten and greatly Enlarged. 2 vols. 8vo, £3, 3s.
  The Ancient Life-History of the Earth. An Outline of the
    Principles and Leading Facts of Palæontological Science. Crown 8vo, with 276
    Engravings, 10s. 6d.

NICHOLSON.
On the "Tabulate Corals" of the Palæozoic Period, with Critical Descriptions of Illustrative Species. Illustrated with 15 Lithographed Plates and numerous Engravings. Super-royal 8vo, 21s.
Synopsis of the Classification of the Animal Kingdom. 8vo, with 106 Illustrations, 6s.
On the Structure and Affinities of the Genus Monticulipora and its Sub-Genera, with Critical Descriptions of Illustrative Species. Illustrated with numerous Engravings on Wood and Lithographed Plates. Super-royal 8vo, 18s.

NICHOLSON.
Thoth. A Romance. By JOSEPH SHIELD NICHOLSON, M.A., D.Sc., Professor of Commercial and Political Economy and Mercantile Law in the University of Edinburgh. Third Edition. Crown 8vo, 4s. 6d.
A Dreamer of Dreams. A Modern Romance. Second Edition. Crown 8vo, 6s.

NICOL. Recent Archæology and the Bible. Being the Croall Lectures for 1898. By the Rev. THOMAS NICOL, D.D., Professor of Divinity and Biblical Criticism in the University of Aberdeen; Author of 'Recent Explorations in Bible Lands.' Demy 8vo, 9s. net.

OLIPHANT.
Masollam : A Problem of the Period. A Novel. By LAURENCE OLIPHANT. 3 vols. post 8vo, 25s. 6d.
Scientific Religion; or, Higher Possibilities of Life and Practice through the Operation of Natural Forces. Second Edition. 8vo, 16s.
Altiora Peto. Cheap Edition. Crown 8vo, boards, 2s. 6d.; cloth, 3s. 6d. Illustrated Edition. Crown 8vo, cloth, 6s.
Piccadilly. With Illustrations by Richard Doyle. New Edition, 3s. 6d. Cheap Edition, boards, 2s. 6d.
Traits and Travesties ; Social and Political. Post 8vo, 10s. 6d.
Episodes in a Life of Adventure; or, Moss from a Rolling Stone. Cheaper Edition. Post 8vo, 3s. 6d.
Haifa : Life in Modern Palestine. Second Edition. 8vo, 7s. 6d.
The Land of Gilead. With Excursions in the Lebanon. With Illustrations and Maps. Demy 8vo, 21s.
Memoir of the Life of Laurence Oliphant, and of Alice Oliphant, his Wife. By Mrs M. O. W. OLIPHANT. Seventh Edition. 2 vols. post 8vo, with Portraits. 21s.
POPULAR EDITION. With a New Preface. Post 8vo, with Portraits. 7s. 6d.

OLIPHANT.
The Autobiography and Letters of Mrs M. O. W. Oliphant. Arranged and Edited by Mrs HARRY COGHILL. With Two Portraits. Cheap Edition. Crown 8vo, 6s.
Annals of a Publishing House. William Blackwood and his Sons; Their Magazine and Friends. By Mrs OLIPHANT. With Four Portraits. Third Edition. Demy 8vo. Vols. I. and II. £2, 2s.
A Widow's Tale, and other Stories. With an Introductory Note by J. M. BARRIE. Second Edition. Crown 8vo, 6s.
Who was Lost and is Found. Second Edition. Crown 8vo, 6s.
Miss Marjoribanks. New Edition. Crown 8vo, 3s. 6d.
The Perpetual Curate, and The Rector. New Edition. Crown 8vo, 3s. 6d.
Salem Chapel, and The Doctor's Family. New Edition. Crown 8vo, 3s. 6d
Chronicles of Carlingford. 3 vols. crown 8vo, in uniform binding, gilt top, 3s. 6d. each.

OLIPHANT.
  Katie Stewart, and other Stories. New Edition. Crown 8vo, cloth, 3s. 6d.
  Katie Stewart. Illustrated boards, 2s. 6d.
  Valentine and his Brother. New Edition. Crown 8vo, 3s. 6d.
  Sons and Daughters. Crown 8vo, 3s. 6d.
  Two Stories of the Seen and the Unseen. The Open Door —Old Lady Mary. Paper covers, 1s.

OLIPHANT. Notes of a Pilgrimage to Jerusalem and the Holy Land. By F. R. OLIPHANT. Crown 8vo, 3s. 6d.

OMOND. The Romantic Triumph. "Periods of European Literature." By T. S. OMOND. In 1 vol. crown 8vo. [*In the press.*

O'NEILL. Songs of the Glens of Antrim. By MOIRA O'NEILL. Square fcap. 8vo. [*In the press.*

PATON.
  Spindrift. By Sir J. NOEL PATON. Fcap., cloth, 5s.
  Poems by a Painter. Fcap., cloth, 5s.

PATON. Castlebraes. Drawn from "The Tinlie MSS." By JAMES PATON, B.A., Editor of 'John G. Paton: an Autobiography,' &c., &c. Cheap Edition. Crown 8vo, 3s. 6d.

PATRICK. The Apology of Origen in Reply to Celsus. A Chapter in the History of Apologetics. By the Rev. J. PATRICK, D.D., Professor of Biblical Criticism in the University of Edinburgh. Post 8vo, 7s. 6d.

PAUL. History of the Royal Company of Archers, the Queen's Body-Guard for Scotland. By JAMES BALFOUR PAUL, Advocate of the Scottish Bar. Crown 4to, with Portraits and other Illustrations. £2, 2s.

PEILE. Lawn Tennis as a Game of Skill. By Lieut.-Col. S. C. F. PEILE, B.S.C. Revised Edition, with new Scoring Rules. Fcap. 8vo, cloth, 1s.

PERIODS OF EUROPEAN LITERATURE. Edited by Professor SAINTSBURY. *For List of Volumes, see page 2.*

PETTIGREW. The Handy Book of Bees, and their Profitable Management. By A. PETTIGREW. Fifth Edition, Enlarged, with Engravings. Crown 8vo, 3s. 6d.

PFLEIDERER. Philosophy and Development of Religion. Being the Edinburgh Gifford Lectures for 1894. By OTTO PFLEIDERER, D.D., Professor of Theology at Berlin University. In 2 vols. post 8vo, 15s. net.

PHILLIPS. The Knight's Tale. By F. EMILY PHILLIPS, Author of 'The Education of Antonia.' Crown 8vo, 3s. 6d.

PHILOSOPHICAL CLASSICS FOR ENGLISH READERS. Edited by WILLIAM KNIGHT, LL.D., Professor of Moral Philosophy, University of St Andrews. In crown 8vo volumes, with Portraits, price 3s. 6d. [*For List of Volumes, see page 2.*

POLLARD. A Study in Municipal Government: The Corporation of Berlin. By JAMES POLLARD, C.A., Chairman of the Edinburgh Public Health Committee, and Secretary of the Edinburgh Chamber of Commerce. Second Edition, Revised. Crown 8vo, 3s. 6d.

POLLOK. The Course of Time: A Poem. By ROBERT POLLOK, A.M. New Edition. With Portrait. Fcap. 8vo, gilt top, 2s. 6d.

PORT ROYAL LOGIC. Translated from the French; with Introduction, Notes, and Appendix. By THOMAS SPENCER BAYNES, LL D., Professor in the University of St Andrews. Tenth Edition, 12mo, 4s.

PRESTWICH. Life and Letters of Sir Joseph Prestwich, M.A.,
D.C.L., F.R.S. Formerly Professor of Geology in the University of Oxford.
Written and Edited by his WIFE. With Portraits and other Illustrations.
Demy 8vo, 21s.

PRINGLE. The Live Stock of the Farm. By ROBERT O.
PRINGLE. Third Edition. Revised and Edited by JAMES MACDONALD. Crown
8vo, 7s. 6d.

PUBLIC GENERAL STATUTES AFFECTING SCOTLAND
from 1707 to 1847, with Chronological Table and Index. 3 vols. large 8vo, £3, 3s.

PUBLIC GENERAL STATUTES AFFECTING SCOTLAND,
COLLECTION OF. Published Annually, with General Index.

RAMSAY. Scotland and Scotsmen in the Eighteenth Century.
Edited from the MSS. of JOHN RAMSAY, Esq. of Ochtertyre, by ALEXANDER
ALLARDYCE, Author of 'Memoir of Admiral Lord Keith, K.B.,' &c. 2 vols.
8vo, 31s. 6d.

RANJITSINHJI. The Jubilee Book of Cricket. By PRINCE
RANJITSINHJI.
ÉDITION DE LUXE. Limited to 350 Copies, printed on hand-made paper, and
handsomely bound in buckram. Crown 4to, with 22 Photogravures and 85
full-page Plates. Each copy signed by Prince Ranjitsinhji. Price £5, 5s. net.
FINE PAPER EDITION. Medium 8vo, with Photogravure Frontispiece and 106
full-page Plates on art paper. 25s. net.
POPULAR EDITION. With 107 full-page Illustrations. Sixth Edition. Large
crown 8vo, 6s.

RANKIN.
Church Ideas in Scripture and Scotland. By JAMES RANKIN,
D.D., Minister of Muthill; Author of 'Character Studies in the Old Testament,'
&c. Crown 8vo, 6s.
A Handbook of the Church of Scotland. An entirely New
and much Enlarged Edition. Crown 8vo, with 2 Maps, 7s. 6d.
The First Saints. Post 8vo, 7s. 6d.
The Creed in Scotland. An Exposition of the Apostles'
Creed. With Extracts from Archbishop Hamilton's Catechism of 1552, John
Calvin's Catechism of 1556, and a Catena of Ancient Latin and other Hymns.
Post 8vo, 7s. 6d.
The Worthy Communicant. A Guide to the Devout Obser-
vance of the Lord's Supper. Limp cloth, 1s. 3d.
The Young Churchman. Lessons on the Creed, the Com-
mandments, the Means of Grace, and the Church. Limp cloth, 1s. 3d.
First Communion Lessons. 25th Edition. Paper Cover, 2d.

RANKINE. A Hero of the Dark Continent. Memoir of Rev.
Wm. Affleck Scott, M.A., M.B., C.M., Church of Scotland Missionary at Blantyre,
British Central Africa. By W. HENRY RANKINE, B.D., Minister at Titwood.
With a Portrait and other Illustrations. Cheap Edition. Crown 8vo, 2s.

ROBERTSON.
The Poetry and the Religion of the Psalms. The Croall
Lectures, 1893-94. By JAMES ROBERTSON, D.D., Professor of Oriental Languages
in the University of Glasgow. Demy 8vo, 12s.
The Early Religion of Israel. As set forth by Biblical Writers
and Modern Critical Historians. Being the Baird Lecture for 1888-89. Fourth
Edition. Crown 8vo, 10s. 6d.

ROBINSON. Wild Traits in Tame Animals. Being some
Familiar Studies in Evolution. By LOUIS ROBINSON, M.D. With Illustrations
by STEPHEN T. DADD. Cheaper Edition. Demy 8vo, 6s.

ROPER. A Claim on Klondyke. A Romance of the Arctic El
Dorado. By EDWARD ROPER, F.R.G.S., Author of ' By Track and Trail through
Canada,' &c. With 10 Full-page Illustrations. Crown 8vo, 6s.

RUTLAND.
Notes of an Irish Tour in 1846. By the DUKE OF RUTLAND,
G.C.B. (LORD JOHN MANNERS). New Edition. Crown 8vo, 2s. 6d.
Correspondence between the Right Honble. William Pitt
and Charles Duke of Rutland, Lord-Lieutenant of Ireland, 1781-1787. With
Introductory Note by JOHN DUKE OF RUTLAND. 8vo, 7s. 6d.

RUTLAND.
Gems of German Poetry. Translated by the DUCHESS OF
RUTLAND (LADY JOHN MANNERS). [*New Edition in preparation.*
Impressions of Bad-Homburg. Comprising a Short Account
of the Women's Associations of Germany under the Red Cross. Crown 8vo, 1s. 6d.
Some Personal Recollections of the Later Years of the Earl
of Beaconsfield, K.G. Sixth Edition. 6d.
Employment of Women in the Public Service. 6d.
Some of the Advantages of Easily Accessible Reading and
Recreation Rooms and Free Libraries. With Remarks on Starting and Main-
taining them. Second Edition. Crown 8vo, 1s.
A Sequel to Rich Men's Dwellings, and other Occasional
Papers. Crown 8vo, 2s. 6d.
Encouraging Experiences of Reading and Recreation Rooms,
Aims of Guilds, Nottingham Social Guide, Existing Institutions, &c., &c.
Crown 8vo, 1s.

SAINTSBURY.
Matthew Arnold. "Modern English Writers." By GEORGE
SAINTSBURY, M.A., Professor of Rhetoric and English Literature in Edinburgh
University. Crown 8vo, 2s. 6d.
The Flourishing of Romance and the Rise of Allegory (12th
and 13th Centuries). "Periods of European Literature." Crown 8vo, 5s. net.

SCHEFFEL. The Trumpeter. A Romance of the Rhine. By
JOSEPH VICTOR VON SCHEFFEL. Translated from the Two Hundredth German
Edition by JESSIE BECK and LOUISA LORIMER. With an Introduction by Sir
THEODORE MARTIN K.C.B. Long 8vo, 3s. 6d.

SCOTT. Tom Cringle's Log. By MICHAEL SCOTT. New Edition.
With 19 Full-page Illustrations. Crown 8vo, 3s. 6d.

SELKIRK. Poems. By J. B. SELKIRK, Author of 'Ethics and
Æsthetics of Modern Poetry,' 'Bible Truths with Shakespearian Parallels,' &c.
New and Enlarged Edition. Crown 8vo, printed on antique paper, 6s.

SELLAR'S Manual of the Acts relating to Education in Scotland. By J. EDWARD GRAHAM, B.A. Oxon., Advocate. Ninth Edition. 8vo, 12s. 6d.

SETH.
Scottish Philosophy. A Comparison of the Scottish and
German Answers to Hume. Balfour Philosophical Lectures, University of
Edinburgh. By ANDREW SETH (A. S. Pringle Pattison, LL.D.), Professor of
Logic and Metaphysics in Edinburgh University. Third Edition. Crown
8vo, 5s.
Hegelianism and Personality. Balfour Philosophical Lectures.
Second Series. Second Edition. Crown 8vo, 5s.
Man's Place in the Cosmos, and other Essays. Post 8vo,
7s. 6d. net.
Two Lectures on Theism. Delivered on the occasion of the
Sesquicentennial Celebration of Princeton University. Crown 8vo, 2s. 6d.

SETH. A Study of Ethical Principles. By JAMES SETH, M.A.,
Professor of Moral Philosophy in the University of Edinburgh. Fourth Edition. Revised. Post 8vo, 7s. 6d.

SHARPE. Letters from and to Charles Kirkpatrick Sharpe.
Edited by ALEXANDER ALLARDYCE, Author of 'Memoir of Admiral Lord Keith, K.B.,' &c. With a Memoir by the Rev. W. K. R. BEDFORD. In 2 vols. 8vo. Illustrated with Etchings and other Engravings. £2, 12s. 6d.

SIM. Margaret Sim's Cookery. With an Introduction by L. B.
WALFORD, Author of 'Mr Smith: A Part of his Life,' &c. Crown 8vo, 5s.

SIMPSON. The Wild Rabbit in a New Aspect; or, Rabbit-
Warrens that Pay. A book for Landowners, Sportsmen, Land Agents, Farmers Gamekeepers, and Allotment Holders. A Record of Recent Experiments conducted on the Estate of the Right Hon. the Earl of Wharncliffe at Wortley Hall. By J. SIMPSON. Second Edition, Enlarged. Small crown 8vo, 5s.

SIMPSON. Side-Lights on Siberia. Some account of the Great
Siberian Iron Road: The Prisons and Exile System. By J. Y. SIMPSON, M.A., B.Sc. With numerous Illustrations and a Map. Demy 8vo, 16s.

SINCLAIR.

Mr and Mrs Nevill Tyson. By MAY SINCLAIR. Crown 8vo,
3s. 6d.

Audrey Craven. Second Edition. Crown 8vo, 6s.

SKELTON.

The Table-Talk of Shirley. By Sir JOHN SKELTON, K.C.B.,
LL.D., Author of 'The Essays of Shirley.' With a Frontispiece. Sixth Edition, Revised and Enlarged Post 8vo, 7s. 6d.

The Table-Talk of Shirley. Second Series. With Illustrations. Two Volumes. Second Edition. Post 8vo, 10s. net.

Maitland of Lethington; and the Scotland of Mary Stuart.
A History. Limited Edition, with Portraits. Demy 8vo, 2 vols., 28s. net.

The Handbook of Public Health. A New Edition, Revised by
JAMES PATTEN MACDOUGALL, Advocate, Secretary of the Local Government Board for Scotland, Joint-Author of 'The Parish Council Guide for Scotland,' and ABIJAH MURRAY, Chief Clerk of the Local Government Board for Scotland. In Two Parts. Crown 8vo. Part I.—The Public Health (Scotland) Act, 1897, with Notes. 3s. 6d. net.
Part II.—Circulars of the Local Government Board, &c. [*In preparation.*

The Local Government (Scotland) Act in Relation to Public
Health. A Handy Guide for County and District Councillors, Medical Officers, Sanitary Inspectors, and Members of Parochial Boards. Second Edition. With a new Preface on appointment of Sanitary Officers. Crown 8vo, 2s.

SMITH. The Transition Period. "Periods of European Literature." By G. GREGORY SMITH. In 1 vol. crown 8vo. [*In the press.*

SMITH. Retrievers, and how to Break them. By Lieutenant-
Colonel Sir HENRY SMITH, K.C.B. With an Introduction by Mr S. E. SHIRLEY, President of the Kennel Club. Dedicated by special permission to H.R.H. the Duke of York. Cheaper Edition, enlarged. With additional Illustrations. Paper cover, 1s. net.

SMITH - WILLIAMS. The Magic of the Desert. A Romance.
By W. SMITH-WILLIAMS. Crown 8vo, 6s.

SNELL. The Fourteenth Century. "Periods of European
Literature." By F. J. SNELL. Crown 8vo, 5s. net.

"SON OF THE MARSHES, A."
From Spring to Fall; or, When Life Stirs. By "A Son of the Marshes." Cheap Uniform Edition. Crown 8vo, 3s. 6d.
Within an Hour of London Town : Among Wild Birds and their Haunts. Edited by J. A. Owen. Cheap Uniform Edition. Cr. 8vo, 3s. 6d.
With the Woodlanders and by the Tide. Cheap Uniform Edition. Crown 8vo, 3s. 6d.
On Surrey Hills. Cheap Uniform Edition. Crown 8vo, 3s. 6d.
Annals of a Fishing Village. Cheap Uniform Edition. Crown 8vo, 3s. 6d.

SORLEY. The Ethics of Naturalism. Being the Shaw Fellowship Lectures, 1884. By W. R. Sorley, M.A., Fellow of Trinity College, Cambridge, Professor of Moral Philosophy, University of Aberdeen. Crown 8vo, 6s.

SPIELMANN. Millais and his Works. By M. H. Spielmann, Author of 'History of Punch.' With 28 Full-page Illustrations. Large crown 8vo. Paper covers, 1s ; in cloth binding, 2s. 6d.

SPROTT. The Worship and Offices of the Church of Scotland. By George W. Sprott, D.D., Minister of North Berwick. Crown 8vo, 6s.

STEEVENS.
In India. By G. W. Steevens. With Map. Second Edition. Crown 8vo, 6s.
With Kitchener to Khartum. With 8 Maps and Plans. Nineteenth Edition. Crown 8vo, 6s.
Egypt in 1898. With Illustrations. Crown 8vo, 6s.
The Land of the Dollar. Third Edition. Crown 8vo, 6s.
With the Conquering Turk. With 4 Maps. Demy 8vo, 10s. 6d.

STEPHENS.
The Book of the Farm ; detailing the Labours of the Farmer, Farm-Steward, Ploughman, Shepherd, Hedger, Farm-Labourer, Field-Worker, and Cattle-man. Illustrated with numerous Portraits of Animals and Engravings of Implements, and Plans of Farm Buildings. Fourth Edition. Revised, and in great part Re-written, by James Macdonald, F.R.S.E., Secretary Highland and Agricultural Society of Scotland. Complete in Six Divisional Volumes, bound in cloth, each 10s. 6d., or handsomely bound, in 3 volumes, with leather back and gilt top, £3, 3s.
Catechism of Practical Agriculture. 22d Thousand. Revised by James Macdonald, F.R.S.E. With numerous Illustrations. Crown 8vo, 1s.
The Book of Farm Implements and Machines. By J. Slight and R. Scott Burn, Engineers. Edited by Henry Stephens. Large 8vo, £2, 2s.

STEVENSON. British Fungi. (Hymenomycetes.) By Rev. John Stevenson, Author of 'Mycologia Scotica,' Hon. Sec. Cryptogamic Society of Scotland. Vols. I. and II., post 8vo, with Illustrations, price 12s. 6d. net each.

STEWART. The Good Regent. A Chronicle Play. By Professor Sir T. Grainger Stewart, M.D., LL D. Crown 8vo, 6s.

STEWART and CUFF. Practical Nursing. By Isla Stewart, Matron of St Bartholomew's Hospital, London ; and Herbert E. Cuff, M.D., F.R.C.S., Medical Superintendent North-Eastern Fever Hospital, Tottenham, London. With Diagrams. In 2 vols. crown 8vo. Vol. I. 3s. 6d. net.

STODDART.
John Stuart Blackie : A Biography. By Anna M. Stoddart. With 3 Plates. Third Edition. 2 vols. demy 8vo, 21s.
Popular Edition, with Portrait. Crown 8vo, 6s.
Sir Philip Sidney : Servant of God. Illustrated by Margaret L. Huggins. With a New Portrait of Sir Philip Sidney. Small 4to, with a specially designed Cover. 5s.

STORMONTH.

Dictionary of the English Language, Pronouncing, Etymological, and Explanatory. By the Rev. JAMES STORMONTH. Revised by the Rev. P. H. PHELP. Library Edition. New and Cheaper Edition, with Supplement. Imperial 8vo, handsomely bound in half morocco, 18s. net.

Etymological and Pronouncing Dictionary of the English Language. Including a very Copious Selection of Scientific Terms. For use in Schools and Colleges, and as a Book of General Reference. The Pronunciation carefully revised by the Rev. P. H. PHELP, M.A. Cantab. Thirteenth Edition, with Supplement. Crown 8vo, pp. 800. 7s. 6d.

The School Dictionary. New Edition, thoroughly Revised. By WILLIAM BAYNE. 16mo, 1s.

STORY. The Apostolic Ministry in the Scottish Church (The Baird Lecture for 1897). By ROBERT HERBERT STORY, D.D. (Edin.), F.S.A. Scot., Principal of the University of Glasgow, Principal Clerk of the General Assembly, and Chaplain to the Queen. Crown 8vo, 7s. 6d.

STORY.

Poems. By W. W. Story, Author of 'Roba di Roma,' &c. 2 vols. 7s. 6d.

Fiammetta. A Summer Idyl. Crown 8vo, 7s. 6d.

Conversations in a Studio. 2 vols. crown 8vo, 12s. 6d.

Excursions in Art and Letters. Crown 8vo, 7s. 6d.

A Poet's Portfolio : Later Readings. 18mo, 3s. 6d.

STRACHEY. Talk at a Country House. Fact and Fiction. By Sir EDWARD STRACHEY, Bart. With a portrait of the Author. Crown 8vo, 4s. 6d. net.

STURGIS. Little Comedies, Old and New. By JULIAN STURGIS. Crown 8vo, 7s. 6d.

TAYLOR. The Story of my Life. By the late Colonel MEADOWS TAYLOR, Author of 'The Confessions of a Thug,' &c., &c. Edited by his Daughter. New and Cheaper Edition, being the Fourth. Crown 8vo, 6s.

THOMAS. The Woodland Life. By EDWARD THOMAS. With a Frontispiece. Square 8vo, 6s.

THOMSON.

The Diversions of a Prime Minister. By BASIL THOMSON. With a Map, numerous Illustrations by J. W. Cawston and others, and Reproductions of Rare Plates, from Early Voyages of Sixteenth and Seventeenth Centuries. Small demy 8vo, 15s.

South Sea Yarns. With 10 Full-page Illustrations. Cheaper Edition. Crown 8vo, 3s. 6d.

THOMSON.

Handy Book of the Flower-Garden : Being Practical Directions for the Propagation, Culture, and Arrangement of Plants in Flower-Gardens all the year round. With Engraved Plans. By DAVID THOMSON, Gardener to his Grace the Duke of Buccleuch, K.T., at Drumlanrig. Fourth and Cheaper Edition. Crown 8vo, 5s.

The Handy Book of Fruit-Culture under Glass : Being a series of Elaborate Practical Treatises on the Cultivation and Forcing of Pines, Vines, Peaches, Figs, Melons, Strawberries, and Cucumbers. With Engravings of Hothouses, &c. Second Edition, Revised and Enlarged. Crown 8vo, 7s. 6d.

THOMSON. A Practical Treatise on the Cultivation of the Grape Vine. By WILLIAM THOMSON, Tweed Vineyards. Tenth Edition. 8vo, 5s.

THOMSON. Cookery for the Sick and Convalescent. With
Directions for the Preparation of Poultices, Fomentations, &c. By BARBARA
THOMSON. Fcap. 8vo, 1s. 6d.

THORBURN. Asiatic Neighbours. By S. S. THORBURN, Bengal
Civil Service, Author of 'Bannú; or, Our Afghan Frontier,' 'David Leslie :
A Story of the Afghan Frontier,' 'Musalmans and Money-Lenders in the Pan-
jab.' With Two Maps. Demy 8vo, 10s. 6d. net.

TIELE. Elements of the Science of Religion. Part I.—Morpho-
logical. Part II.—Ontological. Being the Gifford Lectures delivered before the
University of Edinburgh in 1896-98. By C. P. TIELE, Theol. D., Litt. D. (Bonon.),
Hon. M.R.A.S., &c., Professor of the Science of Religion, in the University of
Leiden. In 2 vols. post 8vo, 7s. 6d. net. each.

TRANSACTIONS OF THE HIGHLAND AND AGRICUL-
TURAL SOCIETY OF SCOTLAND. Published annually, price 5s.

TRAVERS.
Windyhaugh. By GRAHAM TRAVERS (Margaret G. Todd,
M.D.) Fourth Edition. Crown 8vo, 6s.
Mona Maclean, Medical Student. A Novel. Fourteenth Edi-
tion. Crown 8vo, 6s.
Fellow Travellers. Fourth Edition. Crown 8vo, 6s.

TRYON. Life of Vice-Admiral Sir George Tryon, K.C.B. By
Rear-Admiral C. C. PENROSE FITZGERALD. Cheap Edition. With Portrait and
numerous Illustrations. Demy 8vo, 6s.

TULLOCH.
Rational Theology and Christian Philosophy in England in
the Seventeenth Century. By JOHN TULLOCH, D.D., Principal of St Mary's Col-
lege in the University of St Andrews, and one of her Majesty's Chaplains in
Ordinary in Scotland. Second Edition. 2 vols. 8vo, 16s.
Modern Theories in Philosophy and Religion. 8vo, 15s.
Luther, and other Leaders of the Reformation. Third Edi-
tion, Enlarged. Crown 8vo, 3s. 6d.
Memoir of Principal Tulloch, D.D, LL.D. By Mrs OLIPHANT,
Author of 'Life of Edward Irving.' Third and Cheaper Edition. 8vo, with
Portrait, 7s. 6d.

TWEEDIE. The Arabian Horse: His Country and People.
By Major-General W. TWEEDIE, C.S.I., Bengal Staff Corps; for many years
H.B.M.'s Consul-General, Baghdad, and Political Resident for the Government
of India in Turkish Arabia. In one vol. royal 4to, with Seven Coloured Plates
and other Illustrations, and a Map of the Country. Price £3, 3s. net.

TYLER. The Whence and the Whither of Man. A Brief His-
tory of his Origin and Development through Conformity to Environment. The
Morse Lectures of 1895. By JOHN M. TYLER, Professor of Biology, Amherst
College, U.S.A. Post 8vo, 6s. net.

VANDERVELL. A Shuttle of an Empire's Loom ; or, Five
Months before the Mast on a Modern Steam Cargo-Boat. By HARRY VAN-
DERVELL. Second Edition. Crown 8vo, 6s.

VEITCH.
Memoir of John Veitch, LL.D., Professor of Logic and Rhetoric,
University of Glasgow. By MARY R. L. BRYCE. With Portrait and 3 Photo-
gravure Plates. Demy 8vo, 7s. 6d.
Border Essays. By JOHN VEITCH, LL.D., Professor of Logic
and Rhetoric, University of Glasgow. Crown 8vo, 4s. 6d. net.
The History and Poetry of the Scottish Border : their Main
Features and Relations. New and Enlarged Edition. 2 vols. demy 8vo, 16s.
Institutes of Logic. Post 8vo, 12s. 6d.
Merlin and other Poems. Fcap. 8vo, 4s. 6d.

VEITCH.
    Knowing and Being. Essays in Philosophy. First Series.
Crown 8vo, 5s.
    Dualism and Monism; and other Essays. Essays in Phil-
osophy. Second Series. With an Introduction by R. M. Wenley. Crown 8vo,
4s. 6d. net.

WACE. Christianity and Agnosticism. Reviews of some Recent
Attacks on the Christian Faith. By HENRY WACE, D.D., late Principal of King's
College, London; Preacher of Lincoln's Inn; Chaplain to the Queen. Second
Edition. Post 8vo, 10s. 6d. net.

WADDELL. An Old Kirk Chronicle: Being a History of Auld-
hame, Tyninghame, and Whitekirk, in East Lothian. From Session Records,
1615 to 1850. By Rev. P. HATELY WADDELL, B.D., Minister of the United
Parish. Small Paper Edition, 200 Copies. Price £1. Large Paper Edition, 50
Copies. Price, £1, 10s.

WAGHORN. Cricket Scores, Notes, &c. From 1730-1773.
Written as reported in the different newspapers. To which are added two
Poems, with remarks, published in 1773, on Kent *v.* Surrey; also Rules of the
game when betting was permitted. Compiled by H. T. WAGHORN. With a
Frontispiece. Demy 8vo, 6s. net.

WALFORD. Four Biographies from 'Blackwood': Jane Taylor,
Hannah More, Elizabeth Fry, Mary Somerville. By L. B. WALFORD. Crown
8vo, 5s.

WARREN'S (SAMUEL) WORKS:—
    Diary of a Late Physician. Cloth, 2s. 6d.; boards, 2s.
    Ten Thousand A-Year. Cloth, 3s. 6d.; boards, 2s. 6d.
    Now and Then. The Lily and the Bee. Intellectual and
Moral Development of the Present Age. 4s. 6d.
    Essays: Critical, Imaginative, and Juridical. 5s.

WATSON. Sir Sergeant. A Story of Adventure that ensued
upon "The '45." By W. L. WATSON. Crown 8vo, 6s.

WENLEY.
    Socrates and Christ: A Study in the Philosophy of Religion.
By R. M. WENLEY, M.A., D.Sc. D.Phil., Professor of Philosophy in the University of Michigan, U.S.A. Crown 8vo, 6s.
    Aspects of Pessimism. Crown 8vo, 6s.

WHITE.
    The Eighteen Christian Centuries. By the Rev. JAMES
WHITE. Seventh Edition. Post 8vo, with Index, 6s.
    History of France, from the Earliest Times. Sixth Thousand.
Post 8vo, with Index, 6s.

WHITE.
    Archæological Sketches in Scotland—Kintyre and Knapdale.
By Colonel T. P. WHITE, R.E., of the Ordnance Survey. With numerous Illus-
trations. 2 vols. folio, £4, 4s. Vol. I., Kintyre, sold separately, £2, 2s.
    The Ordnance Survey of the United Kingdom. A Popular
Account. Crown 8vo, 5s.

WILLIAMSON. The Horticultural Handbook and Exhibitor's
Guide. By W. WILLIAMSON, Gardener. Revised by MALCOLM DUNN, Gardener
to his Grace the Duke of Buccleuch and Queensberry, Dalkeith Park. Cheap
Edition. Crown 8vo, paper cover, 1s.

WILLS. Behind an Eastern Veil. A Plain Tale of Events
occurring in the Experience of a Lady who had a unique opportunity of observing the Inner Life of Ladies of the Upper Class in Persia. By C. J. WILLS, Author of ' In the Land of the Lion and Sun,' ' Persia as it is,' &c., &c. Cheaper Edition. Demy 8vo, 5s.

WILLSON. The Greek Gulliver. Being a Translation of
Lucian's ' Vera Historia.' By ST J. B. WYNNE WILLSON, M.A. With numerous Illustrations by A. Payne Garnett. In 1 vol. fcap. 4to.   [*In the press.*

WILSON.

Works of Professor Wilson. Edited by his Son-in-Law,
Professor FERRIER. 12 vols. crown 8vo, £2, 8s.

Christopher in his Sporting-Jacket. 2 vols., 8s.

Isle of Palms, City of the Plague, and other Poems. 4s.

Lights and Shadows of Scottish Life, and other Tales. 4s.

Essays, Critical and Imaginative. 4 vols., 16s.

The Noctes Ambrosianæ. 4 vols., 16s.

Homer and his Translators, and the Greek Drama. Crown
8vo, 4s.

WORSLEY.

Homer's Odyssey. Translated into English Verse in the
Spenserian Stanza. By PHILIP STANHOPE WORSLEY, M.A. New and Cheaper Edition. Post 8vo, 7s. 6d. net.

Homer's Iliad. Translated by P. S. Worsley and Prof. Con-
ington. 2 vols. crown 8vo, 21s.

WOTHERSPOON. Kyrie Eleison ("Lord, have Mercy"). A
Manual of Private Prayers. With Notes and Additional Matter. By H. J. WOTHERSPOON, M.A., of St Oswald's, Edinburgh. Cloth, red edges, 1s. net ; limp leather, 1s. 6d. net.

YATE. England and Russia Face to Face in Asia. A Record of
Travel with the Afghan Boundary Commission. By Captain A. C. YATE, Bombay Staff Corps. 8vo, with Maps and Illustrations, 21s.

YATE. Northern Afghanistan ; or, Letters from the Afghan
Boundary Commission. By Colonel C. E. YATE, C.S.I., C.M.G., Bombay Staff Corps, F.R.G.S. 8vo, with Maps, 18s.

ZACK.

On Trial. By ZACK. Second Edition. Crown 8vo, 6s.

Life is Life, and other Tales and Episodes. Second Edition.
Crown 8vo, 6s.

11/99.